Alchemy of the Timeless Renaissance

By

John G. Vibes

TABLE OF CONTENTS

Introduction

Legend

Peace

Shamanism

"In this concrete jungle we live, our survival is love that we give. Now my instinct is guiding my way, it's true what they say, the world is your chance to create" - DubFX

Section 1

Introduction

1. Alchemy of the Timeless Renaissance
2. Disclaimer
3. Alchemy
4. Ethics and the Basic Philosophical Principles of Peace and Freedom
5. Human Struggle for Freedom

"We are unraveling our navels so that we may ingest the sun. We are not afraid of the darkness. We trust that the moon shall guide us. We are determining the future at this very moment. We know that the heart is the philosopher's stone. Our music is our alchemy." — Saul Williams (Poet) [0]

1. Alchemy of the Timeless Renaissance

Today the human race finds itself in a constant state of worry and fear. It seems that humankind has now spiraled so far out of control that no one can grasp the reality that it doesn't have to be this way. A superficial world has been created for us, a world which has corrupted our perception of ourselves and the world around us. Authority, status, countries, centralized currencies, race and organized religion are some of the concepts that govern our world, but these concepts are nothing more than illusions that some human beings use to enslave others. We are conditioned to accept these illusions as absolutes, simply because we do not know any better.

We don't know any better because our perspective is limited. Much like a fish born in an aquarium couldn't imagine the existence of an ocean, it's almost impossible for a human in the 21st century to conceive what lies outside of our conventional reality. With limited perspective comes limited possibility, which is why our species is caught in a cycle of misfortune, never understanding our full potential. This cycle will be broken when the human consciousness as a whole is in a state of peace. Then, and only then, will we be able to live in a peaceful world.

Throughout history there have been many groups that have worked to create a positive shift in consciousness to bring about a peaceful world. Many times these revolutionaries disguised their message in various forms of art and culture so they could still reach the people without being condemned by the state. During the times of ancient Greece they were called "Philosophers", and then towards the end of the Middle Ages into the renaissance they were called the "Alchemists", while today they go by many names. The alchemists were a collection of mystic rebels who studied many forbidden areas of research, which had been banned by the government and church. However, this cunning group of philosophers publicly told the government, and church, that they were not studying forbidden teachings, but were actually learning how to change base metals into gold using science. Since this was a very attractive offer to both the government and church, the alchemists were given complete freedom to research whatever they wanted.

Though their front was gold making, the alchemists were primarily interested in esoteric knowledge about reality, space, society, human psychology, and the supernatural. These are traditions that have been kept alive through various cultures and counter cultures since the times of ancient Egypt and Mesopotamia. This ancient knowledge was later uncovered by the alchemists, through their research into the forbidden teachings, which have many times been called the "mystery schools". These ancient secrets are known and harnessed by both good and evil forces.

Similar to the times of the alchemists of the Middle Ages, humanity is living in a dark age that needs a rebirth in order to correct itself. History is a cycle of dark ages and golden ages, separated by times of rapid intellectual and spiritual growth which we refer to as a renaissance. The word "renaissance" represents the idea that a civilization can be reborn stronger and more conscious than before. During the renaissance of the middle ages, alchemists managed to raise the consciousness level of an entire civilization without knowledge of their oppressive government or religious regimes. They did this by building an underground culture embedded with disruptive ideas, which assimilated with the contemporary culture of the time. Even the most famous artists of the time were deeply involved in the alchemical teachings and used their art to bring revolutionary messages to people.

In present times, the alchemists manifest themselves as artists, musicians, philosophers, entrepreneurs and independent journalists of the counter culture. This is our generation's movement that will carry on the "great work" to transform and uplift the human consciousness, just as the alchemists did before us. As we near the end of this dark age of materialism and oppression, history repeats itself and the counter culture is again beginning to inject its values into the traditional mainstream culture.

The messages of the modern alchemists are reaching the hearts of millions, through the music, art, and philosophy that the counter culture embodies. These are messages that teach peace, personal freedom, and universal connectivity. Our oppressors know that once humanity as a whole accepts peace, that they will no longer be needed and no longer be in control. We will control our own consciousness and our own destiny, as we lead future generations into a more free and positive world.

This book is a call to action for anyone who thinks that a better world is possible. We have the power to make a difference. We outnumber our oppressors by roughly a million to one. They stand absolutely no chance, their power only comes from their control over our thoughts, and thus our actions. We are incarcerated in an invisible prison where our society and learned prejudices act as the bars and prison walls. So in order to free humanity from this rat race, we must first educate and enlighten as many people as possible about the true nature of our existence, just as the alchemists did before us.

"I didn't come here to chill, I came here to rock, to smash the empire with my boom box!" - Michael Franti (Rock Musician) [0]

2. Disclaimer

First and foremost this book is dedicated to you, and every other soul that has been a victim of war, slavery, and genocide. I would also like to acknowledge the people who have made me feel sane and encouraged me to continue with this project, despite the many roadblocks and discouraging situations that I have encountered trying to get this work out to the world.

There are many ideas in this book that may be unpopular. These ideas may question everything you know to be true. Since I am aware that so many of the issues that I touch on are extremely controversial, I make sure to back up my claims with specific examples, that have been proven and are on public record for you to research yourself.

Some of the most damning evidence that I present herein are the direct confessions, and public statements, of the culprits themselves. As you will discover, that which we learned through our "education", media, cultural institutions, and even our family and friends is mostly disinformation that's been handed down by our illegitimate rulers. It is important that you approach this information with an open mind. These essays are best read in order, but the book does start out with some very heavy subject matter. Feel free to use the table of contents to bounce around if you are in the mood to learn about a particular subject.

By providing this research, I am in no way saying that I am any kind of authority, and you are completely welcome to disagree with me all that you wish. This book is simply one of my attempts to speak out about the injustice that is going on in the world, and offer a few ideas that I think would improve the quality of life for our species. You're also welcome to disagree with my solutions, and if you do, I encourage you to organize your ideas to create an alternative to share with the world.

The issues facing our generation are so abundant and so complex that I felt it was best to briefly explain a wide variety of those issues. These short essays will introduce you into the world that has been hidden from our view by the cultural institutions that dominate modern societies. The information you are about to read is only the tip of the iceberg, the very surface of the rabbit hole. This is merely one resource of many, and after you finish reading I urge you to continue your research so you can form your own unique opinions about what's going on in the world. No one source of information should be the foundation of your world view, when that happens you are giving another person the power of thinking for you.

The specifics that I offer up in this book and the confessions that I reveal I will stand by as fact, but I still suggest everyone does their own research to confirm mine. That's not to say that everything contained within this book is absolute truth, especially some of the metaphysical aspects of my philosophy. Metaphysics still plays an important role in what is going on in the world today. In order to branch off into that realm of philosophy it is necessary to venture beyond the limitations of our five senses, and beyond measurable phenomena. My assumptions on spirituality and various legends are simply assumptions based on my research and my own personal experience. I personally believe these things to be true, but I can't prove them because they are in the realm of the supernatural. I feel that these topics are still important to bring up, because they are related to some of the deeper issues that many people are afraid to consider.

For your convenience, I have grouped these more metaphysical discussions into the chapter called "Legend", and there are also two in the "peace" section titled, "future physics" and "positive vibrations". Remember to read with an extra critical eye when you get to these parts of the book. With that being said, when it comes to my research on politics, the history of banking, and the current plan that the ruling class has for global society, I am very

10

confident that these facts are correct. However, all these areas should be read with a critical eye as well, every word that you read anywhere should be approached this way.

In the following pages I will break down how many aspects of modern culture create a prison for the human family. Some of the things I say may challenge your most sacred beliefs and your favorite past times. By revealing this information to you, I'm not telling you to completely change your life, but I want you to be aware that there is more going on then you have been told.

The society that we grew up in was built upon lies so we would be powerless and ignorant of what was actually taking place. If one is able to set aside the cultural assumptions that have been instilled in us by our oppressors, and think for ourselves, the true nature of our struggle will come into focus.

Many of us have a vested interest in maintaining these cultural assumptions because they act as a defense mechanism, protecting us from the harshness of reality. Unfortunately, the longer we ignore the problems that face our species and leave them for someone else to deal with, the more difficult our predicament becomes. At first glimpse these issues may seem overwhelming and insurmountable, but simply knowing that they exist is the first step towards freeing your mind and creating a better world for us to live in. Contrary to what we have been led to believe ignorance is not bliss, it is actually the reason for the majority of the suffering that has taken place throughout history.

If we are not fully aware of what is going on, then there is no way that we can possibly improve the quality of life on this earth, so our children can live in a better world.

Everyone wants to be positive, and it is definitely in our nature to put off things that may be difficult, sad, or painful. However, this is no excuse to ignore legitimate problems that need to be fixed and it is certainly no reason to allow crimes to be committed before our very eyes.

Some of the main things that are standing between humanity and a better future are the corrupt governments and financial systems of the world. Today almost everyone is somehow connected to these systems and depend upon them for survival. Most of the jobs available are related to the government, military, corporations, or other system of control, there aren't many other options.

When I discuss the crimes of the government and aristocracy in this book, I am specifically referring to the evil of the system itself and the people at the very top who have been corrupted by that system. I am not speaking of the average people who are working nine to five jobs for the government, the people who are on unemployment and welfare, or the independently wealthy millionaires who made an honest living. .

When a person initiates violence, theft or fraud, they enter a territory where they can rightfully be exposed and brought to justice for their crimes. So it may seem like I am "attacking" or "slandering" various people throughout this book, but that is only because their actions have justified this sort of reaction. I am simply pointing out their aggressions and suggesting that we do something about it. The ones that I criticize are the ones who are initiating the violence. That's not to say that there aren't many good people who are simply trying to survive, and provide for their family, that are left with no choice but to work a government job or collect a welfare check. Some of these people even understand the failings of the system and do have the good intentions of making changes from within the system. Unfortunately the system is designed to prevent that from happening.

You can't use a broken system to fix itself, it just doesn't make sense. In any event, this book is not an indictment of the average person, who is simply a cog in the wheel and a mere victim themselves. If you are one of these people, remember that just because you are forced to depend on the establishment for survival in some way or another, does not mean that you have to agree with and support their actions. When I criticize these things that we are all forced to do I am no way attacking you. When I say that the education system is corrupt, I am in no way condemning people who didn't know any better and sent their children to public school. By saying that gas and oil is used to control us and is harmful for the environment, I am not condemning the construction worker who is forced to use a gas guzzling truck for work. Car emissions are absolutely nothing compared to the billions of gallons of crude oil or radioactive waste that has been dumped into the ocean, (but I'll get deeper into that later).

Due to the way this whole system has been created, we oftentimes have no choice but to live within the boundaries of the establishment if we wish to survive, I understand that. However, that doesn't change reality, it doesn't change the fact that we are being taken advantage of, and it doesn't change the fact that a better world is actually possible. If we don't fully understand the nature of our reality, then we will be unable to avoid the common social pitfalls and we will fail to create a better world for our children.

There are some of you that will read this and think my ideas are "all over the place, because I don't subscribe to a particular political ideology and adhere to all the ideas of a Republican, Democrat, Communist or Capitalist. Things are much more complicated than simply picking a political party, or social clique, and subscribing yourself to a whole system of beliefs based on other people's ideas. So if you disagree with me about something, that's great! I'm glad that you feel strongly about something that isn't on TV! Please research that topic the best that you can and bring your informed opinion to the rest of us so we can make some progress, which is what a free society is all about!

"The true alchemists do not change lead into gold, they change the world into words." - William H. Gass (Writer) [0]

3. Alchemy

All alchemy starts with the mind, or more specifically, the application of the mind to achieve some kind of productive or creative goal. If this is the case, then it's safe to say that this has probably been taking place in various forms since the beginning of time. Although few facts are known about life in ancient Egypt, we can tell from their ruins that alchemy played a very important role in their society.

After Egypt, the first alchemists in western culture were the early philosophers of ancient Greece. These are the great thinkers who brought the concepts of logic, reason, and philosophy into the realm of mainstream society. Aristotle, Plato, and Socrates were among the most influential of the ancient philosophers because their ideas greatly improved our ability to make sense of reality. Many researchers believe that these great thinkers actually picked up a lot of their ideas from the mystery schools of ancient Egypt, where some of them spent time studying. This is quite possible considering Greece is fairly close to Egypt and the ancient Egyptians had an extremely advanced philosophy which was similar to that of the Greeks.

In ancient Greece, the tools of the alchemist were far more accessible to everyday citizens than ever before. Although there was still aristocracy and slave labor in ancient Greece, there was also a wealth of information that was rarely seen in the ancient world. The use of logic and philosophy were undoubtedly some of the primary factors in the development of this early civilization. Tyrants thrive in times of violent insurrection, as it adds legitimacy to the idea that people need to be controlled. However when their authority is logically examined, it is revealed to be illegitimate and will no longer be tolerated.

Logic was a new way of thinking about the world through closely examining the language that was used to describe reality. By removing contradictions from their beliefs, and exposing lies in their culture, they were eventually able to construct a clearer vision of reality. This resulted in one of the most independent civilizations that this particular part of the world had ever seen. Eventually, this intellectual power and freedom among the commoners pushed the aristocracy to become even more deceptive. It wasn't long before they they conned their way back into power, assuring that the civilization would collapse.

After the fall of ancient Greece, and then Rome, the entire western world descended into a dark age. There was no philosophy, logic, or intellectual self-defense whatsoever for the mass majority of the population. It wasn't until centuries later that the age of enlightenment and European renaissance revived the lost art of philosophy, which then grew into the infamous "Alchemy" that so many are familiar with today.

The early European renaissance was defined by the explosion of art, culture, and expression that took place just after the dark ages. In a short time Western Europe was transformed from a dreary, hopeless wasteland into a thriving center for business, education, and technology. This transformation was a result of the public becoming more informed and aware about history, natural law, and philosophy. Prior to the renaissance, only the aristocracy was able to learn about these subjects, the rest of the population was cut off from this kind of intellectual study. This suppression of information had a profound impact on the world view that most of the public shared throughout the Middle Ages. Once the information spread to the masses, and they became more cultured, it was like a veil had lifted and many people saw the world in an entirely new and different way. These new insights were shared with the peasants through art, music, and other forms of culture. Through this revolutionary subculture, everyday peasants were transformed into artisans and alchemists who brought life to their ideas with their new found knowledge.

Aside from philosophy, astrology is by far the oldest form of alchemy. Some of the earliest civilizations were expert astrologers, who had knowledge that in many cases surpassed today's most accomplished astrophysicists. The modern concept of astrology that is found in tabloids and newspapers is really a cheap knock off when compared to the work of real astrologers.

Expert astrologers have a deep knowledge of how people's moods are affected by the movement of our planet in relation to other celestial bodies. Although the idea of astrology is ridiculed in most mainstream circles, some of the most wealthy and powerful people in the world actually have personal astrologers. Infamous robber baron J.P Morgan had it right when he said *"Millionaires don't have astrologers, billionaires do"*.

It is even rumored that Morgan's astrologer advised him not to get on the Titanic, a voyage that killed many of his friends and business associates. Ronald Regan is another powerful public figure who was obsessed with astrology, as was documented in the Washington post, Time Magazine, and People magazine during his presidential term. The ruling class has long been obsessed with the supernatural, although they typically dismiss this publicly.

One glaring example in recent history is the case of Hitler, who we now know to be obsessed with the occult and the supernatural. However, Hitler kept this fact a secret during his rule. In typical "do as I say not as I do" fashion, Hitler outlawed any kind of literature on the supernatural, while at the same time sending his troops around the world in search of ancient relics from myths and legends.

Sacred Geometry is another extremely old form of alchemy, which is as old as life itself in the natural world, but was discovered by humans sometime in ancient history. In many ways, sacred geometry is being completely rediscovered today and could possibly be the key to some amazing new technologies. Since prior to the rise of ancient Egypt, sacred geometry has been used in advanced art, music, and architecture. In nature, sacred geometry can be seen in shells, flowers, beehives, and even in your own mind in altered states.

Today, the knowledge of sacred geometry has paved the way for the forms of fractals. Fractals are an advanced form of sacred geometry in which there is a *"fragmented geometric shape that can be split into parts, each of which is a reduced sized copy of the whole"*. Today, fractals are used in advanced computer technology, graphic simulations, art, and music. In nature, fractals can be found in snowflakes, spider webs, river networks, clouds, mountain ranges, crystals, leaves, lightning, systems of blood vessels, and even DNA.

DNA itself is an amazing development of modern science that is constantly unraveling deeper mysteries into the nature of life and our existence. Many people don't know it, but psychedelic drugs played a vital role in the discovery of DNA. Francis Crick, the scientist who discovered DNA, was actually on LSD when he made his groundbreaking revelation. Shamanism when combined with critical thinking skills, and a definite purpose, can lead to many more of these unbelievable discoveries.

This forbidden practice is also age old, psychedelic use and deep meditation has been common among alchemists and philosophers in various cultures throughout history, despite its prohibition. The alchemists and philosophers had access to much more information than the rest of society did, but there were still many areas that were forbidden even to them. They still researched these areas anyway, but were met with strict penalties if they were caught.

In the dark ages, any higher education or cultural expression was reserved strictly for the ruling class. In suppressing this knowledge, the ruling class has actually slowed down the evolutionary process for the whole human species as well. If over 90% of the population is not given all the tools and all the information that is necessary for them to do their part in pushing along civilization, then there won't be much of a civilization. Sure the physical labor you get out of the population will bring great roads and palaces, but if their creativity is not fueled, then there will be very little cultural advancement, as can be seen in places like North Korea. That's the kind of society that you have during a dark age, one where a small group of people are responsible for the direction of the civilization while the rest are exploited and dehumanized.

It was the artists and alchemists who brought the renaissance to Europe. They were on the cutting edge of knowledge and would hide sensitive information in their works. This was a way of peacefully bringing revolutionary ideas to average people, who had not yet been exposed to them. It was this spreading of ideas, through art, that was responsible for a complete change in society and upheaval of the old cultural norms. Although the alchemists were not able to bring a completely free and humane society to Western Europe, they were able to greatly improve the quality of life for average people within their civilization just by expressing their ideas.

A revolution of ideas is what these people brought to the struggling society of the dark ages, and it was that revolution which saved that society from total collapse. Without one weapon being drawn, these thought warriors radically changed the whole structure of society.

In Present times, we are on the brink of total collapse because people don't have all the information and aren't given a fair shot to express themselves. Our social institutions have been hiding information from us for ages and it has limited our perception of reality. This is the same sort of knowledge suppression that was occurring in the dark ages. This intellectual oppression lasted for hundreds of years, until the renaissance, when forbidden information was revealed to the masses through art.

"There is no reason why the future generation should be instructed in how to live by an older generation that is committing suicide" - Manly P. Hall (Philosopher) [0]

4. Ethics and the Basic Philosophical Principles of Peace and Freedom

What is morality? This question has been debated by philosophers since the beginning of time. Today, it is one of the most confusing and volatile topics in western culture. Throughout human history, our course of action has been directed by our sense of morality and our code of ethics. In other words our concept of "right and wrong" or "good and evil" has had a direct impact on our behavior.

Ethically speaking, our species has come a very long way since the dark ages, but the progression is far from over, and has unfortunately slowed to a screeching halt in the 20th century. Sure, the slave trade has slowed down, authoritarian psychopaths now have velvet gloves over their iron fists and people are at least starting to pretend that civil liberties have a place in our society, but we still have a very long way to go.

Humanity is at a very interesting crossroads, we now know right from wrong, but we continue to allow immorality to take place for the sake of convenience. This is much in the same way that the cigarette smoker knows that they really should quit, but just can't bring themselves to actually do it. What we are lacking here is an objective and universal code of ethics that holds every human being to the same moral standard and is consistent in all circumstances. Throughout time, there has existed a double standard, in which the masses have been subject to a completely different set of rights and expectations than their rulers experienced.

A double standard is basically the idea that different people are subject to different rules and expectations based on arbitrary characteristics, such as their class position, race, sex or social

19

status. This idea becomes even more complicated when you throw "proxies" into the mix. A "proxy" is basically a group or organization that accepts blame and responsibility for the actions of individual people. To put this term into perspective, many people see the word "proxy" as another way of saying "barrier" or "shield".

Governments and corporations are the most obvious and oppressive examples of this phenomenon in our society. When people do something on behalf of the government or a corporation they are almost never held accountable for their actions, this is one of the primary purposes of governments and corporations to begin with. These proxies legitimize the unethical actions of individual people and protect them from any legal consequences.

The double standards created by governments and corporations are at the very root of human suffering and environmental destruction. We have come to the understanding as a species that murder, theft, kidnaping, and other forms of violence are completely unacceptable human behaviors. Unfortunately it isn't that simple. This is where the double standards come in, because the aforementioned violent acts are excused if they are carried out by agents of the state, or the corporate establishment. This is why none of the people who were responsible for the financial collapse or the murder of civilians in Iraq have been brought to justice. Murder is seen as justified if it takes place on a battlefield; theft is seen as charity if it takes place at the hands of an IRS agent; and kidnapping is seen as justice if the police are locking up a nonviolent offender.

This is the insane world that we have found ourselves in: a world of subjective law and subjective morality where the most heinous atrocities are given a pass if they are ordered or allowed by someone in "authority". Gang members and serial killers account for a very tiny percentage of the violence that takes place on the entire planet, as these people are forced to do their deeds in secret and they are subject to the consequences of law.

20

On the other hand, state-sponsored thieves and murderers like the IRS, the army, or the police are cloaked by the false legitimacy that is created by the proxy of government. Corporations work very much the same way thanks to a little-known legal loophole called "corporate personhood". This is why no one is held accountable when the CEOs at Exxon make decisions that bury tropical islands in crude oil, or when the CEOs at Goldman Sachs make decisions that cause millions to be homeless.

On the other hand, your average citizens are under constant scrutiny and are always 10 steps behind the tiny few who are given a license to murder, cheat, and steal. This is why there is so much inequality and violence in the world, because some people are allowed to cheat, steal, and commit violence without consequence. It really is that simple.

This subjective legal structure is quite effective in keeping people in their place, but it only goes so far because it doesn't control people's behavior when they are in private. This is where morality comes in. Moral arguments have long been used by religious or political organizations to manipulate people and dictate their personal decisions, even when "the law" isn't looking. These various establishments constantly twist the definitions of "right and wrong" depending on the circumstance to suit their own needs and steer human behavior in a direction of their choosing. Strict judgments about victimless actions and obedience to authority have been imposed on us and our ancestors and sold to us as moral virtue. At the same time, those in power and authority have been given a pass to violate these established moral values as a matter of contrived necessity.

Generally, when a violent crime is committed, the suspect is at least sought after to face punishment for their crime. However, if that criminal is sanctioned by the state, their aggression is overlooked and considered to be perfectly moral. This is nothing new, control systems throughout history have used inconsistent moral standards to warp the minds of their subjects. One of the primary objectives of any government is to justify or legitimize their own aggressions and to ultimately develop a monopoly on the use of force so no one is able to challenge their power. This is why the idea of a clear and consistent moral standard is so repulsive to those in power, because they know it will ultimately negate their double standard, hold them accountable for their unjust actions, and revoke their license to threaten and kill.

In short, authority figures establish ethical guidelines based on their own self-interest and then tell the public "*do as I say, not as I do...because I said so*". This is a completely unjust and illogical way of evaluating ethics, because it's NOT intended to evaluate ethics, it is simply a con intended to make obedience a virtue in the eyes of the oppressed. Obedience is never a virtue. When ideas about morality are forcefully imposed and are not practiced by those who enforce them, it is not just those particular ideas that are rejected by the population, but the whole concept of morality altogether is rejected with it. This is a natural reaction to counter the cognitive dissonance that has been created by years of contradictory ethical standards and inconsistent moral codes. After so many generations of suffering under the false moral codes of different ruling classes, many people nowadays just shut off and roll their eyes at the mere mention of morality.

This multi-generational corruption of morality has left the majority of people generally confused and frustrated with ethical concepts, thus giving way to the philosophies of pragmatism and solipsism. Both of these philosophies basically equate to moral relativism, the idea that there is no such thing as objective morality. This has been the doctrine of solipsism for ages, while pragmatism is just a newer reformatted version of this same philosophy. These ideas did not naturally develop in the human consciousness, but were implanted into mainstream culture through the media and education system. When adopted in the early 20th century, pragmatism implicitly justified state violence and actively demoralized future generations by ruling that ethics

22

were subjective, and a matter of opinion.

Moral relativism is essentially the idea that morality does not exist and cannot be defined, but rather is only a matter of agreed upon social convention. This is the core principle which was embodied in the philosophical Trojan horse of pragmatism. Pragmatism is one of the most popular and misunderstood concepts in western thought. It sounds nice, if you look up the definition of "pragmatism" you will see the word "practical" used multiple times without establishing exactly what that means. Let's take a look, here is the definition of "pragmatism" from the Merriam Webster online dictionary.

" An American movement in philosophy marked by the doctrines that the meaning of conceptions is to be sought in their practical bearings, that the function of thought is to guide action, and that truth is preeminently to be tested by the practical consequences of belief" [1]

This definition is rather confusing, but when you sift through the newspeak you will find a philosophy that doesn't really stand for anything, but just "goes with the flow" and disregards the search for truth and morality. The pragmatist blindly seeks out the path of least resistance without attempting to properly understand how that path came to be. This mentality is obviously reckless, irrational, and nihilistic, yet is unbelievably popular because it allows people to take a passive role in reality without feeling any guilt or shame.

If a person believes that there are no moral absolutes they are then able to justify their own unethical actions, as well as turn their back on the unethical actions of others, if that's what feels good for them at the time. This is obviously a very appealing philosophy for people who have been trained from birth to accept authority and feel incapable of achieving any good in this world even if they tried. It is also somewhat understandable that people would adopt this mindset, considering they been through a lifetime of watching various religious sects battle over subjective moral standards. Likewise, they have seen corrupt political organizations use moral arguments to oppress nonviolent people and justify their own violence at the same time.

Most peaceful and rational people get very turned off by these kinds of situations, and rightfully so. Unfortunately, this is the very reason that pragmatism and ideas of moral relativism are so attractive to the current generation, because people are understandably sick and tired of having their personal lives governed by irrational and subjective moral edicts. This is most likely the same reason why many of the philosophers and academics who got any attention during the 20th century embraced these ideas, but there were still a few rebels who saw these ideas for what they really were.

One such rebel was author and philosopher Ayn Rand. In her book "For the New Intellectual" she gives a brilliant description of the pragmatist philosophy and its implications on ethics in society. She said:

"They [The Pragmatists] declared that philosophy must be practical and that practicality consists of dispensing with all absolute principles and standards—that there is no such thing as objective reality or permanent truth—that truth is that which works, and its validity can be judged only by its consequences— that no facts can be known with certainty in advance ……whatever one wishes to be true, is true, whatever one wishes to exist, does exist, provided it works or makes one feel better….. and anyone who holds any firm convictions of his own is an arbitrary, mystic dogmatist, since reality is indeterminate and people determine its actual nature."[2]

While I don't personally agree with every single aspect of Ayn Rand's work (specifically her blind loyalty towards big business and promotion of egoism), she did have a lot of great ideas that have made it a lot easier for future generations to understand philosophy. More recently, in 2011 a world renowned scholar and educator named John Taylor Gatto shared similar thoughts in an interview with Richard Grove of Tragedy and Hope media.

Gatto Said *"If you now connect pragmatism with the concept of justified sinning, you have an absolute blank check in any situation, to invent truth, invent justice, sacrifice biologically inconsequential people and invent any excuse for doing anything that you want. It seems to me that's been the driving force in American affairs for a long long time, but interestingly enough it's been the driving force of an intellectual elite, I believe, through history."* [3] So in other words, people in power use these philosophies to control the minds of the entire human population, in order to justify their crimes and rationalize the twisted civilization that they have created.

The philosophy of moral relativism has been embedded in our culture for several generations, so by now it has become an unquestioned and unconscious convention. Today children grow up learning this philosophy without even realizing it, much in the same way that they learn other cultural traits like accents, slang terms or even personality traits. These are all things that we pick up unconsciously from the culture we grow up in, as we are constantly exposed to these ideas through the media, education, family and our peers.

Many children who adopt this philosophy still manage to become intelligent adults who openly reject culturally imposed dogma, without realizing that their whole worldview is corrupted by the subliminal dogma of pragmatism. Our lives are filled with encounters where people use pragmatic arguments to explain their actions or defend the status quo, so naturally this mindset becomes quite popular without ever being explicitly described or understood. Unfortunately, moral relativism, solipsism and pragmatism are the dominant ethical philosophies of the modern age, which has rendered our generation, and several before it demoralized, hedonistic and apathetic.

If a consistent moral standard is necessary to create a truly free and civilized society then those standards must apply to everyone equally. Interestingly enough, such a standard has already been proposed and is practiced by freedom seekers worldwide. That standard is known as the Non-Aggression Principle or NAP for short. The common law institute describes the non-aggression principle as "*do not initiate force or fraud*", or "*if it harms none, do what you will*", or "*treat others as you'd like to be treated*", or *"live and let live"*. In more detail, *"Do not initiate force or fraud against anyone else's person or property."* In other words, *"except for self-defense, don't harm others, don't harm or steal their property, don't break your word, and don't try to coerce anyone by threatening to do any of these things, and don't delegate or encourage anyone to do any of these things."*

This principle, in large part, makes up the philosophy known as natural law. When one speaks of natural law, they are referring to the universal moral code of non-aggression. However, natural law is a deeper philosophy that covers a lot more territory, while the non-aggression principle is a very specific concept within the realm of natural law.

Don't hurt anyone, be honest and don't take anything that doesn't belong to you. In reality, this is all common sense to most average people, and the good majority of the world's population would prefer to live their lives according to these principles. Some people will even argue that our society is already functioning according to these principles, and for the most part they would be right. However, those who claim positions of authority over others are the most likely to violate these principles, because they are given a pass to do so.

By this non-aggression standard we can say *"if you initiate the use of force and harm another person, or you violate their property you are acting immorally"*. This rule applies to every human being regardless of what title they happen to have or costume they happen to be wearing. This is a moral standard that aims to protect the individual rights and personal property of every human being, regardless of class or social position. This

26

would be recognized as fair, only customs that are seen as fair will actually be respected by society, which is why subjective and inconsistent standards are never fully respected and encourage chaos.

Subjective ethical standards are seen as optional by most people, so they fail to create any kind of social order, which is apparently what they are intended to do. The reason that most people see these standards as optional is because they are rarely obeyed by those in power. If the most powerful people in the world are behaving like savages, then that sends a message to the rest humanity that behaving like a savage will bring you power, wealth and happiness. This seems like a natural psychological reaction to me, as disturbing as it is, it does make a lot of sense.

No one wants to be a victim of violence, theft or fraud, it is these fears that are responsible for the development of law and morality in philosophy to begin with. Unfortunately, neither law nor morality is currently achieving this goal because their honest intention is not to protect people but to fleece and control them.

QUOTE SOURCES AND SUGGESTED READING
[0] Manly P. Hall – personal collection of audio lectures
[1] Merriam Webster Online Dictionary
[2] For the New Intellectual –By Ayn Rand
[3] Peace revolution 43 john Taylor Gatto

"Conventional wisdom would have one believe that it is insane to resist this, the mightiest of empires, but what history really shows is that today's empire is tomorrow's ashes; that nothing lasts forever, and that to not resist is to acquiesce in your own oppression. The greatest form of sanity that anyone can exercise is to resist that force that is trying to repress, oppress, and fight down the human spirit" - Mumia Abu Jamal (Activist/Political prisoner) [0]

5. Human Struggle for Freedom

Since the beginning of civilization the majority of the world's population has been in a constant fight for freedom from oppression. It has been the same story all along in many different cultures, a small group of people have been obsessed with dominating the rest of us, and have successfully done so by using force, words and mind games.

Many steps have been made in the right direction since the days of slavery, human sacrifice or the witch hunts, but we really haven't come all that far. Consumerism and taxation represent the new slavery, and war is the new form of human sacrifice, where billions of souls are wasted in the name of conquest. We still live in an inhumane world where a ruling class dominates and enslaves the rest of us, in every country across the earth it works the same way.

Through all the hardships that our ancestors have endured over the past few millennia we have realized that the kind of life that we were being offered before was unacceptable. In the past few hundred years, people have voiced this realization and rebelled against the ruling class. This kind of situation usually presented itself as a revolution where whoever is in power is removed and replaced with another tyrant and the system stays completely the same.

If there are ever any changes after a revolution they are very small, although the "leader" may change, the concept of authority

28

and the "justified" violence that comes with it continues. If any rights are granted to the population it is a very select few liberties given to a small portion of society. We have seen this all throughout history, the establishment has told the public that everyone will finally be given rights, but that they were only entitled to those rights if they met certain criteria. Additionally, those rights could be easily taken back on a whim, as a result of extenuating circumstances. Usually their criteria will leave out over half of the population. This trick is tragically obvious when looking at the aftermath of the European monarchies collapsing or the end of slavery in America.

Before all of the revolutions took place, no one had any rights except for the monarchy. Then after various revolutions broke out all over Europe the monarchy was forced to give a small percentage of the population some kind of say in how the ruling class behaved.

When the aristocracy finally felt threatened enough, they gave small amounts of freedom to certain people and made minimal concessions on their social policy, but again not much changed, the elite still had an immense amount of power and control over everyone on the planet. Even though they allowed the public to have limited rights, they didn't give up their taste for control that easy. History tells us that despite what they say, the ruling class is not particularly in favor of the commoners having any measure of freedom.

Now the public will no longer accept the kind of conditions that our ancestors dealt with. Since those in power can no longer tell us to our faces that they believe they are our "divine rulers", they must instead pretend to be the voice of reason, so we will still listen to them, and they have done a very good job at fooling most of us. They have made most of us think that we are free and that our liberty has already been won, but this is far from the case.

Additionally, how can we say that we are living in a "civilized" society when war, genocide, slavery and other forms of exploitation are taking place all over the globe? These atrocities are unfortunately still a sad reality for the majority of the people on this planet.

Although most of history has been a cycle of oppressive, dominating societies, there have been those times when we managed to win freedom from the aristocracy. Those emancipating times have led to some of the most impressive civilizations seen in the human story. Unfortunately as we saw with the Greek and Roman Empires, after a few generations of flourishing under self-governance a civilization comes to a crossroads. The wealth and progress of the society attracts corrupt souls that wish to use the region's power to create an empire. This process is inevitable when centralized control and the belief in authority is present, because it is then easy for a psychopath to come along and hijack the civilization simply by gaining political power and establishing themselves as a so called "authority".

The struggle for human rights is a struggle against the exploitation of people. It is a struggle towards the freedom of autonomy and self-ownership, the right for people to live as they wish without bothering anyone else. We are all important and vital to the essence of this planet, none of us deserve to be killed, oppressed or marginalized because of the color of our skin, the language we speak, the size of our bank account or the politics of our so called "leaders".

This kind of mentality where small groups of people are given the power to use force on others without consequence is depraved and is responsible for the dismal state of our civilization. We are making progress, but we must continue to demand that we are given the freedom that we deserve. Many generations of our ancestors have fought to end inequality and oppression, it is our responsibility to carry on that legacy so our children will live in a more peaceful and free worlds then we see today.

"Religion is a common motion and is like a river that may flow through one country, but may have its headwaters in another." – Manly P. Hall

Section 2

Legend

**Note: This whole section is just my interpretation on the historical research that surrounds these particular religions and the statements of the holy books themselves, I encourage you to do your own research and come to your own conclusion

6. -Mythological Origins of Modern Religion
7. -Your Prophets Were Shaman Revolutionaries?
8. -Jesus the Peaceful Revolutionary
9. -The Birth of Islam and the Arabian Empire
10. -Holy Wars
11. Living the Dream Awake
12. Synchronicity

"There is only one religion, though there are a hundred versions of it."-George Bernard Shaw (Writer) [0]

6. Mythological Origins of Modern Religion

In the ancient world, human spirituality was guided by mythology, mysticism and alchemy. In ancient Egyptian, Hindu and Sumerian mythology there were countless legends and tales of the gods and ancient people that paved the way for their civilization. The legends laid the foundation for all of these ancient societies, and eventually over many generations these legends would splinter into various different spiritual traditions. The stories were spread throughout the known world by merchants who traveled from empire to empire, trading fabric, drugs and spices.

Many of these legends were identical aside from the names, dates and places, which led many researchers to believe that they are all copies of a much older tradition that lies outside of our historical view. These are very sensitive subjects that happened very long ago, and have very distorted histories, so it is difficult to nail down the true origin of these stories. However, many researchers are starting to agree that all of these ancient myths are simply allegories with astrological references. In other words, they are stories that have been designed to represent and symbolize the passing of the days, seasons, equinoxes as well as other natural earth and space functions. This is most likely how all of these legends started out, until civilization became more complex and the astrological myths began to take an earthly form with human characters that were loosely based on historical figures.

As Centuries passed, the Roman, Greek and Babylonian philosophies all developed the same themes as the traditional myths, but many of the details and language within the stories were changed to fit the geography and culture of these civilizations. So as time went on the ancient myths still played a role in shaping religions around the world, but they were

32

constantly changing and adapting based on the political and cultural influences that ruled each empire. These cultural differences are responsible for creating an array of seemingly different religious philosophies that all have the same historical origin. As time progressed even further, each culture became more and more familiar with the unique language of their own cultural myths, until they were unable to recognize the similarities between their belief structures and that of their neighbors. This process is referenced in the biblical tale of the tower of babel, where the people of the world are separated by the splintering of language.

The leaders of these empires also frequently changed the spiritual teachings within their civilizations, which resulted in further perversion of the ancient myths. As different kings and emperors added laws to the religious philosophy, the divide between each empire's spiritual structure began to grow. As the cultural differences between these empires deepened, it became more and more difficult to distinguish the origin of their religious traditions. Eventually, due to different styles of governance and different cultural prejudices, a once small collection of ancient myths morphed into several full blown dogmatic religions. It's important to remember that all aspects of spirituality in our early development were totally controlled by the literate ruling class, and then dictated to the rest of the civilization. The different "leaders" of these ancient cultures molded the traditional myths to fit their own political and cultural agendas.

The Babylonian empire and their rendition of the ancient myths would change the face of civilization for centuries to come. An ancient ruler named Hammurabi developed a complex set of laws and rules based on the "Sumerian Family Laws" and "the Egyptian book of the dead", which governed the ancient societies that came before the Babylonians. This set of laws came to be known as the "Code of Hammurabi". Although the Babylonian codes were not religious in nature they originated from the Sumerian and Egyptian spiritual traditions that were practiced before the time of Hammurabi. He simply collected ideas from past civilizations that he felt would be best for ruling a society and adopted those ideas to form the basis of his empire.

All of this historical information is extremely important when considering the biblical character of Moses who is the basis for the Old Testament. According to biblical historians, Moses was a prophet that came into the picture a few hundred years after Hammurabi, and was the first to dictate "the ten commandments" to humanity. Because of this apparent historical incident, Moses came to be known as "the law giver". There have been many other "law givers" in ancient spiritual mythology that have strikingly similar stories to that of Moses. Different renditions of this character appeared in many other cultures, "Menu" in India, "Mises" in Syria, "Menes" in Egypt and countless others with similar names are found throughout ancient history. All of these characters were considered by their cultures to be "law givers" who brought the law of god to their people on stone tablets. Each one of these characters was also pulled out of a basket floating in a river, had a rod in which they performed miracles, including parting waters and leading armies across the sea, the parallels are unending. While the laws may differ slightly between cultures, the basic ideals remain the same throughout every civilization. The code of Hammurabi, the Sumerian family laws and the Egyptian book of the dead all predate these religious traditions and all have the same basic intentions. So it is safe to say that the Egyptian and Sumerian philosophies are in fact the origin of the bible and everything that came after it.

These basic ancient origins of the world's mainstream religions are among the best kept secrets on the planet. If everyone realized that their beliefs were not different from one another at all, it would be more difficult for dominating cultural institutions like churches or governments to maintain control over their subjects. This mentality is typical of the classic "divide and rule" strategy of governance, where societies are divided into smaller sections or cliques so they are easier to control and manipulate. While different cultures fight and bicker over their petty philosophical differences, their "leaders" exploit that cultural bias

34

so they can start wars and expand empires. However, this deception can be easily put to rest with a comparative look at religious history. Once we compare the language and situations depicted in the different spiritual traditions, we can see that they can all be traced back to Egyptian or Sumerian roots. This fact is right under our noses in many cases, especially in Christianity, Judaism and Islam. For example, at the end of every prayer, Christians pay homage to the Egyptian god Amen-Ra when they say "Amen". The vast majority of our modern astronomy, architecture and politics originated from these ancient cultures, so it would make perfect sense that a lot of our religious philosophy came from these civilizations as well.

" All major religious traditions carry basically the same message; that is love, compassion, and forgiveness are the important things that should be part of our daily lives. " Dalai Lama (Buddhist Monk) [0]

7. Your Prophets Were Shaman Revolutionaries

There are many established religious orders spread throughout the world, all of them claiming to have a different perspective from the rest. In addition to all of these faiths having the same mythological origins, the traditional figures that represent these different sects have all preached the same message and would not be very happy to see that there is spiritual segregation going on in their name. The "prophets" of the mainstream religions all opposed organized religion and authoritarian government in their time. Historical records of these figures show that they spoke out against the great injustices that were occurring in their lifetimes, and condemned the social institutions that propagated those injustices. The injustices that they spoke out about were mainly war, poverty and slavery. The social institutions that these teachers spoke out against included organized religion. Even though they were very religious people they understood that to create a social system out of a belief structure was spiritual tyranny. They also understood that corrupt political and religious orders would use spirituality as a tool to control and manipulate people, so they were all advocates of a more personal, less authoritarian religious tradition.

The message that all these prophets brought to us was that we should live in peaceful societies and respect and love one another. They told us not to lead aggressive lives and live in harmony with nature. They also warned us not to trust dominating control systems like government, banking or the church because they were responsible for the separation of human beings and unhappiness within civilization. It was no surprise that every single one of these religious figures was persecuted by establishment authority figures of the time. This is

36

always the part that is left out of the holy books, because the holy books were all written by the establishment. Many times accounts of these prophets were written hundreds of years after their deaths by people who had absolutely no connection to them or their cause. At the time that most of the major religious texts were produced, the only people that could read and write were the aristocracy, so they were the people that ended up writing the holy books.

The prophets of every religion were true revolutionaries, and for their eras they became a great threat to the establishment. Although they all sprang up in different times and places, their shared message of equality and peace made their local authority figures very nervous. Their teachings were groundbreaking for human rights and they were in complete defiance of the established orders of the time. The fact that the ruling class was responsible for recording and handing down the history and philosophies of these religious figures is absolutely insane, because they were the forces that these revolutionaries were working against. There is an obvious conflict of interest on the part of the ruling class to manipulate the message, in order to suit their political needs. The establishment knew that these figures had made such a profound impact during their lives that their legends were never going to go away. So instead of trying to erase the revolutionaries from history, the ruling class merely corrupted their message. When translating these stories into the traditional religious texts, the established orders of the time presented the information in a way that would reflect ideals which were favorable to their agenda of social dominance.

Both mainstream prophets Jesus and Muhammad believed in the same general philosophy and were promoting the same ideas. The only reason why their messages appear to be somewhat different is because they were recorded at different times, by different rulers, in different cultures all over the world. Due to the difference in language, culture, and politics between the rulers who passed along the messages, there have arose divisions between the various religious sects. If one looks at the

37

works that these different revolutionaries carried out throughout their lives, one can see that they were all very much on the same page. These were people who brought a message of peace and equality to a system gone mad with greed and corruption. These figures fought against the established orders of the time in hopes to put an end to poverty and social control. They were so strong in their lifetimes that the establishment saw them as a threat and in most cases they suffered extreme persecution at the hands of their local political and religious institutions.

QUOTE SOURCES AND SUGGESTED READING
[0] The Greatest Quotations of All-Time - Anthony St Peter (2010)

"Archbishop - A Christian ecclesiastic of a rank superior to that attained by Christ" - H. L. Mencken (Writer) [0]

8. Jesus the Peaceful Revolutionary

The biblical accounts of Jesus were not consolidated and printed until roughly 300 years after his death. In that time, his followers had caused a massive social upheaval which threatened the established religious institutions of the time. Even in his own time, Jesus was an enemy of the state and an enemy of the church for his radical views of peace, freedom and equality. The established religious order of the time was the Roman church and they were so threatened by his philosophy that they had him silenced. However, his death did not silence his message and his ideas were starting to spread all over the empire. Fearful that this antiestablishment movement would break down their spiritual monopoly, the church developed a plan to corrupt the message of Christ and use his cult status as a banner for their religious institution. The religious institution that was in fact responsible for the death of Christ and persecution of his followers was now planning to merge the popular image of Christianity with the dogmatic tradition of the church.

In 325 AD the Roman Church held "The Council of Nicaea", a meeting of ranking church figures, where they discussed how they would deal with the explosion of the Christian philosophy in their society. The church knew that if they let things continue as they were, that all of their subjects would convert to Christianity in a very short time. They had to find a way to change this trend and convert the Christians back to the traditional structure and control of the church. To achieve this goal, the establishment decided to merge Christianity with their religious teachings in such a way that the radical messages of peace and freedom were replaced with the hierarchy of the existing church.

The outcome of the Council of Nicaea stated that Jesus Christ was the son of god and that he was to be treated as a divine figure, even though during his life he insisted that he was only a messenger and that people should not worship him, only follow his message. Christian followers who mostly belonged to the working illiterate class were deceived by the church and felt that this was a cause to be celebrated, because their savior was finally formally recognized by the church. Most Christians did not know the true implications of the terms that their rulers laid out at the council of Nicaea. The church then used "the divinity of Christ" as supporting evidence for all of their philosophies, even though the issue of divinity was decided by them at the conference. With the image and following of Jesus now a part of their church, the establishment was able to neutralize the social movement of Christianity from within.

Once the church molded the Christian ideologies to fit its own political agenda, they were also able to dictate an "official" but corrupted recording of history. The church focused only on their fabricated depictions of Christ's birth and death and gave very little mention of what he actually stood for and what he did throughout his life. Many historical accounts of Jesus have been suppressed by the religious institutions, because the reality of his political struggle would expose many of the primary falsehoods of our authoritarian society. This is the way that they have "watered down" and misdirected Jesus' revolutionary message. This is the most successful strategy to silence and corrupt revolutionary movements, which is used by the ruling class when they are backed up against a wall. They know that attempts to fully eradicate a social movement will only make that movement stronger and give it more credibility, so they simply corrupt the message and turn it into a tool of social control.

Even in the accounts of Jesus that have not been destroyed by the church, his opposition towards the oppressive system of government, banking and organized religion is extremely obvious. In all of the biblical depictions of Christ he has a peaceful state of mind, except when he is dealing with "the money changers". According to biblical writings, he used physical force to throw these people out of a temple, which was the only account of him ever getting physical with anyone. The money changers were an ancient banking cartel that ruled the ancient world by lending money to governments and applying interest. Just like today, the money changers of biblical times were deeply embedded in the government.

There is a great deal of controversy surrounding the divinity of Christ, and many say that he didn't want organized churches in his name. Behind the fabricated image of Jesus that the church has been perpetuating for centuries, there was most likely a revolutionary who vehemently opposed the ruling class and fought for the rights of the oppressed throughout his entire life. His whole life was a struggle for peace, equality and human rights, yet the religions that have sprung up in his name have distorted his message, because it stood up against the kind of blind obedience to authority that they all require.

"There hasn't been a religious organization in the world that wasn't a little bit political, and there hasn't been a political organization that wasn't a little bit religious." - Jordan Maxwell (Researcher) [0]

9. The Birth of Islam and the Arabian Empire

Islam is one of the most misunderstood religions in the world today, like most of the other mainstream religions it is even misunderstood by its own followers. The origins of this religion are shrouded in mystery, and the government has had total control of the direction of the faith in most of the Arab world for centuries. The faith of Islam sprang up in the 7th century during the reign of the Arabic empire. The introduction of this belief structure into the Arabic society was largely due to the revelations of a man named Muhammad, the prophet of Islam. This was a man who committed many great acts and prompted positive social reform just as many different prophets of different faiths did before him.

Prior to the time of Muhammad, the Arabic world was mostly nomadic tribes that traveled the desert. A prominent group of Arabs called Bedouins were among the most cultured of these nomadic people. The Bedouins invented the camel saddle which allowed them to travel throughout the known empires working as merchants. In their trade journeys, the Bedouins learned all the poetry, philosophy and science that the modern world had to offer. It was Bedouin culture which gave rise to the first Muslim cities, including Mecca. From the age of six, Muhammad had grown up and traveled with caravans of Bedouin traders, so he had the advantage of a philosophical and historical background, but like most of the world's population he was still illiterate. Muhammad remained a merchant until the age of 40 when he had a vision that inspired him to preach about the need for social and religious reform in Mecca. After a few years of preaching he got involved in politics and became a voice and prophet for the people.

42

Muhammad did bring many of the reforms to Mecca that he intended to, but he never assembled a structured set of religious beliefs. He had nothing to do with the writing of the Quran, that actually took place hundreds of years after his death. It is agreed that he was a strict monotheist and also had some very egalitarian social philosophies as well. His insistence on monotheism was a sign of the times, the authoritarian government in the Arabian world at that time was strictly pagan so he associated that religion with the establishment's policies. It is also very possible that Muhammad was actually referring to the Christian or Jewish deity when he was talking of the "one god". Remember, Muhammad spent most of his life along the Bedouin trade routes, where he had a lot of contact with western monotheism, which would have been Christianity or Judaism.

Some of the social reforms that he was able to put into place show his revolutionary antiestablishment philosophy. Just as Jesus Christ "expelled the moneychangers from the temple" several hundred years before the birth of Islam, Muhammad actually managed to make "money changing" illegal in the Arab world. The act of "usury" or charging interests on loans was deemed to be a sadistic trick by Muhammad and remains illegal in most of the Middle East to this day. Perhaps that has something to do with why international bankers have made them an enemy, and created constant war in their homelands. Muhammad was an advocate of social equality and human rights. During his time he was able to make incredible political changes which shifted power from wealthy aristocrats to common people. He did this by demanding that people have the right to vote instead of being ruled by bloodlines. Muhammad made many attempts to develop thriving classless societies and his ideas began to assimilate into political systems all over the ancient world. Unfortunately, just as many teachers to come before and since, Muhammad's message fell on deaf ears and his social vision was overpowered by the status quo.

Muhammad died in 632 AD with a whole civilization under his control and left no successor. This situation resulted in years of battles between different royal classes that wished to take his kingdom. Over the years, different tyrants have continued to fight over the lands that Muhammad once ruled and continually use his name to push their own political agenda, although their philosophies are nothing alike. Just as in the case of Christianity, oppressive cultural institutions have been responsible for handing down the holy book. The Quran has very little to do with Muhammad's philosophy and was produced by authoritarian regimes many years after his death.

The Quran is just a different retelling of the same ancient myths depicted in the bible, just with different cultural and political twists that suited the Arab establishment. Christians, Jews and Muslims are all praying to the same god, just with different names, being described by different cultures. If Muhammad or any of the other prophets, for that matter, experienced divine intervention we may never know, but we can be sure that they did not want religions in their name and they had nothing to do with the production of the holy books of their faiths. The Quran in fact was never really an important part of Islamic tradition until "the renewal movement" of the 19th century. The renewal movement was a push by the authoritarian rulers of the Middle East to integrate the Quran into everyday Islamic teachings. It was only after this movement that the words of the Quran were expected to guide the lives of everyday citizens. Muhammad himself strictly opposed authoritarian political and spiritual institutions so the current dictatorial trend in the Middle East is completely against the teachings of Muhammad and the true intent of Islam.

"Anarchy is to statism what spirituality is to religion" –Derrick Broze (Activist) [0]

10. Holy wars

Spirituality is one of the many great paradoxes of the human story. Nothing in the world is responsible for so much joy yet at the same time responsible for so much pain and destruction. Even now in the apparently "civilized" world that we are living in today, millions are killed in the name of religion. After centuries of fighting there has been no progress, it hasn't gotten us anywhere. Different Cultures have different belief structures because we come from different areas of the earth. We use different words to communicate our ideas, so of course the names dates and places in each culture's sacred stories are not going to be the same. Every religion tells basically the same story, just with different words to accommodate whichever culture the book is coming from.

A positive spiritual movement usually turns into a violent control mechanism when it is corrupted by a figure of authority. It is at this point when everything changes, the goals are no longer to discover the future, but to fear the future and cling to the past in order to serve said authority. At our current stage of evolution we have about the same chances of understanding the spirit realm as a gold fish has of understanding quantum physics, so it's absolutely insane for us to be killing each other in the name of god. At the heart of this ignorance is fear, fear that has been stirred up and manipulated by our oppressors for many generations. They have preyed upon our natural fears of the unknown, of change, and the progression of time, while only giving us fractions of information about our existence.

We can now look back throughout history and see that most wars and "crusades" in the name of religion were really over land, resources and empire expansion. The Rulers of the time used their subject's deep fear of god to manipulate them into going on crusades, just as our rulers today use fear tactics to

45

con us into fighting and dying in wars. Just like pawns on a chess board, time after time we are sent out to war by the king, and seen as if we were completely expendable. This kind of senseless carnage is still taking place without anyone really stopping to question it. Insignificant differences among common people of all nations are still used by those in power for the sake of conquest. Whether those differences are religion, race, economic status or culture, they are used as justifications to commit atrocities.

Our fear of being wrong has pushed us away from our brothers and sisters and thrown us all into a world of confusion and pain. We spend all of our time worrying about, and planning for our destruction, while we lose sight of the beautiful complexity and infinite mystery of life. Accepting life as a mystery, only to be solved upon the turning of the final page will allow us to progress spiritually.

What is needed is a more open ended spiritual culture that can grow with our evolutionary path, instead of keeping us chained to ridged ideologies. None of us even have a fraction of a clue what lies beyond, and accepting that fact is the first step towards discovering truth. If different religions would have been seriously open to the fact that they had more to learn, and shared information with each other instead of going to war, imagine the positive impact it would have on our spiritual development and safety here on this planet.

QUOTE SOURCES AND SUGGESTED READING
[0] Derrick Broze Spoken live at Anarchy in the NYC 4/20/13

"A dream you dream alone is only a dream. A dream you dream together is reality" – John Lennon (Rock Musician of The Beatles) [0]

11. Living the Dream Awake

The human psyche is one of the most mysterious frontiers of modern science. The study of consciousness has been developing in the west for the past few hundred years and we have not been able to catch up with the knowledge of our indigenous ancestors. Our knowledge of the brain consists of mostly observational or recordable information. For example, we know which parts of the brain are responsible for our mechanical functions and we know which parts of are brain are responsible for creativity. However, there are still many brain functions such as dreaming, telepathy, intuition and meditation that still remain a mystery to modern science. The material world of the west does their best to ignore the more mystic and unexplainable realms of the human psyche, which is why their knowledge in these areas is so mundane.

The dream realm was always held sacred by indigenous cultures, it was believed that dreams held the key to not only our inner struggles but also gave us a glimpse into the future and a connection to the spirit world. Throughout the centuries, most mystic traditions have been lost in the overwhelming materialistic cultures that dominate our world, and the spiritual connection to dreams is no different. Many of us pay very little attention to our dreams, and when we do pay attention we don't know enough about the dream realm to understand what's going on and put things into context. Recent studies have found that dreams and even near death experiences may be traced to a specific region of the brain. This region of the brain is known as the pineal gland and to this day it remains an anomaly to modern medicine. The pineal gland is located in the very center of the brain and is extremely delicate, but it is well protected by the rest of the brain and skull.

47

Although there has been little mainstream interest in the pineal gland in modern times, advanced civilizations of the past all recognized this gland as the "3rd eye". The 3rd eye represented the source of consciousness to these cultures and linked the human body with the spirit world. Egyptian tombs were decorated with animals coming out of the center of the pharaoh's head, to depict the power of the 3rd eye or pineal gland. Art all over Asia and ancient America also show countless depictions of the 3rd eye and its connection to other realms. What makes matters more interesting is that in the past few decades some western scientists are actually conducting studies on the pineal gland and its effects on the human condition.

Over the past 20 years a doctor from the University of New Mexico, named Rick Strassman, has been conducting experiments on a chemical called DMT, or dimethyltryptamine, which is produced naturally in the pineal gland. Strassman's 5 year study included test subjects from all backgrounds and gave new insight into the pineal gland and its role in the human body, as well as possible links between DMT and consciousness. Strassman's studies do not conclusively prove a relation between the pineal gland and DMT, but does show a strong correlation. Based on the research so far, many believe that the pineal gland releases stored DMT in times of REM sleep and at the time of death, this could explain the popular phenomenon known as a "near death experience". If this chemical really is released every night when we sleep, and at the time our soul passes onto the next life, than this reconfirms what our ancestors believed about the pineal gland being the source of consciousness. This relationship also tells us that dreaming is very much an important spiritual experience just as passing to the next life is.

The DMT research study was extremely difficult to fund and there were many bumps along the way, but they ironically received a large grant from some high up places to start their work. The Scottish Rite Freemasons actually made a considerable donation towards Rick Strausmans work. There is

48

no doubt that secret societies and ruling class organizations are interested in occult knowledge, so it makes perfect sense that they would be interested in knowing more about this pathway to the dream realm. More on secret societies and occult organizations will be revealed later in the book.

Now that we understand the importance of the dream realm to our human psyche, we must cherish the times spent away from our material consciousness. For all we know, every night our souls could be transported to a universal dream world, where all the great mysteries of life are revealed.

The same cultures that knew about the importance of the pineal gland also shared spiritual systems that were deep rooted in meditation and other realms of consciousness. In these meditative states people would learn about their inner selves as well as their relation to the rest of the world and their impact on it. Our ancestors paid close attention to the lessons they were taught in the dream realm and while in meditative states. On a mass scale adopting this kind of mentality could help people make better decisions that are more centered on the progression of our planet instead of the progression of our current self-destructive ideologies.

QUOTE SOURCES AND SUGGESTED READING
[SR1] DMT: The Spirit Molecule by Rick Strassman

"Synchronicity hints at the unified world behind the illusory veil of the material universe." – (Roger S. Jones, associate professor of physics at the University of Minnesota) [0]

12. Synchronicity

Since Human beings were able to contemplate the nature of their existence in the universe they have asked for signs from beyond to aid them in their spiritual journey. These signs have always come in the form of "synchronicities" which are also known as "cosmic coincidences". This takes place when something that you are thinking about actually presents itself in the real world as a result of your thought. Over the generations our limiting cultural institutions have led us to believe that these signs from beyond are merely randomly occurring events and that our mind has no impact on, or relation to, the physical world around us. These events are passed off as insignificant and are largely ignored by the general population. However, if one pays close attention to what is going on around them, they will find that nothing is random and that everything happens for a reason.

Carl Jung was one of the most well respected figures of modern science, and was the first person to use the term synchronicity. He used it to describe the significant coincidences that occur when something in a person's psyche manifests in the physical world. Jung was inspired to this concept when treating a patient in his psychology firm. The night before a therapy session, the patient had a dream about a golden scarab. The next day during the session when he was discussing this dream with his patient, a real golden scarab randomly hit against the cabinet window. This strange occurrence was the basis for Jung's "acausal connecting principle" which linked mind and matter through the process of synchronicity. The synchronicities that take place every day demonstrate that there is a connection between our consciousness and the physical world around us. Every one of us experiences this phenomena on a daily basis, whether we realize it or not.

When someone is actively looking for synchronicities in their daily lives, every day becomes a new meaningful adventure where magical things happen all the time. The magic is always there, in every event that everyone encounters, but it's only visible to those who are actually looking for it. The modern idea of this is more commonly recognized through a principal called "the butterfly effect". This is the observation that every action that someone takes, no matter how small, has a direct and profound impact on how the future will unfold. Synchronicity just takes it a step further and recognizes that thoughts as well as actions are somehow related to future events.

The most visible occurrences of synchronicity in our everyday lives are surrounding the important relationships that we develop and important places that we encounter. When you meet a best friend or significant other through an odd circumstance or a new job drops into your lap just when you need it the most, you are witnessing synchronicity take place. I'm sure you can think back through your past and remember a few unbelievable circumstances that were in no way just coincidences. Now in the future when these events occur you will understand that they are significant and you will pay close attention to what you are feeling, thinking and what is taking place around you. Taking in as much information at this pivotal moment is important because it will give you the intuition that will lead you down the right path. That path may not present itself immediately, but whatever was learned through your synchronistic experience will prove to be vital at some point in the future.

Synchronistic experiences teach us that the world is more complex then we can imagine and that our psyche has an unseen relation to the events that unfold in our everyday lives. The alchemists of the European Renaissance paid close attention when these events would manifest because they believed that synchronicities occurred during important moments that would significantly change the future. This acted as a sort of a guide for many philosophers who were seeking to solve the

51

world's mysteries. If a synchronicity were to occur which had a relation to something that the philosopher was studying, then that was taken as a sign that they were on the right track and to follow their intuition.

This kind of mystical approach to life was not limited to just the alchemists, many indigenous tribes throughout the world also observed synchronicities as signs from their gods. Tribal elders would use these signs to choose where to set up their village, where to hunt or for guidance in times of struggle. Nothing has changed since our ancestors took this path, the universe still behaves in the same way, even if many cultures have forgotten this fact. We may never fully understand these phenomena or their origins but they are so apparent in our everyday life that it would be careless to ignore them. Synchronicity shows us that the universe is not just a collection of random events thrown together in a meaningless space, like today's pop culture would lead you to believe. The universe is a place of cosmic intelligence where every thought and every movement has a deeper meaning then we can perceive.

QUOTE SOURCES AND SUGGESTED READING
[0] 'Time and Time Again' American Theosophist, The (Dora Kunz, Executive Editor)
[SR2] The Collected Works: Civilization in transition by Carl Gustav Jung (1964)
[SR3] The Sync Book: Myths, Magic, Media, and Mindscapes

"Remember this revolution is born out of love for my people not hatred for others." –Immortal Technique

Section 3

Peace

"Political language is designed to make lies sound truthful and murder respectable, and to give an appearance of solidity to pure wind" - George Orwell (Writer)

13. An Error in Communication

Language is without a doubt the most important and profound development in human history. It has allowed us to describe the world we live in and express ourselves to one another. Language lays the foundation for our belief systems, possibilities and also our idiosyncrasies. Our view of the universe is shaped by the words that we use to describe what we see and experience. Written language is especially important because it immortalizes information and makes it possible for humans to record an extremely detailed history.

Before the renaissance of the middle ages, reading and writing was a secret art mainly reserved for the ruling class. Thus, it was the story of the elite that got passed down through the generations and presented as history. The slaves and peasants were not able to contribute their perspective to history because their messages wouldn't last many generations as an oral tradition. With no true past and no frame of reference, our oppressed ancestors were unable to recognize the inhumane conditions that they suffered at the hands of their rulers. In many feudal societies throughout medieval Europe it was actually a punishable offence if someone from the underclass was caught with personal reading material, or even calendars. The authoritarian rulers feared that if the peasants were to become educated then they would no longer be content with their slavery. The current view of history would be drastically different if the people who lived through slavery, poverty and political tyranny had an equal chance to pass their message to future generations.

In addition to literacy suppression, our entire vocabulary has been manipulated to carry subliminal implications. This hijacking of the vocabulary affected not only written language but the

54

spoken word as well. Language manipulation was highly effective for the early establishment and is still used by governments all over the world today. In the United States, our vocabulary has been crafted to support a male dominant, white, upper class perspective. By setting the parameters of our linguistic possibilities, they can to an extent control the direction of the dialogue. They have been in wars all over the world, but have called these wars everything from "police actions" to "peacekeeping missions". America is apparently an equal and free society, yet everyone who is not a rich white male is considered a "minority". The "patriot act", has set up a carefully named "homeland security" agency to act as a modern day Gestapo. This "newspeak" that I will explain in detail later, is found everywhere in American culture, especially in the political arena, because if they actually straight up said what was going on, in plain English, there would be a huge public uproar.

Many people don't think of it this way, but human language is a technology, and like any form of technology it can be used for good or for evil. Language can be used to enlighten and inspire or imprison and control, just as nuclear energy can be used to heat homes or destroy the planet. However, language that helps people describe the true nature of their reality has been long suppressed and discouraged. It is absolutely absurd that there is a book of terms to describe the different parts inside a computer, but only a handful of words to describe human emotion or other natural phenomena. This is why it is so difficult to describe unexplained phenomena or articulate the difference between something like religion and spirituality, because the words are simply not there.

What we must do to counteract this problem is to expand the limits of our vocabulary and create new terms and new words to describe the indescribable. If you come up with a new word or new way of explaining something in your day to day conversations then by all means continue to use it! If it sounds good to you than you are probably right and your addition to the language will most likely catch on, as long as it works. Terms like vibe, synchronicity, ego trip or civil liberties have revolutionized philosophical dialogue just as terms like inertia, gravity or relativity have revolutionized scientific dialogue. Imagine how hard it would be to have a conversation about the state of our society without words like "freedom", "oppression" or "autonomy". These philosophical terms are all fairly new to our vocabulary and allow us to better describe things that were at one time just beyond our descriptive possibilities. Some of these terms were created by philosophers, scientist and psychologists, others by college students and hippies. Anyone can contribute to the positive expansion of their cultures vocabulary, and tear down the linguistic barriers set by those who keep us mentally enslaved.

Advancing our communication skills is an essential step towards achieving world peace, one man who proved that fact in our lifetime is a traveler and psychologist by the name of Marshall Rosenberg. Rosenberg is responsible for developing a new way of speaking which he calls Non Violent Communication (NVC) or Compassionate Communication. This method of communication is simple and has had profound success all over the world, from the feuding tribes of the southern hemisphere to the broken homes of modern America. Marshall recognized that all human language is filled with traps that inevitably lead to conflict, these traps are trigger words which he referred to as "jackal language".

Jackal language consists of words that imply guilt, humiliation, shame, blame, coercion, or threats. Marshall believes that this kind of language and interaction is not a natural process, but is a byproduct of the "culture of domination" that he believes has consumed our species for at least eight thousand years. I would tend to agree with his assertion. To resolve conflicts it is necessary for us to avoid using jackal language, and learn to be empathetic when working out our problems. According to NVC, conflict arises between two or more people when someone in the equation has needs which aren't being met. This is the root cause for humans acting out and the reason why some people are oftentimes unhappy with the actions of others. In most

56

conflicts these issues are never addressed, instead of identifying everyone's feelings and needs to work towards a solution, the two parties begin a battle of blaming, which neither side can ever truly win.

Nonviolent communication is a very easy method to explain, but can be difficult to master. One of the most difficult parts of the process to actually grasp is the very first step, observation. In times of conflict many of us are very quick to confuse judgments with observations. An observation would be *"our project is due next week"*. In this case you are only stating the facts of the situation, you are not making any judgments. A judgment relating to this observation would be *"our project is due next week and you haven't done a damn thing, I have done all of the work, you are lazy"*. This is an example of the kind of judgments that cause a lot of arguments and miscommunication. It is very common for conflicts to be filled with judgments and labels that only push the conversation into a more negative direction. Don't get discouraged with yourself if you find it difficult to speak without passing judgments or using jackal language, these are both things that are fundamentally woven into our language and seem natural to most people. A wise eastern Philosopher once said "*Observation without judgment is the highest form of intelligence*".

The philosopher was right, this is an amazing achievement but with some practice it can become second nature. Once an observation is made, it's time for the parties involved to express their feelings on the subject to establish a mutual understanding. Relating to our example scenario, to include the feeling aspect we could say the following: *"our project is due next week, and I'm very worried about our grade, what can we do to make sure we pass?"* In situations of conflict it is an unmet need that is causing discontent, so the objective of the conversation is to identify the needs which are causing the feelings. Once everyone's needs are on the table it becomes very easy to see a possible solution in which everyone's needs are met and the conflict can be resolved.

This was a very quick and basic introduction to nonviolent communication but there are many books written by Marshall Rosenberg that discuss this in greater detail, so it can be better understood. Marshall Rosenberg is just one great mind in a sea of millions, and it is very possible for his method to be someday improved upon, or for an entirely different communication method to develop. In fact, it is probably necessary for each generation to constantly be working to improve our language, so it can be a tool of expression rather than a tool of oppression.

"The Matrix is a system, Neo. That system is our enemy. But when you're inside, you look around, what do you see? Businessmen, teachers, lawyers, carpenters. The very minds of the people we are trying to save. But until we do, these people are still a part of that system, and that makes them our enemy. You have to understand, most of these people are not ready to be unplugged. And many of them are so inured, so hopelessly dependent on the system, that they will fight to protect it. –
Morpheus (The Matrix)

14. Peer Pressure in a Divided Culture

In modern democracies such as the United States, the establishment's top priority is to mold public opinion in a way that suits the goals of the establishment and preserves the institutionalized control systems that keep the people in check. This is often referred to as "social engineering", which basically just means large scale social manipulation. There are a variety of ways that this is done but the most basic fundamental step is creating false divisions amongst the public, this is known as the "divide and rule" political strategy. They know that if all of the impoverished, downtrodden people of the world, or even in a single country were to band together to fight for equality, then their stranglehold on the human race would literally topple within days. So it is essential for them to keep the masses divided and in disagreement so they don't join together and overrun the empire. This has been the policy of many different political systems all over the world for many centuries.

In American culture, women are played off against men, blacks against whites, Jews against Catholics and so on. Sadly, even the many civil rights struggles that sought to bring equality to this nation were all eventually co-opted and used to further divide the public. Oppressed African Americans were led to mistrust the white man down the street instead of the white men in congress and on Wall Street. Likewise women were led to mistrust the men in their families and communities, instead of the men in government who had long labeled them as second class citizens.

Many white males have been led to mistrust everyone that doesn't look like them, while at the same time blindly respecting authority. Every so called "social group" has been played off against each other, which keeps everyone distracted from the true source of their oppression. Everyone is convinced that the problems in their society are caused by their neighbors, instead of the few crooked members of society that claim positions of "authority".

The Middle East has been tormented with authoritarian governments and oppressive "caste" systems for generations. Different castes relate to different classes within the social structure, creating a hierarchy that ranges from the poorest of the poor to the ruling elite. Every caste within these societies is oppressed by the ruling class, but they never rise up because of the mistrust and stereotypes that have been created between the lower and middle castes. For centuries the elite in the west and middle east alike have lived in luxury while the other 99.9% of the population lives in different levels of poverty constantly fighting and bickering over the small rations that are handed down to them by their rulers. This is just a culture where the class system is divided in a painfully obvious way, but it is certainly not the only area of the world where this policy is in place.

Early on in American history even before the revolutionary war, colonial governments used this tactic to keep their slave and working poor populations at bay. In colonial America the disparity of wealth was just as great as it is today and there was a very large population of working poor whites, many of which were considered "servants". There was a great fear among the so-called "masters" that the white servants would join up with the massive African slave population and revolt against the ruling class. Most of the servants at this time had no racial hatred whatsoever towards African slaves, but had an extreme animosity towards the white aristocrats, who were responsible for the difficulty of everyday life. So to prevent the coming insurrection, the ruling class gave the white servants a limited amount of freedom and respect. They were given the "privileges" of owning property, weapons and the right to vote for which aristocrat would rule over them. This created a divide between the lower class and the slaves and made the whole population easier to manage for the establishment. This was how caste systems worked in early America. When the poor whites were able to have a certain level of freedom, they became more loyal to the ruling class and developed a false sense of superiority towards the slaves. These conditions would ensure that there would be no insurrection.

This divisive strategy was also used to prevent organization within the plantations as well. The so-called "masters" imposed a class system on the slave populations that they held in captivity. Some slaves were given a limited amount of freedom and treated with a bit more respect. They were allowed to stay inside the mansion and were well fed and clothed in comparison to their brothers and sisters, who were subject to the most cruel of conditions just outside the walls of the mansion. This is where the term "house slave" comes from. Whenever one of the slaves in the field would start talking about escape, they were usually told by one of the house slaves that "they have it good and they should stay where they are at".

These strategies were used to keep enough of the population comfortable, so that the comfortable portion of society would be convinced to protect the riches of their masters from the less fortunate, while thinking that they were protecting their own. This also worked to divide any groups that threatened or questioned those riches. It is the Native American and African races, who have suffered more than anyone at the hands of the Anglo aristocracy, but this oppression transcends color lines, it even transcends class lines. Rich, poor, black, white, woman and man all experience oppression and manipulation from this very tiny portion of society. These people that call themselves the "masters", they have wronged us all and they have been frantically hiding the truth for generations.

61

The divide and rule strategy is still a vital part of American politics to this day and has corrupted the foundation of our social structure. All of the issues that are sensationalized in politics create divisions by design and turn the working class against one another. The division that exists in our culture creates a deep need within most people to be accepted and to belong to some kind of social group. While this is obviously a positive thing and something that we should all strive to achieve, this desire often pushes us further away from the truth. Many people who understand the injustice that is taking place and realize that the status quo is insane are too afraid to speak out because they are afraid of what their parents, friends or even what total strangers will think of them.

Deep down most people don't accept the status quo, but since it's socially unacceptable to question it, everyone goes on thinking that they are alone, weak and powerless. Most self-respecting people can't go on feeling like that, so they rationalize what's going on around them, tell themselves it's the only world that's possible and then proceed to ridicule anyone who challenges their unconsciously created facade. This is why many people go on putting up with circumstances that they find to be intolerable, they are afraid of being alienated from their peers. Unfortunately, if your peers are ostracizing you for talking about peace and freedom then you might want to think about the company your keeping.

Remember that most of these people are just afraid. Just like a battered child who cries when being taken away from the safety of their abusive parents, we also feel comfort in unacceptable situations simply because we are familiar with them. Much like that child, we need to break free from the familiar confines of our abuse and oppression. This situation is actually so common that the condition is classified medically as "Stockholm syndrome". Stockholm syndrome is typically used to describe hostages who develop positive feelings for their kidnapper, because they are dependent upon them for sustenance. When we apply this concept to the macrocosm of our civilization we find that people living under a system of authoritarianism exhibit these exact same characteristics.

Our political and economic systems have been structured to protect the wealth of the ruling class and to add to it. It seems to be only simple logic that over enough time they will control just about all of the land and resources in the world and everyone will be dependent upon them for their basic needs. Under those circumstances we would be indebted to these people just for attaining our basic needs as human beings, and they have spent their whole lives creating a political environment where the only path to survival is through them. This is obviously some sort of slavery or serfdom, but it is tolerated by the masses because they place the blame amongst each other instead of where it really lies.

"The whole deal's like some crazy game. They put you at a starting line, and the name of the game is "Make It Through Life," only everyone's looking out for themselves and looking to do you in at the same time." - Frank Armitage (They Live - Film) [0]

15. Inhuman Nature?

Our culture has molded us into manipulative, envious and self-destructive souls, we are so confused and out of touch with our origins and our purpose that we write this depraved mentality off as "human nature" or "just the way it is". Billions of people on this planet now accept war, poverty, corruption and greed as "human nature" but no one really stops to think about how we got here and where these ideas came from. Even as we look into history, one must be careful, because the history books were still mostly written, edited or published by tyrants, monarchs and politicians. This is just one small example of how the ruling class controls the information that a population receives, in order to keep them satisfied with the distorted reality that they are living.

For thousands of years authoritarian rulers have suppressed knowledge on a mass scale through rewriting religious texts, wartime propaganda or when subtle forms of manipulation didn't work, they would simply wipe out entire civilizations. By keeping everyone ignorant of where we came from and where we're headed, these empires have actually held back the natural process of human development. We have been led to believe that the meaning of life is to fight with one another, to climb on top of your brothers and sisters, and to benefit from the misfortunes of others. Obviously, they have it all wrong, the meaning of life is to overwhelm people with love and respect, to learn from one another, learn from our environment and see where it takes us. Sure, that's very different from what we're experiencing today, but it is still within our reach.

The idea that violence and dominance is a part of our genetic makeup is obsolete and stifling the process of evolution. It is these kinds of assumptions about the nature of our species that justifies the most horrific behavior. For example, war is the most inhumane and unnatural phenomena on the planet, yet due to endless propaganda and indoctrination, it is revered as honorable and unavoidable in most cultures. Dehumanizing programs such as the American "boot camp" are used by governments to remove any traces of empathy, compassion or free thought from the minds of potential soldiers. During these programs, the military conditions soldiers into accepting violence through imposing racist and hateful ideologies. This kind of psychological manipulation coupled with the horror of war often results in what doctors describe as post-traumatic stress disorder, a severe emotional condition in which extreme circumstances cause severe depression and panic attacks. If violence was a natural part of the human condition then soldiers would not be coming home from war with post-traumatic stress disorder.

In the rest of this chapter I'm going to be discussing the concept of human nature using the terms "competition" and "cooperation". These are vague terms that can have very different meanings for different people, so to avoid confusion I'm going to redefine these terms for the purpose of this discussion. Competition will be defined as a mindset where one *"achieves their goals by violating the rights of others, using force or fraud"*. Cooperation will be defined as a mindset where *"everyone achieves their goals by their own merit, without violating the rights of others"*. In the case of cooperation it would be common for people to achieve their goals with the voluntary help of others, since it is completely possible to have situations where everyone wins. Cooperation by this definition doesn't necessarily require all parties involved to be on the same team working towards the same goals, it simply requires them to be civil and honest with one another in their interactions.

It is the cooperative nature of our species that is responsible for our technological way of life and our understanding of the world. Language and communication has allowed humanity to pass information between one another and to future generations, which results in a steady increase in knowledge over time.

Much more progress can be made through positive human interaction and cooperation, than through fighting and coercion. In reality, it is this kind of aggressive lifestyle which has held us back in so many ways. The time and resources spent on war are wasted, if applied towards something productive, instead of something destructive these efforts could bring unimaginable positive change to the world.

Some argue that our aggressive tendencies may have been necessary during the beginning stages of humanity, but even if that is the case they are now obsolete because we are no longer living in the wilderness and we have the capabilities of avoiding conflict by using our intellect. Most of the popular ideas about a violent human nature have been handed down by power seekers to justify their immoral plan. It is these people who stand in the way of us achieving freedom and peace, so we must not look to them for answers about the nature of our species. Their assumptions are loaded with ulterior motives and they have not once throughout the course of history led us in a positive direction with their limiting and self-destructive ideologies.

The human mind is a very malleable thing and is dramatically affected by propaganda, indoctrination and other environmental factors. Therefore, how can anyone form assumptions about human nature by observing human behavior, when human behavior has been manipulated on a mass scale for centuries? If people were naturally brutal and violent then they would not have to be trained to deal with killing people in boot camp. Likewise, people back home wouldn't need constant pro war propaganda to convince them that violence was virtuous, they would naturally admire this kind of activity.

Even in today's world, with seemingly limited resources we can still all get by without slaughtering each other. Frankly, the reason why we are still dealing with limited resources and possibilities is because we are constantly trying to take from one another instead of actually focusing on fulfilling our needs and using our imaginations. Isn't it possible for everyone to just do their own thing, and use their intellect to work things out when they get in each other's way? This seems like a far safer and more productive way of doing business than we see today, where many people think that the only way to get ahead is to cut others down. The mainstream culture has yet to catch onto this concept, but that doesn't mean that we have to stagnate with them. In our everyday encounters, business interactions and especially our conflicts, we can take the high road by using our intellect to meet our needs without violating the rights of others.

"I don't care if you're gay, black, Chinese, straight. That means nothing to me. It's all an illusion." – Joe Rogan (Comedian) [0]

16. The Illusion of Race

Every human being is a unique individual. We each have different thoughts, different inspirations, different hair, eye and skin color. These differences should all be embraced as it shows that everyone is bringing a unique and enlightening perspective to the table for humanity. Sadly, those who seek to control us use these differences to put us against each other, and take the heat off of themselves. Throughout the history of imperialism our "leaders" have conditioned us to be frightened and hostile towards those who are not under their rule. That is because our rulers either wish to enslave these other people, or take their land and resources, or both.

In order to carry out war and conquest it was necessary for rulers to infect their subjects with blind nationalistic ideologies. People were trained from birth to think of their nationality as being superior to all others. Citizens were taught that people who lie outside the domain of their ruler were sub human, their lives were said to be less valuable than those that were inside of the kingdom. Imposing this kind of twisted world view made it possible for kings and emperors to use their citizens as mercenaries and gate keepers. This is how racism was invented, as a mental justification for conquest and the brutality of the ruling class. By using fear tactics and generalizations, those in power have managed to turn everyone in the world against one another so they can play war games amongst themselves, using us as the pieces.

Some of the darkest moments in human history were the result of mob frenzies fueled by racist ideologies. The crusades, the German holocaust, the Native American holocaust, the African holocaust, and various forms of slavery have all been carried out under the racist visions of various ruling class psychopaths. Each time it has been a different control freak, from a different corner of the earth, with the same list of excuses and a similar set of dehumanizing epitaphs. This is happening in any country with an imperialistic, dominating system of government, just as it has for centuries. Although the mass majority of people are more conscious now and are opposed to racism, the elite still project a very racist message through the media and through their social policies. This influence has a very serious impact on the acceptance of the current occupation in the Middle East and the corporate rape and pillaging of the 3rd world.

Humanity as a whole wants to move past this barbaric self-destruction but the aristocracy and their dominant political systems create a social environment where certain groups are at a disadvantage due to their ethnicity. The establishment is constantly promoting racism and creating social injustice under the radar, regardless of what they say in the public arena. This has been the policy of the ruling class for centuries and is still very much alive today just in a more subtle subliminal form.

Unfortunately, racism is alive and well today in the form of ethnocentrism and nationalism. Both of these words mean the same thing, but ethnocentrism would be a more realistic description that carries a more negative stigma. The Merriam Webster Dictionary defines ethnocentrism as *"the belief in the inherent superiority of one's own ethnic group or culture"* and defines Nationalism as *"loyalty and devotion to a nation; especially : a sense of national consciousness exalting one nation above all others and placing primary emphasis on promotion of its culture and interests as opposed to those of other nations or supranational groups"*. Both of these definitions sound like a dressed up form of racism to me. These ideologies are an attempt to justify or rationalize aggression against another group of people. These are cultural assumptions which are rooted in falsities and continue due to a lack of understanding.

Regardless of the color of our skin, the language we speak or the cultural ideologies we subscribe to, we are all a part of the same human family. In every country throughout the ages we

69

have been deceived by our oppressors. People of all nationalities struggle and suffer at the hands of conniving sophists, who tell us that other oppressed people in some far away land are the reason for our unhappiness. In reality, the oppressed people of all nations have more in common with each other than they do with the people in charge of their governments. Unfortunately, we have all been lied to and conditioned to be suspicious of our brothers and sisters. Our real enemies are the snakes that promote subversive racist political systems and put the human organism on a path of self-destruction.

"Our society is run by insane people for insane objectives. I think we're being run by maniacs for maniacal ends and I think I'm liable to be put away as insane for expressing that. That's what's insane about it." - John Lennon [0]

17. Who Are You Callin Crazy?

We live in a crazy world, a world where war is peace, lies are truth and ignorance is wisdom. Our species as a collective is speaking the language of hate, with its wars and its divisions and all the other injustice we have come to accept. So I guess it only makes sense for those who speak the language of love to be written off as "crazy", "irrational" or "idealistic". Most of the greatest thinkers to walk the earth have been called "lunatics", simply for questioning the status quo. It is important for us to pay close attention to these people, they are the greatest teachers that we have and without their contributions we would understand even less about the world around us than we do now.

Now in modern times, when we hear of Socrates, we think of him as being the father of philosophy, one of the first great thinkers recorded in this age. Though in death his achievements have been respected and remembered, in life this was unfortunately not the case. Socrates spent his whole life asking questions, as most philosophers find themselves doing, and towards the end of his life those questions led him to some politically forbidden answers. Ancient Athens had a democracy much like the governments we see today in the west today, where a ruling class were actually the ones running the country, not "the people" as was advertised. This ruling class was not very fond of Socrates because he saw through their game and was always questioning their authority, and even worse encouraging the public to question it as well.

Eventually the aristocracy grew very afraid of this great teacher and like many other great teachers before him, Socrates was put to death by the ruling class. This all happened in ancient

Greece, the birthplace of democracy, where slavery was still common and a great thinker was killed because he wanted people to have freedom over their own minds. 2000 years later an Italian astronomer and mathematician by the name of Galileo Galilei was condemned to medieval house arrest for his radical ideas. What was this heresy that Galileo committed? He insisted that earth revolved around the Sun and that the Earth was not the center of the universe.

Even in contemporary American culture it is easy to find rebellious free thinkers that have made their mark on history, and changed the way we look at the world around us. For example let's take a look at Mark Twain, the legend of American literature. In his own time Mark Twain was a rebel, who was constantly speaking out against authority. He seemed to have a pretty good idea about where our government might have been heading and was always dropping underhanded knowledge in his writings. Closer to our generation we saw John Lennon, a pop music icon that would sacrifice everything, even his own life in the fight for peace. In the years before his death, Lennon was extremely outspoken when it came to the war in Vietnam and was very critical of the government and corporations that were impoverishing the world. He became such a threat to the establishment that they actually deported him from the U.S and then finally assassinated him when he was able to reenter the states. Another great musician that fought the struggle was Bob Marley, one of the most popular recording artists of all time. All that one needs to do is listen to any album by "The Wailers" with an open mind, and it will become obvious that this is very revolutionary music. It's almost eerie to see how much of Bob Marley's music is relevant in today's world. Despite their popularity, many of these artists were seen as eccentric at best, and heretical at worst, by their contemporary culture.

If you were watching the news in the 1960's you would have seen that Martin Luther King was out to destroy America and that the good policemen were doing their jobs beating and arresting civil rights protesters. At that time the civil rights movement was a serious threat to the establishment, so much so that the C.I.A developed a program to target and silence civil rights leaders, this program was called "COINTELPRO". It is this program that many researchers believe is responsible for the deaths of Martin Luther King, Malcolm X and other civil rights activists. The fact that Martin Luther King was an enemy of the state did not silence his message, and even in his death that message was not silenced. Kings message is so strong because he was undeniable, he was so positive and non-violent that it demanded respect not only from his followers, but his oppressors as well. It is possible that King was inspired by another great teacher of the past few hundred years, Mahatma Gandhi. Gandhi brought a whole imperial nation to their knees without a single gun being fired, he did this through promoting peaceful resistance. It is interesting that Gandhi was one of the most radical people of the 20th century, an "idealistic extremist" and at the same time was someone who preached peace for his entire life. What would the world be like if we were all a bit "crazy" like Gandhi was? I'd say it would be a world worth living in, and a world worth working towards.

The alchemists, artists and revolutionaries such as Gandhi, Socrates, Martin Luther King and others who have risked their lives to speak a message of peace were far from mentally unsound, if anything they were true examples of human sanity. They were only labeled as insane because they represented ideals that were radically different from those of the existing power structure. If we actually look at the definitions for various forms of insanity we can see that being different, radical or out of the ordinary has absolutely no relation to mental illness. In modern clinical terms aggressive insanity is described as psychopathic behavior.

Characteristics of a psychopathic mind would be selfishness, ruthlessness and a lack of empathy for other people. Psychopathic behavior is often confused with psychotic behavior, but these are actually two very different things. A psychotic person is more prone to violence and overt aggression because they have little self-control and no regard for consequence. Meanwhile a psychopath is well aware of his or her actions and their possible consequences, so they display more subtle, but equally destructive violent behavior. The actions of a cunning psychopath can actually be far more destructive than that of a person who is psychotically deranged, because they are better able to conceal mental instability, thus allowing them to impact more victims over greater periods of time without getting caught.

Psychopaths are known to be dishonest, manipulative, and impulsive, and they have a completely different thought process then the rest of society. Most of us make our decisions with the wellbeing of other people in mind while, psychopaths are not only incapable of doing this, but they actually realize this fact and see their cold mentality as an advantage that they have over their peers. They actually view empathy as a weakness and with this perspective they manipulate people by playing on their natural concern for others. Psychopaths never accept responsibility for their cruel actions and always blame others, especially their victims, to further justify the negative situations that they have created.

Psychopaths make up a very small percentage of the human population but they come from various walks of life and many times their ruthless and manipulative disposition lands them in positions of great power. In reality the only thing that separates a serial killer from a wartime tyrant or Wall Street robber baron is social status, opportunity and intellectual capabilities. Unfortunately it is actually quite common for psychopaths to come into positions of power simply due to the fact that they are obsessed with dominating their peers and will stop at nothing to get what they want.

It is so typical for our "leaders" to be manipulative, deceitful, callous and ruthless that most people actually expect this kind of behavior from a politician or aristocrat. Yet these are the very personality traits that characterize the most violent and dangerous element in our society, so this means that

74

psychopathic behavior is actually accepted simply because it is being exhibited by those with authority. To make matters worse, the general public actually begins to mimic the psychopathic behavior displayed by their "leaders", since it has been established as acceptable. This is why our values are demoralized and twisted, because they have been established by control freak rulers, based on their psychopathic worldviews. They make sure that their perception of reality is the dominant view within the culture, so they can use that culture to impose their will on the general population.

Only a deranged person with no empathy for other human beings would take place in starting wars, carrying out genocide or neglecting suffering people, but these are the kind of things that our so called "leaders" do on a regular basis. Yet, unfortunately many of these acts are carried out through a proxy such as a government or corporation. In other words, these psychopaths hide behind a group or organization and basically say "*I am committing all of these horrors on behalf of this group of people and if you want to come after me then you have to get through them first*". Many people on both sides are convinced by this argument, even those who are being used as human shields. In the case of America, the American people are convinced that their "leaders" are carrying out wars of conquest in their best interest, when in reality they are being used as workhorses, scapegoats and political pawns. Sadly, the insanity doesn't end with political and social violence, many of these aristocrats lead extremely depraved private lives that are hidden from the mainstream culture. Some of the things they do are so downright careless and sick that in today's connected world their deranged behavior is starting to see the light of day.

The most common trait that psychopathic elites share is sexual predatory behavior. There have been countless stories that have surfaced in recent memory where some of the most powerful people in the world are caught up in a rape case, human trafficking ring or child prostitution racket. The most recent and high profile rape case involving a member of the

75

aristocracy occurred in the spring of 2011 when the chief of the International Monetary Fund, Dominique Strauss-Kahn was charged with sexually assaulting a hotel maid while he was staying in New York. When the story broke, women from all over the world came forward with similar stories about Kahn, saying that it was dangerous to be alone in a room with him. Aristocrats like Kahn are so arrogant because most of the time they suffer no consequences for their depraved actions, even when they are caught.

A perfect example of this came less than a year before Kahn's now infamous hotel maid encounter, when British banker and close friend of the royal family, Jeffrey Epstein got off with a 13 month sentence after being convicted of sex crimes including pedophilia. Conchita Sarnoff writing for the online newspaper "The Daily Beast" explained the horrific background of Epstein's sex crimes. According to her article "*Some of the most shocking allegations against Epstein surfaced only after the conclusion of an FBI probe, in civil suits brought by his victims: for example, the claim those three 12-year-old French girls were delivered to him as a birthday present. But the feds did identify roughly 40 young women, most of them underage at the time, who described being lured to Epstein's Palm Beach home on the pretense of giving a "massage" for money, then pressured into various sex acts, as well as the "Balkan sex slave" Epstein allegedly boasted of purchasing from her family when she was just 14. More recently, a big cash payment from Mail on Sunday coaxed one of Epstein's main accusers out of anonymity to describe what she claims were her years as a teenage sex toy. This victim, Virginia Roberts, produced a photo of her with Prince Andrew in 2001 and reported that Epstein paid her $15,000 to meet the prince. Then 17 years old, she claims that she was abused by Epstein and "loaned" to his friends from the age of 15.*"

After hiring some of the best lawyers in the world and using ruthless witness intimidation tactics, Jeffrey Epstein was able to escape any serious charges like so many others in his position.

Epstein was closely connected with the British royal family who also has a scandalous history in human trafficking. Recently, one of the royal family's victims, William Arnold Combes, was able to get away from the situation and tell the world about the horrors he was subject to by some of the world's most powerful people.

The human trafficking industry is so elusive and difficult to prosecute because trials are shut down, cases are dropped or the investigation is completely diverted whenever evidence surfaces that implicates the aristocracy, which happens more often than not. The elite has been organizing and profiting from the human slave trade for many centuries, so it really doesn't take a stretch of the imagination to consider that they are still behind the business today, especially when the evidence is constantly implicating them. There are almost too many cases to list in which high profile public figures or organizations were accused in pedophilia or human trafficking cases, but quickly dodged any prosecution or public scrutiny due to their control of the legal system and media. The rampant child molestation accusations that have been brought upon catholic priests are by far the most obvious examples of how people in positions of power claim the moral high ground while at the same time leading a predatory lifestyle.

There have been many cases in recent memory where establishment figures have been caught up in child prostitution rings, but quickly had the story swept under the rug. One such case was on June 29 1989, when the Washington Times' Paul M. Rodriguez and George Archibald reported on a Washington D.C. prostitution ring that had intimate connections with the White House and President George H.W. Bush. It was suspected that this was connected with the Franklin prostitution ring that was being exposed at the same time, in a different part of the country. That story involved the manager of the Franklin Community Federal Credit Union in Nebraska. His name was Lawrence "Larry" King and he was also a prominent republican politician. Various unconnected victims accused him of transporting them around the country to be used as sex slaves for politicians. When the accusations finally came to light, the victims were railroaded out of court and threatened into recanting their statements, thus making themselves guilty of perjury in the process. This was unfortunately enough to drop the case and actually send some of the victims to jail. The truth of the matter didn't come out until former Nebraska State Senator John DeCamp went back to reexamined the case and discovered that the accusations were indeed true.

Human trafficking is an industry of the ruling class, it always has been. Your average blue collar, white collar people aren't buying slaves, and they certainly aren't selling them either! This is still very much a part of western culture, even companies with major government contacts have been accused of organizing full scale slave rings. These companies have not only been protected by their governments, but they were also able to keep the contracts and subsidies that they had prior to the accusations.

Some of the world's largest multinational corporations such as DynCorp and Halliburton were exposed as major players in the global human trafficking market. These companies did not work alone, but cooperated with each other through various subsidiaries and had the luxury of government protection. When suspicion was brought upon these companies it was swept under the rug by government officials. Even high ranking members of the establishment such as Donald Rumsfeld were implicit in covering up this scandal. On March 11th 2005, he was questioned by Congresswoman Cynthia McKinney and he admitted on the record that the allegations did have credibility, but he pushed the blame off onto a few "rogue" employees. He used the "few bad apples" line that the government always dishes out when they are caught up in scandal. Although Rumsfeld and other high ranking officials claimed that they would look into the situation, they actually prevented any serious investigations from taking place. This happens every day, even organizations like the UN and NATO have come under fire for running slave rings out of third world countries when they are on "peacekeeping missions"

The things I have just discussed are absolutely crazy and depraved, but they are sadly true, and what I'm about to talk about is actually even more disturbing. What is more cruel and disgusting than human trafficking? I'm talking of course about, human sacrifice, mass murder and cannibalism. I know it sounds too outrageous to be true, but these horrific practices have been commonplace among aristocrats in various different cultures throughout history. In most modern cultures, mass murder and human sacrifice still takes place out in the open under the cover of warfare, while cannibalism also still takes place but behind closed doors. It is only in the past few hundred years that the practice of cannibalism among royals was forced underground. In Europe around the time of the American Revolution "corpse medicine" was very popular among the ruling class, Charles II even brewed his own. Today this aspect of royal life has been kept secret, but many other bizarre practices of the elite have been exposed to the public. Strange rituals have been infiltrated and videotaped at prestigious country clubs such as "The Bohemian Grove".

For most people this information is a lot to take in and may be very hard to believe because it is just so sick and extreme. This level of insanity and cruelty is very hard for most people to understand, because most people are kind hearted individuals that wouldn't like to see anyone get hurt. The majority of the general public also believes the great myth that people in authority are to be trusted and can do no wrong. If history has shown us anything, it shows us that power makes people do very crazy and illogical things, pretty much across the board. When people are in positions of power and have authority over others it literally changes their whole psychological process and seems to make them far less empathetic than they were before they attained their power. Authority seems to make it easier for people to justify or rationalize immoral actions and it tends to create a mentality in which the lives of others are less valuable.

Deborah Gruenfeld, a psychologist at the Stanford Business School did a study that analyzed over 1,000 decisions made by the United States Supreme Court between 1953 and 1993. She found that as the judges ascended the power structure of the court, or became part of a majority coalition, their written opinions became vague and they also became less considerate of outside perspectives. Many psychologists refer to this phenomena as "the paradox of power" and its characteristics are visible anywhere you find authority. That's not to say that every person who ever had authority over someone else was a pedophile and a cannibal, that's only in very extreme cases. There are many good people involved in the establishment who do genuinely believe that they are doing the right thing, but unfortunately most days they are taking orders from complete lunatics.

Every president, chairmen of the Federal Reserve, corporate CEO, decorated general and many other agents of the aristocracy lead lifestyles of violence and deceit with a total lack of empathy for the people whose lives are negatively impacted by their actions. Yet when someone speaks out against the cruelty of these traditions they are the ones who are written off as mentally unstable. Sanity is not something that should be judged by observing ones thoughts or opinions, rather it should be judged by observing their actions. If ones actions are detrimental to the wellbeing of others and there are no signs of remorse then there is a pretty good chance that you are dealing with a person who is mentally unsound. On the other hand just because someone is unusual, or different doesn't mean that they are insane, as long as they are still peaceful in their interactions.

"Evolution has exponential timing. It'll be half as long 'til the next breakthrough that blows our mind. It's up to people to brave on with experimentation. Move forth the species by using our imagination." – 311 (Rock/Reggae Group) [0]

18. Future physics

Many of us who have been brought up in the technological age of satellites and wireless communication, take for granted the impossible feats that are taking place right before our eyes every day. In just a few generations our knowledge of the universe has grown at a pace never seen before in the history of humankind. This new knowledge has allowed us to do things which were unthinkable just a short time ago. If someone 50 years ago were to be shown today's cutting edge technology, it would appear to them as magic.

As intelligent of a species that humans are, it is surprising to see how arrogant they can be when it comes to the limits of their own knowledge. Yet, time after time our theories about the nature of existence are proven wrong by those who come after us. Even brilliant scientists in the past that were bold enough to call something "impossible", were eventually proven wrong. In 1825 the philosopher Auguste Comte declared in his "course de philosophie" that it was impossible to determine what the stars were made of. Lord Kelvin, the prominent Victorian scientist who is buried next to Sir Isaac Newton insisted that airplanes, X rays and radio were absolutely impossible.

Many life changing technological advances have been made possible by complex mathematics and a new revolutionary field of science called "quantum physics". Quantum physics represents a new and more imaginative era in scientific research. Science as we know it at the beginning of the 21st century is a very materialistic and close minded institution. As a result of hundreds of years of religious oppression, the scientific community would immediately dismiss any kind of paranormal or spiritual answers to their questions. This kind of arrogant

81

approach is certainly not scientific or unbiased. In the long battle of wits against the Catholic Church, the scientific community had become exactly what they were trying to destroy. Science has become a dogmatic, mind imprisoning institution itself. Luckily, quantum physics has forced the mainstream scientific dialogue to be somewhat less rigid, but that's not to say that the scientific establishment isn't still a completely dogmatic and mind imprisoning institution to today, even with the recent addition of quantum physics.

It is true science has brought us many great things, and the scientific method specifically has helped us decode our reality in unimaginable ways. However, the direction of scientific progress and research has been misdirected and tightly controlled by the ruling class. This is the point that I am making, I am in no way attacking science itself or the scientific method. The Soviet government in Russia used falsified "science" on a regular basis as a means of distorting reality and controlling the public discourse. This is still happening in Russia today but to a lesser degree, and it is definitely happening in the west at an ever increasing rate. This does not mean that that there is something wrong with science, it just means that science can be used as a weapon of oppression and control when it is directed by such a small sect of society.

There are a lot of positives though, the discoveries within Quantum Physics put serious doubt on the *"if I can't physically touch it, it doesn't exist"* philosophy taken on by conventional science. String Theory, The Uncertainty Principal and studies involving extremely small atoms and very complicated mathematics have torn down a lot of the barriers that were separating conventional science from a clear picture of reality. Through these studies we have learned that there is an endless world of life and energy that is not detectable by our 5 senses. Quantum physics show us that the world is far more complex and unpredictable then conventional science believed it to be.

"Our senses enable us to perceive only a minute portion of the outside world. Our hearing extends to a small distance. Our sight is impeded by intervening bodies and shadows. To know each other we must reach beyond the sphere of our sense perceptions." - Nikola Tesla (Inventor)

19. Positive Vibrations

Modern science has finally begun to catch up with the sacred knowledge that was possessed by the ancients thousands of years ago. Ancient people may not have had the advanced technology that we do today but they had a far greater understanding of consciousness, energy fields, astrology and other mysteries of the natural world. Indigenous Cultures were aware that there are many invisible layers of our existence that are not detectable by our 5 senses, as we have recently been shown through the discovery of atoms, germs and energy. Just a few hundred years ago, most of these ideas would have come across as either completely insane or would have been labeled as black magic. Through quantum Physics we have learned that energy waves of all kinds play a huge role in how the world around us works. We have also learned that our consciousness has a profound impact on how our reality unfolds. The idea of "waves" transmitting information is actually very common in modern science. Our technological society is made possible by invisible vibrations such as radio waves, or satellite transmissions, for example. The room that you are sitting in right now is filled with many different vibrations or "waves". Some of these vibrations are synthetic and come from machines that our species have created, then others come from the human consciousness. The natural "Vibes" that occur as a result of consciousness travel from person to person in waves, just as WIFI waves travel from transmitter to transmitter.

Brain waves are organic vibrations that originate in our psyche and are constantly being projected out to the universe. It is these brainwaves that are responsible for mysterious phenomena like telepathy. Telepathy is not reserved for

83

psychics and gurus, every human being is capable of telepathy. It is simply the transmission of signals from one consciousness to another. Have you ever thought about someone then right away got a phone call or email from that person? Has someone ever taken the words right out of your mouth when the words weren't even relevant to the conversation?

These situations come up often in most of our day to day lives and are made possible by the sending and receiving of brain waves. Right now our world is in danger because too many people are operating on a low vibrational frequency, it is these negative vibrations that are responsible for the destructive forces we see around us. The power to manifest a better reality is hidden within every soul, but in order to uncover that potential one must be operating on a higher vibrational frequency. This higher frequency can be achieved by living in accordance with natural law and making a positive impact on the world around you.

"There is a spiritual obligation, there is a task to be done. It is not, however, something as simple as following a set of somebody else's rules". -
Terence McKenna

Section 4

Shamanism

"Prohibition will work great injury to the cause of temperance. It is a species of intemperance within itself, for it goes beyond the bounds of reason in that it attempts to control a man's appetite by legislation, and makes a crime out of things that are not crimes." -Abraham Lincoln (Politician) [0]

20. The Psychedelic Inquisition

It is a matter of provable fact that psychedelics are the safest compounds within the modern drug culture. The strongest hallucinogen known to man dimethyltryptamine, is actually less damaging to the human body than Americas favorite fix, caffeine. Many substances that are deeply embedded in American culture such as alcohol, caffeine, nicotine or pharmaceutical narcotics are in fact toxins, while psychedelic compounds are actually physically benign and many times already occur naturally in human metabolism. What this means is that the chemicals which make psychedelics do what they do are actually naturally occurring compounds that are chemically suited for your body.

Study after study confirms the safety and natural composition of these substances, yet psychedelics are vilified in our media, politics and other cultural institutions. This massive public smear campaign exists because the establishment fears the impact that psychedelics would have on the materialistic society that keeps them rich and powerful. You see, these drugs are not dangerous to the individual or the community, but they make us seek our own answers about the world around us, instead of swallowing the line of garbage that we have been fed by the establishment. Psychedelics will break down the personal ego and cultural barriers that our materialistic society has corrupted us with and will make negative cultural norms such as war, poverty and oppression seem completely insane. This kind of social clarity could be very dangerous for the establishment and their control system, which is why they insist that these substances are bad and cannot be introduced into society.

The government isn't against all drugs, they shove drugs down

86

your throat every day through your food, drinking water, prescriptions and the street drugs that they smuggle into the country via the CIA. What the government is against is the practice of shamanism, the oldest religion in the world which connects the practitioner to his environment and his fellow human beings. Shamanism is a possible antidote for the cultural poison that plagues this age. Whether it is through meditation, psychedelic journeying or spiritual healing, the practice of shamanism can very quickly free a person from the mental restrictions of a dominating culture.

Terrence McKenna, one of the frontrunners of the modern psychedelic age, understood the nature of this situation very well and toured around the world to speak with audiences about the wonders of psychedelic shamanism. In one of his lectures, Terrence articulated the psychedelic inquisition quite well by saying "*all cultures are involved in the culture game and psychedelics transcend the culture game, and whether you're a citizen of Jerusalem, a Tokyo stock broker or a tribal islander when you take psychedelic substances your cultural values will suddenly be much more relativistically revealed to you. And that is political dynamite. Psychedelics challenge the assumptions of any cultural or political system and that makes them dangerous to every culture or political system. So if there's anything a Marxist dictatorship, a high tech industrial democracy or a theocracy, they can all get together on one thing which is that psychedelic drugs are a knife poised at the heart of community values, well this is just simply nonsense and all the reasons brought forth are a red herring. Psychedelics are among the safest substances known for human ingestion. Considering the depth of their impact on human mental functioning the fact that you pick yourself up 6-8 hours later and go on about your business with an expanded point of view is quite remarkable.*"[1]

McKenna's point is highlighted in recent American history by the counter culture explosion of the 1960s. Psychedelic research began in the late 1950s and became a regular part of the youth culture by the mid-1960s. The explosion of psychedelic use interestingly coincides with the explosion of cultural freedom and antiestablishment sentiments of that decade. It is for this reason that the American government took quick action to make these substances illegal and to vilify them in the public arena. Laws were passed which imposed strict penalties on anyone involved in psychedelic use, manufacture or even scientific study. Yea that's right, psychedelic drugs are actually the only subject that science is almost completely forbidden to explore, only recently have any serious studies into psychedelics been able to take place. The establishment knew that the psychedelic movement was a threat to their control system, and that if enough of the population were exposed to this experience then their whole system would be in jeopardy. If psychedelics were tolerated and further explored they knew that they would see more counter culture movements, protests and overall more questions on their ill-gotten authority.

Luckily there have been some brave researchers over the years. Psychiatrist Dr. John Halpern, of Harvard medical school did a study of people with cluster headaches and discovered that the majority of patients who took LSD or psilocybin noticed a drastic reduction in their pain. In the past few years more and more of these studies have developed all over the world, researching the possible therapeutic uses for psychedelic compounds. From Rick Strassman's experiments into consciousness and DMT to the many other experiments that have conclusively shown LSD and Psilocybin to be beneficial for people with anxiety, substance abuse problems and troubles with creativity. Yet despite the mounting evidence that they can be used for positive means, research into psychedelics has remained extremely taboo in most mainstream circles. And remember, the mainstream isn't just completely disregarding all this scientific and anecdotal evidence, but they are also completely ignoring the recent history of psychedelics influencing important technological breakthroughs.

Without the creative application of psychedelic drugs it is very possible that the personal computer never would have been invented and DNA may have never been discovered. This isn't rumor or speculation, Steve Jobs, the mind behind the first Apple computers, ipods, iphones and other revolutionary inventions, has frequently said that his experience with psychedelics were among the most important events in his life. Steve Jobs wasn't the only technological pioneer who was using psychedelics to boost creativity, Douglas Englebart, the inventor of the computer mouse was also a psychedelic user. Likewise, Francis Crick, the scientist credited with discovering DNA was taking psychedelic drugs when he made his groundbreaking revelation. Years later, another scientist and LSD user by the name of Kary Mullis advanced our knowledge of DNA even further with the development of the polymerase chain reaction (PCR) technique, a process that made it possible for scientists to better study how DNA works.

These psychedelic compounds are so important that we cannot let them be suppressed in the extreme manner that we see in western culture. Psychedelics offer us a glimpse into the final frontier of humanity, the consciousness. With these substances we can explore the human imagination for profound insight that will help us in our own personal lives and the bigger picture as well. We must push for new legitimate scientific research into the therapeutic uses for these drugs. These studies will prove, as they have in the past, that psychedelic compounds have many medical and spiritual uses that are necessary for our species to continue the evolution of our consciousness.

QUOTE SOURCES AND SUGGESTED READING
[0] Abraham Lincoln (1809–1865), U.S. president. Speech, December 18, 1840, to the Illinois House of Representatives.
[1] Terrence McKenna - Personal Collection of Recorded Lectures

"This is my simple religion. There is no need for temples; no need for complicated philosophy. Our own brain, our own heart is our temple; the philosophy is kindness." - Dalai Lama (Buddhist Monk) [0]

21. Why Shamanism?

Shamanism may be a taboo subject in today's society, but it was actually the world's first religion. Before royal oligarchies gave spirituality a strict set of rules and guidelines, indigenous cultures had a much more personal and open religious tradition. Through shamanism these cultures were able to advance their spiritual knowledge with every age that passed, because each generation would play an active role in building their culture's understanding of the universe. This happens much like our scientific research is conducted today, generation after generation puts in work to slowly chip away at the mysteries that they are trying to uncover. Shamanism does the same thing but it deals with exploring the realm of the spirit, instead of the material realm which science deals in. Generations worth of scientific research has allowed our species to create incredible technology, but our spiritual growth seems absolutely crippled due to lack of exploration.

What has happened in the modern world in the past few thousand years is that the exploration into the spirit realm has ended. The religious institutions that have had control of the spiritual dialogue for the past few millennia have made any kind of research into these realms completely forbidden. They tell us that no new questions need to be asked because they already have all the answers, and to ask any questions is heresy. It is this kind of strict stubbornness and arrogance that has caused so much of our generation to be completely uninterested in spirituality at all. The fact that these institutions are trying to keep us from asking questions and preventing us from thinking philosophically should tell us that they are not to be trusted. They do not want us to study these matters because it could threaten their political power and influence. This should come as no surprise, because let's face it, religious institutions are and always have been power and capital seeking political organizations that have very little honest interest in spirituality.

Shamanism is different from our modern religious institutions because there is no agenda or hierarchy. There are no cloaked figures to tell you that you are not worthy and then take your money. There is no inquisition to condemn you to death if you happen to disagree with the metaphysical conclusion that other people have come to. There are no politics or heretics either, no one is going to benefit from you financially or tell you how to think. No one is going to call you evil and demand that you be killed because you don't comply with their edicts. Shamanism is less of a belief system and more of an advanced form of philosophy. Belief systems many times claim to have every single correct answer in the universe, and this approach can have a negative impact on people and society. If people really believe that there are no intellectual frontiers then they will stop looking and stop questioning, and when this happens they are cutting themselves short. Any major human advancement has come from individuals trying to expand the collective pool of knowledge. Not by recycling information that has been in constant circulation for centuries and handed down by authoritarians.

Life is a forever unraveling mystery, every time a question about our universe is answered, ten more pop up in its place. Even if someone were to live for a hundred years in daily research and meditation they will still have questions, there will still be more left to uncover. Every great teacher that has walked this earth has recognized the infinite mystery of life. This is the kind of attitude that is necessary to investigate the spirit world through shamanism. This path will not give you a prepackaged set of ideals and convictions wrapped with a bow and carried by a savior. You will be forced to create your own belief structure that will change every day with every new situation you encounter. Really it shouldn't even have a name, the fact that I even call it shamanism is merely because I have to attach a term to the philosophy to be able to articulate the idea. Spirituality is a personal, individual thing that should be a mutual respect and interest between everyone, instead of a division or a barrier.

The fact that various groups of aristocrats from different cultural backgrounds have managed to stamp a copyright on spirituality is itself a complete sacrilege. Everyone should have their own religion that they ponder on and share with one another. The good ideas would be shared more often and become more popular while the bad ideas would dwindle off pretty easily. The best ideas would be passed along to the next generation to be changed and molded based on whatever new information came in during their lifetime. This would essentially be a constantly changing collective religion that was actively being built by everyone in the society. This is the kind of social structure that a shamanic culture would have. This would eliminate a lot of the spiritual segregation that is caused by modern religion because participants are encouraged to learn from one another instead of look down on one another. If people were actually talking to each other philosophically on a regular basis and reaching into the spirit realm using meditation and psychedelics we would be able to achieve the same kind of breakthroughs in the spirit realm that we have in the material realm, and we would be much closer to peace.

"The mind is constantly talking. If the inner talk can drop even for a single moment you will be able to have a glimpse of no-mind. That's what meditation is all about. The state of no-mind is the right state. It is your state." - Osho (Spiritual Philosopher) [0]

22. Meditation

The art of meditation dates back many thousands of years, and is just as natural as dreaming. Throughout history, the practice of meditation has had a profound impact on the intellectual and spiritual growth of billions. Even in today's materialistic societies many people still meditate. A 2005 Newsweek study showed that one in three adults meditate on a daily basis. Yet in our modern institutions of control like the education system or the media we see a very sarcastic and even negative attitude towards meditation. Meditation is presented by the establishment as a sort of tribal ritual that has no place in the so called "civilized" world. Many people buy into this mentality not knowing what meditation is and go through their whole life with an unclear perspective of their own consciousness.

Meditation is a much simpler and more natural act then most people realize and can be extremely therapeutic in the fast paced, high stress world we are living in. It is simply the act of taking personal time to relax, focusing your attention and clearing your mind, no "witchcraft" or "voodoo" involved. Anyone that has counted sheep to fall asleep before has meditated. All that you have to do is set aside some time to yourself, in a quiet comfortable area, somewhere away from distraction. Once you have found this place, sit or lay down in a comfortable position. The traditional lotus posture seen in most kung-fu movies works for a lot of people, but many find that uncomfortable and prefer laying down or sitting in a different posture. As long as you're comfortable that's all that matters. Now instead of thinking about the daily dramas or your aspirations just put your mind at ease. This may be difficult for you at first, some find it helpful to count their breaths or repeat meaningful phrases, this can help you center your focus.

That is really all that you have to do to get started. There are many techniques which go beyond this to bring the practitioner into deeper states of meditation and there is a lot of free material out there that help teach these techniques. OHSO is perhaps one of the most well-known meditation experts of our time. He has his own "meditation resort" in India where people visit from all over the world to learn the inner workings of meditation. He has written many books and has a very informative website that I would highly recommend (osho.com). If meditation is an idea that is foreign to you then it is really important to look into it and do some research for yourself. There are countless different techniques that work for different people and which technique works for you is a very personal thing. So it is best for you to discover your own style of meditation using the techniques that you are most comfortable with.

There are many advantages to meditation, which are now being confirmed by scientific studies. We have learned through scientific research that meditation can relieve pain, enhance creativity, relieve stress and boost immune systems. In 1998, a breakthrough study published in the Journal of the American Medical Association, by a DR. Dean Ornish showed that meditation can actually reverse heart disease. This study lasted for over 5 years and involved various control groups that all had coronary artery disease, and only one of these groups practiced meditation. Amazingly the group that practiced meditation had actually managed to reverse the effects of the illness.

Meditation can also help to heal mental disturbances and correct psychological issues. In 2006 a doctor by the name of Ron Cavanaugh started a meditation program at Donaldson high security prison in Alabama. His course was called "Dhamma Brothers" and included a 10 day session in which inmates refrained from speaking and took on 100 full hours of meditation during the session. The results of this program were profound and greatly improved the lives and attitudes of the inmates. You can feel the sincerity in their words. One man named Omar

Rahman says *"For the first time, I could observe my pain and grief. I felt a tear fall. Then something broke, and I couldn't stop sobbing. I found myself in a terrain where I had always wanted to be, but never had a map. I found myself in the inner landscape, and now I had some direction."*

Another man named Edward Johnson says *"On the third day of meditation, I began to feel calm. And then and there, for the first time in my life, I was really ready to deal with me. A lot of guys was afraid to deal with Big Ed. And now I was ready to take him on, right there on that meditation mat."* Yet another Dhamma brother Benjamin "OB" Oryang says *"Well, it is over. But the vibrations are still here. The memories of those last 10 days on the mat, the experiential wisdom which was gained, and all the prospects of peace which were found here, that is always going to linger."* Many of the inmates said that they wished that they only would have known about meditation before they made the decisions that landed them in prison.

Even in light of all the positive findings that would encourage meditation, the subject is still approached with sarcasm and ignorance in most mainstream circles. This taboo exists because meditation is a path toward the spirit realm and the far reaches of the human imagination. This whole process is a great threat to the established cultural institutions because it opens a connection to deeper levels of the psyche. The establishment wants the public to be cut off from their higher realms of consciousness. These higher realms of consciousness actually have the capability of showing people the insanity of the status quo. These realms also give people the insight and the tools to devise real solutions to the problems created by the establishment. This is the same reason why they made psychedelic drugs illegal, but they cannot outlaw meditation like they did psychedelics, so instead they create social taboos to discourage people from practicing it. Just as they have dumbed down our education and passed legislation to keep us away from psychedelics, they have created social stigmas to discourage us from reaching meditative states of consciousness.

95

"I think psychedelics play a major part in what we do, but having said that, I feel that if somebody's going to experiment with those things they really need to educate themselves about them. People just taking the chemicals and diving in without having any kind of preparation about what they're about to experience tend to have no frame of reference, so they're missing everything flying by and all these new perspectives. It's just a waste. They reach a little bit of spiritual enlightenment, but they end up going, 'Well, now I need that drug to get back there again.' The trick is to use the drugs once to get there, and maybe spend the next ten years trying to get back there without the drug." - Maynard James Kennan (Rock Musician of TOOL) [0]

23. Responsible Shamanism in the 21st Century

Long before the days of western medicine and pharmacists sponsored by multibillion dollar drug companies, indigenous cultures had a sacred understanding of the plants that shaped our evolution. The knowledge that ancient cultures had about the complexity of our reality make our current spiritual conceptions look primitive at best. It was this deep knowledge and understanding of the universe which led these ancient tribes towards the path of shamanism. Meditation, yoga, psychoactive plants, herbs and various philosophical traditions allowed indigenous people to look far beyond the limits of our conventional wisdom. Shamanic cultures oftentimes held rituals where dancing, storytelling and psychedelic intoxication took place, but there was a sacred respect for the psychoactive plants and the earth from which they came. Many of these tribes still exist today and practice these methods in various places throughout the world, although their numbers are far less due to the Indigenous genocide that has been going on since the Middle Ages.

The Traditional indigenous perspective of psychedelics is drastically different from the current western view. Due to the overindulgent lifestyle that is prevalent in the west, psychedelics are grossly misunderstood throughout most of the so-called "civilized" world. In modern western cultures intoxication is not about connecting with the depths of consciousness, instead it is seen as a method of sedation, a way to escape the troubles of life. Our culture teaches us from a very young age that there is time for work and time for play, and most of us work so hard throughout the week, that come Friday we just want to forget everything before it all starts over again on Monday. When work time is over, westerners play hard and they usually put their bodies through a great deal of torment in the process. The substances available to most westerners are far more damaging to the mind, body and spirit than most shamanic psychedelics and they are also far more addictive.

Alcohol and Tobacco companies spend billions of dollars every year to target their future customers, these future customers being impressionable kids. If there was ever such a thing as a gateway drug, alcohol and tobacco would be the primary drugs in that category, they are widely accepted, easily available and some of the leading causes of death and social problems in this country today. These drugs in their modern forms don't just diminish ones consciousness, but are also extremely addictive and will build up a habit of abuse that will go unchecked because of the ignorant acceptance of these substances by the general population. These substances are largely responsible for misconceptions about shamanism because they teach entire civilizations that altered states of consciousness are "playgrounds", and as a result people have absolutely no respect for the psychedelic experience. Today, many see the psychedelic experience as just another high, another variation of uppers, downers, whatever's and this couldn't be farther from the truth. Indigenous cultures understood that their ancestor's souls were somehow imprinted into the psychedelic experience, so they treated these altered states with great care and dignity. I'm not trying to attack anyone who might enjoy alcohol or tobacco products, but it is a fact that their excessive use is encouraged in our society and they are far more damaging to body and mind than any psychedelic.

The overindulgent nature of a consumerist culture typically results in a lack of respect for many sacred things, including the psychedelic experience. Beginning with the discovery of LSD and reemergence of psilocybin in the later part of the 20th century, the sheltered youth of America began to handle psychedelic drugs much like they handled a bottle of whisky. Children that grew up with shopping malls, liquor stores, infomercials and Marlboro now have access to the shaman's tools, but they do not have access to the shaman's teachings, so it is near impossible for them to use these tools correctly and have the proper respect for their power. During the cultural revolutions of the 1960s this is exactly what happened, suburban teenagers were using psychedelics to "get high" and oftentimes were taught a very harsh lesson in the process. The youth of this generation entered the psychedelic realm expecting a front row seat at a Hollywood movie, but what they got was a rude awakening. That rude awakening was a conscious flow of ideas that told them things that their culture did not prepare them for, a lot of times they were told things about themselves and their society that their ego did not want to hear. Without the Shaman present to explain the lessons and to put what's going on into context, this kind of experience results in what is now days called a "bad trip".

Although his wares were free for all who sought after them, the shaman kept a very watchful eye over his stash. He was well aware that if someone without the proper knowledge and assistance were to go into the psychedelic experience blindly, it would be taken out of context and the whole village would have an interesting problem on their hands for the next few hours. Today things are unfortunately much different, young people have easy access to intoxicants and are given all the wrong information about them. Sure there may be laws and social taboos to keep young people away from intoxicants, but this only results in stimulating more curiosity. It isn't even all that difficult for young people to get illegal drugs, all that they have to do is go looking for long enough. Since psychedelics are outlawed their care and distribution responsibilities fall on the black market. Unlike the shaman, the black market has no interest in the people who are consuming their products. Whether it is legal or illegal intoxicants, they are easy to come by in the western world and overindulgence is encouraged either way.

There are pockets of various counter cultures in the west that have a more well-rounded understanding of shamanism than mainstream society does. Those who are in the rave and festival scenes are more familiar with psychedelics, but some of them still don't have a proper respect for the experience. This is because they have come from a materialistic consumer culture which teaches them that everything is a competition and reinforces that it is not important to take care of your body, mind and spirit. The same opportunity for discovery and expansion of consciousness that existed in the 60s & 70s is reemerging again today, but a lot of the same obstacles are still standing in the way.

There are still many who escape the mainstream to seek refuge in the counterculture, but in doing so they bring along a lot of the baggage that is associated with mainstream thinking. Most of us are introduced to intoxicants through drinking games, frat parties or other situations that encourage excessive drinking and drug use. The rave and festival scenes are intended to create a different kind of atmosphere, one of peace, freedom and creativity. Some who are brought up in a culture of gluttony are given personal freedom and feel that they are no longer required to be responsible for themselves, when in reality it is then actually much more important for them to be responsible for themselves.

In times of struggle the counter culture experiences explosions in popularity, because there are so many people who become fed up with the mainstream and seek out new ways of living so they can be more fulfilled personally. When these times of growth occur there is an excess of people who don't properly understand the meaning behind the events that they are attending and sometimes their irresponsibility can cause trouble

99

for the entire culture. Such is the case when a misinformed teenager goes overboard and hurts themselves at a show, like we saw in Los Angeles in 2010 at Electric Daisy Carnival. That was the biggest event in the US and it can no longer take place in the city of Los Angeles because overindulgence was causing a problem for the city and a concern for local parents. The victims in these situations aren't necessarily to blame, many of them don't even know what they are doing and were raised in a society that has taken away their ability to be responsible for themselves. Still, this is a serious issue that needs to be addressed or more people can be needlessly hurt.

Since the brain goes into overdrive when under the influence of psychedelics, it's important to enter the experience with a process of critical thinking so we can accurately decipher the messages contained within the psychedelic experience. When critical thinking is applied, there is no need for a shaman to be present, you become the shaman and are able to make proper sense of your experience. Within the psychedelic experience you will be subject to an onslaught of emotions, intuitions and opinions that you will never have any hope of understanding without some method of organizing and analyzing the incoming data. Establishing a clear goal for the experience and finding the appropriate setting are some extremely important steps for getting the most out of psychedelics. Setting is vital to having a good experience, if you are in a place that is going to make you feel uncomfortable or with people who aren't going to respect your state of mind, then you are setting yourself up for bad times. Keeping journals and records of experiences are also helpful when using psychedelics to figure out long and complex problems.

It is not my business or the business of anyone to tell you what to do with your body and what decisions to make in your life, but it is still important that people know how to take care of themselves. People should be free to do what they want but there are some general things that everyone should know in order to keep themselves safe. It is generally a bad idea to mix drugs with alcohol. It is important for people to understand that overindulgence and habitual use is not only dangerous but it also makes it impossible to get any kind of shamanic value out of the experience. Psychedelic drugs are tools, and just like any tool they can help us if we use them correctly, but they can also harm us if we misuse them.

Well, as I understand it, the main supporters (of prohibition) are beer companies and the pharmaceutical companies. I'd like them to show me the dead bodies from marijuana. But they can't, because there aren't any. Jack Herer (Activist) [0]

24. Marketing Illness and Addiction

In western society our school systems fail to educate, our businesses have corrupted our economy and our "elected" "representatives" don't represent the people that elect them. Everywhere that you find powerful cartels providing a public service you will also find policies that are extremely oppressive to the consumer. Energy companies have had the ability to break away from fossil fuels for decades, but continue using them because it is easier to manage and exploit a controlled commodity. So it should come as no surprise that the pharmaceutical industry has destroyed the nation's health and wellbeing, in order to provide themselves with steady flow of income.

Like many of the business issues we are facing today, the problem with the drug industry is that it is controlled by a government protected corporate cartel. This allows a select few mega corporations to dominate the market, preventing entrepreneurs from developing new products that could threaten this monopoly. Without having to worry about any kind of competition, this cartel can make their products as harmful and ineffective as they like. Thanks to government protections, they are able to make their products more addicting and less effective so they can create return customers and extend their profits. If a medication is effective in curing a patient then they won't continually use and purchase that drug because they will have no need to do so. However, if the drug is mediocre and has addictive properties then it will become a regular part of the patient's monthly budget.

This deceptive strategy proved to be quite lucrative so the drug companies launched a massive advertising campaign to peddle a wide variety of ineffective and unnecessary drugs to a trusting and ignorant public. This industry actually spends more money on advertising then they do on research and development every single year. That fact alone shows that they are more interested in making sales than producing a well-researched and effective drug. Today's television and radio commercial spots are dominated by advertisements for mediocre pharmaceuticals. Companies pay billions of dollars per year on advertising alone and their investment comes back many times over. This advertising budget includes "incentives" for personal care providers to overwrite prescriptions, or in other words bribes for doctors to sell more drugs.

The arrogance and carelessness of the pharmaceutical industry has had a detrimental effect on society since its inception. This industry is responsible for creating and marketing the most toxic substances that our species has ever seen. In the 19th century morphine and cocaine were being peddled by pharmacists as wonder drug cure all's. Patients were told that these drugs were not addictive if they were injected directly into the bloodstream. I know it sounds unbelievable, but this kind of stupidity actually passed for medical science less than 200 years ago. This act of ignorance resulted in widespread addiction all throughout America and Europe, because drugs are in fact more addictive and potent if they are injected.

A Scottish physician by the name of Alexander Wood was the first to inject morphine directly underneath the skin with the hypodermic syringe, almost immediately after it was invented. Ironically, his wife became the first needle addict and the first person in the western world to overdose and die from injected opiates. When morphine addiction finally became recognized as an issue, doctors rushed to find a cure for this problem, so they invented heroin. Wrong again doc! This creation was many times worse than morphine and spawned a drug problem more ferocious then any seen in the world. Sadly, even a century later doctors are still peddling toxic drugs containing amphetamines, opiates and other addictive chemicals.

The most over prescribed, unnecessary and problematic drugs on the market today are antidepressants, ADHD medication and opiate based painkillers. Clinical depression and attention deficit disorder are both fabricated conditions that were made up by the pharmaceutical industry to create a new market where they could push more of their dangerous and ineffective drugs. The medications that are currently on the market for these conditions have extremely harsh side effects and very low rates of success, yet they are still over prescribed by thousands of doctors.

People are depressed because they live in a society where injustice and exploitation run rampant, not because they are "sick and need medication". This medication is even known to make people feel more depressed and in extreme cases even lead to suicide or violent outbursts. Clinical ADHD is also a myth, children are supposed to be hyperactive, playful and disorderly, this is no "sickness". The drug companies wish to create a culture where everyone can be labeled with some kind of sickness that will require them to be on maintenance medication. On an even deeper level, the establishment promotes these drugs because it makes the population easier to maintain, especially if they are drugged from an early age.

Prescription painkillers are among the most abused narcotics in the United States. These drugs are just as addictive and harmful as the hardest street drugs, but because they are legal and prescribed by doctors, they are greatly underestimated by our society. This is what makes these drugs so dangerous, since they are somehow socially acceptable, many people ignore or overlook their addiction until it's become a serious problem. In most cases when someone finally faces their problem they go right back to the doctor that got them hooked on the drugs in the first place to ask for help. At that point they are actually given more drugs that are supposed to wean the patient from their original addiction. This is seen in the popular but ineffective methadone and suboxone programs, which are responsible for keeping millions of addicts dependent on synthetic drugs. Many of the drug programs in the United States are actually designed to keep people disempowered and dependent. People fighting addiction are told that they are helpless and have a "disease" which they will suffer with for their entire lives, regardless of their ability to overcome their current habitual drug use. This kind of rhetoric makes it more difficult for people to channel their will power and lays the foundation for future relapse.

The pharmaceutical industry has created a dependent pill popping generation that is riddled with addiction issues. People are taught from a very young age to over consume mass produced drugs at the slightest sign of physical or mental discomfort. While the medication that is available on the market is typically far less effective than a healthy diet, exercise and natural remedies. These options are never mentioned in mainstream circles because they would put the pharmaceutical monopoly in danger. However, due to a growing public distrust of the industry, many people are taking a more holistic approach to their healthcare.

In 2010 a consumer reports study showed that a staggering 80% of patients felt that their doctors were so influenced by the drug industry that they would deliberately write a drug prescription even if a better, safer, non-drug option was available. This blatant corruption has resulted in a renewed interest in herbal medicine, there are many cures and remedies waiting to be discovered deep in the rainforests. This is one of the many reasons why it is so important to preserve the world's rainforest, because they contain plants that can cure every ailment known to us. The solutions to the pathological threats that humanity faces lay within nature, not a corrupt multibillion dollar industry.

Our national drug is alcohol. We tend to regard the use any other drug with special horror. - William S. Burroughs [0]

25. Fundamentals of Firewater

Throughout the course of history, the human mind has been constantly sedated by alcohol. In our modern society this poison elixir is the only option that most people have in legally reaching an altered state of consciousness. Unfortunately, this altered state is a far lower realm of consciousness where confusion and aggression run rampant. It is this state of consciousness that the ruling class wants us to experience, because we are much weaker and don't think very deeply under the influence of alcohol. A weak and uncreative population is much easier to control and they are far less likely to complain about the unfair conditions that they are forced to experience on a day to day basis.

The alcohol issue is far more complicated than most people realize. In 2010 the "Centre for Crime and Justice Studies", based out of London, did some research to discover which drugs were the most harmful on an individual and the people around them. This study concluded that alcohol was the most damaging controlled substance in our society. Illegal poisons such as meth and heroin actually ranked just below alcohol, but showed to be close to equal in destructive potency. At the end of the list were psychedelics, they were found to be the least dangerous drugs in the study, ranked far below alcohol, tobacco and poisonous street drugs such as heroin or meth.

The findings in this British study only confirm what many of us already knew. The legal drugs are far more dangerous than the illegal ones! Why is this? Why do drugs like DMT, LSD or MDMA carry strict legal penalties while more harmful substances like alcohol and tobacco are available in every storefront? It has nothing to do with health and has everything to do with social control. They know that a person on alcohol may wrap their car around a tree, abuse their family and squander their paycheck.

106

Of course, this isn't the kind of behavior that is exhibited by all drinkers, but alcohol does increase the risk of violence, accidents or foolishness, that much we must admit. Oddly enough, this is exactly the kind of behavior that the establishment finds acceptable! These are the traits of a subservient consumer who needs to be told what to do in order to survive, or perhaps a citizen who causes enough trouble to keep the government in business. This is the kind of population that the aristocracy and the governments that they support are looking to create. It may sound kind of crazy, but this is how they stay in business.

On the other hand how will a person react after a shamanic experience with DMT? Maybe that person will feel a deeper connection to their true self and turn their back on the sick culture that they have fed. Maybe after someone has a profound experience on psychedelics they will be less likely to march off to war! Imagine, someone who does not want to take another human life! What a problem he has made for the establishment! It would be far easier to convince a regular alcohol user that war is somehow a good idea, as opposed to someone who uses psychedelics.

The "Fire Water" as the natives called it, took away their sense of spirit and allowed them to be easily manipulated by the conquering Europeans. To this day alcohol remains a serious problem for the few Native American communities that have not been eradicated by early Europeans or the US Government. In fact, this issue is commonplace in most native cultures that were colonized by the Europeans and Americans. In South Africa the situation is far more blatant under a policy known as the "DOP" system. This is a system of employment that developed during apartheid where native farm workers were actually paid in alcohol for their labor.

Overindulgence in alcohol can cause people to become tired, unimaginative and extremely easy to manipulate by the powers that be. The substance is also very addictive which serves to keep people in the same imprisoned state, until they are able to break the chains of addiction on their own. Due to the seemingly endless supply of revenue that this substance creates for the people that manufacture it, and the sedative properties that is has on the population, alcohol has been chosen as one of the favorite weapons of the ruling class.

From a young age we have seen our elders and our media set the stage for future alcohol use. While we have been taught to stay away from mind expanding psychedelics, the poison firewater remains a part of our culture leaving a nation completely helpless and sedated. There is nothing wrong with relaxing with some friends and enjoying some drinks, but when that happens don't lie to yourself and think that you aren't partaking in drug use. Alcohol is a drug just like any other and is actually one of the most dangerous and addictive drugs out there, so it should be treated as such despite its legality. If you're going to drink there's nothing wrong with that, but don't judge someone that decides to relax or party in a different way. It is possible to use alcohol responsibly, but the misconceptions about its effects on the body and mind in relation to other chemicals needs to be understood and came to terms with in our society.

"If the words "life, liberty and the pursuit of happiness" don't include the right to experiment with your own consciousness, then the Declaration of Independence isn't worth the hemp it was written on." - Terence McKenna (Philosopher) [0]

26. Marijuana: Miracle not Menace

Marijuana has been proven to be one of the safest drugs known to man, less harmful than alcohol or anything you will find in a pharmacy. This plant has been called a miracle drug by many and is quickly growing in popularity for its medicinal properties. Yet despite the growing evidence of the incredible advantages and benign nature of cannabis, there are powerful business and political interests that are very intent on keeping this drug illegal.

The system that incarcerates people for using marijuana is a multi-billion dollar industry. Politicians, law enforcement and prison developers all see great financial benefits from the prohibition of marijuana. These agencies as well as other government and corporate interests all share in the profits made from the seizure of drugs and cash, as well as the fines imposed on the victim for breaking said law. Police officers get bonuses for these arrests, politicians get campaign donations to keep this harmless substance illegal, prison developers get paid a cash amount for every human being that they put in a cage. This is a huge business, where the cash crop happens to be human lives.

The law enforcement system is its own unique scam as I cover in detail in another chapter, but there is also a long list of financial reasons behind the prohibition of this plant. The primary lobby groups you will find supporting laws that criminalize marijuana are alcohol companies, oil companies, tobacco companies, prison developers and pharmaceutical manufacturers. These companies are threatened by the many industrial and medicinal uses that the marijuana/hemp plant has. If marijuana were to be made legal, many of these industries would lose their monopolies because their products would no longer be necessary or practical for widespread use. A plant that can grow almost anywhere and is in completely limitless supply cannot be used to exploit people and is difficult to control, therefore it is not in their best interests for this plant to be legal.

We all know politicians don't really do what they believe in, they do what they are told and what they are paid to do. Every single piece of legislation that goes through our government has "special interest groups" on both sides of the argument. Whichever side is most "persuasive" or donates the most money to the politician is the side that ultimately decides whether the legislation passes or not.

The pharmaceutical drug industry spends an incredible amount of money to ensure that marijuana remains illegal. This is because marijuana is much safer and more effective than synthetic prescription drugs in treating a wide variety of illnesses. There are many conditions that marijuana can improve greatly without risk, even cancer. A study by Manuel Guzmán of Madrid Spain showed that THC, the active chemical in marijuana can actually inhibit tumor growth. Dr. Ethan Russo , a neurologist and world authority on medical cannabis explains the process in which THC fights cancer in this statement. *"Cancer occurs because cells become immortalized; they fail to heed normal signals to turn off growth. A normal function of remodeling in the body requires that cells die on cue. This is called apoptosis, or programmed cell death. That process fails to work in tumors. THC promotes its reappearance so that gliomas, leukemias, melanomas and other cell types will in fact heed the signals, stop dividing, and die. But, that is not all. The other way that tumors grow is by ensuring that they are nourished: they send out signals to promote angiogenesis, the growth of new blood vessels. Cannabinoids turn off these signals as well. It is truly incredible, and elegant."*

This extreme breakthrough has been known about by the establishment since at least 1974 when studies at the Medical College of Virginia showed the ability that THC had in fighting

110

cancer. The results of these tests were reported in the Washington Post on august 18th 1974 and then completely disappeared from the news due to a media blackout. Despite the media blackout many independent scientific investigations have been carried out over the past 20 years that reconfirm the healing power of cannabis. If these details were presented to the public, the pharmaceutical industry would lose billions of dollars.

The alcohol and tobacco industries have an obvious conflict of interest when it comes to marijuana prohibition. Alcohol and tobacco are Americas top vices and both of them are extremely addictive, unhealthy and honestly pretty repulsive when considering the natural cannabis plant as an alternative. These companies are well aware of the threat that marijuana legalization poses on their yearly earnings so they lobby for politicians to vote for prohibition just like many other industries have. There are a lot of corporations and government entities in addition to the ones I mentioned putting a lot of money through the government to keep the drug laws as they are. That includes the oil, cotton and paper industries all of which would lose their cash crops at the hands of industrialized hemp.

Marijuana can cure cancer, heal countless other physical ailments, reduce our dependence on oil based products and prescription pharmaceuticals. All research shows that this plant is not only harmless, but can be extremely beneficial to our environment and our society. Hemp was even used to clean up radiation after the Chernobyl disaster in 1986. The current social stigma against marijuana is only the result of the propaganda put forth by those industries that benefit financially from marijuana prohibition as well as the overarching control system that wishes to keep our minds enslaved. By exposing the corrupt nature of the drug laws and the system that is enforcing them we can shatter that unjust social stigma and have a fair and sensible dialogue regarding legalization.

Section 5

The Past

27. -Occult History and Nationalistic Folklore

28. -Powerful people commit crimes and lie to you about it…. This is no theory

29. -The Banking Backstory of Friday The 13th

30. -America Was Not Discovered, It Was Stolen

31. -The Nazi Agenda Reborn

32. -Darwinism, Eugenics and the Silent Genocide

"History will be kind to me for I intend to write it." - Sir Winston Churchill (Politician) [0]

27. Occult History and Nationalistic Folklore

Having an accurate view of history is extremely important in making sense of what's going on around the world today. Every situation that is taking place today is the result of something that happened in the past, and those past situations are the result of something that happened before that. This may seem very simple, but among the politicians and the general public there is no respect for the great lessons of history.

If there was a proper respect for the lessons that history has taught us, then most people's opinions about global events would change drastically. Without a clear picture of how we got here, it is completely impossible to figure out how to get to where we need to be, which is why everyone is so confused about the state of the world. Think back to our discussion on pragmatism while reading these next two chapters. It is extremely relevant because pragmatism basically insists that history and causation have no value whatsoever.

In school and in the media, history is generalized by random and mostly trivial stories. This results in a mainstream view of history, where there is a disconnected series of events that seem to take place for absolutely no reason. Many of the extremely important events in history that had a big impact on the world have been left completely out of the history books. This shortsighted historical dialogue in the public arena causes people to have a distorted vision of why things are the way they are. If you are going to see a movie and you arrive to the theater late and miss the beginning, then the middle and the end of the film will make no sense to you.

The history that is acknowledged by our schools, media and other social institutions is a very superficial and biased account of what actually happened. There are countless stories that

113

have been intentionally hidden from our view for many ages. These stories make up what many have called our "occult history", as the word "occult" means hidden.

When hidden information is revealed, the dots of the past are connected and history is no longer a confusing blur. If the occult history is the version of events that is factual and hidden, then the version of events that is false and presented to the general population through the media and education system should be considered "nationalistic folklore". This idea of nationalistic folklore goes back before the times of Plato, who used the phrase "noble lies" to describe the false reality that is presented to society by the ruling class. The purpose of a noble lie is to maintain social order and keep the working class in their place. This same idea was prevalent in Nazi Germany, only Hitler referred to the noble lie as "the big lie".

"Voting allows the people a say in how society works", "taxes are spent on public services, not war and bureaucratic budgets", "the government always acts in the best interest of the public", "the government cares about the public and is here to protect them" and "financial success is the only route to happiness".

These are just a few of the blatant noble lies that work to maintain the social structure of western civilization. Possibly one of the worst noble lies to infect our generation is the idea that *"there is no such thing as truth or morality"*. It does not take much investigation to discover that those statements are untrue, but due to intimidation, social engineering, peer pressure and other methods of coercion, the lies are never exposed so they continue to perpetuate.

Throughout the generations, the world has been constantly torn apart by war, poverty and corruption. The politicians tell us that we only have ourselves to blame for these hellish circumstances. We are told that we should hate and fear our neighbors, but our neighbors aren't to blame and neither are we. There are many times throughout history that we can look back on and see where

114

specific political organizations and financial dynasties are completely responsible for the chaotic world that we are seeing develop. To cover up their responsibility, these dynasties and organizations create nationalistic folklore in which they are the protectors of humanity, who no one can live without, when in reality the complete opposite is true.

With all the manipulation that takes place in shaping our view of the past it, is apparent that what has happened in history is still open to debate in many cases. It is also a widely accepted idea that those in power write history in a way that makes them seem honorable, and if that is true it would reaffirm that mainstream history is only one side of the story. The establishment is very open about the fact that they are in control of the public perception of reality. George W. Bush blatantly lied to the American public about Iraq developing weapons of mass destruction, and when news came to light that there were in fact no weapons of mass destruction. Bush simply accused anyone who criticized him of attempting to "revise history". During his presidency, while giving a speech about that very issue, Bush said *"Now there are some who would like to rewrite history; revisionist historians is what I like to call them"*[1]

He made this statement knowing full well that it did not match up with the facts that had recently been made public. This is because the facts are completely irrelevant to the establishment; the only version of events that is accepted in discussion is their side of the story. Karl Rove, one of the top aides in the Bush white house took this idea a step further when he described to a New York Times reporter how the establishment literally controls reality. The Reporter Ron Susskind happened to be critical of the dishonest Bush administration, and Rove responded by claiming that Susskind belonged to *"the reality-based community,"* which he defined as people who *"believe that solutions emerge from your judicious study of discernible reality. That's not the way the world really works anymore. We're an empire now, and when we act, we create our own reality. And while you're studying that reality—judiciously, as you will—we'll act again, creating other new realities, which you can study too, and that's how things will sort out. We're history's actors ... and you, all of you, will be left to just study what we do."* [2]

What Rove is saying here is that he and the rest of the establishment decide what reality is and what fiction is, using absolutely no logical process and basing none of their stories on verifiable facts.

Most Americans are extremely confused about the plummeting economy and an ever growing unemployment rate because the history of money has been neglected by our education systems and completely rewritten by the mainstream media. If we look back at the history of the US economy and banking system which has been hidden from us, then everything makes a lot more sense. Our economic downfall is a direct result of the establishment of the Federal Reserve central bank over a hundred years ago. Because of the pyramid scheme that they have created in our economy, it is impossible for our country to get out of debt. These banking cartels have been around since before the discovery of the new world. Since well before the days of the American colonies, they have been obsessed with controlling this nation's economy just as they do throughout many different parts of the world.

Throughout American history these banks have been very unpopular, and some politicians have even been forced to strike out against them, in order to avoid revolution. Andrew Jackson may have been a slave owning aristocrat and he is far from a champion of the common people, but he was one of the biggest challengers of the English banking cartels in his time. In the 19th century Jackson gave us a warning about the banks that puts the current crisis into focus, he said *"The bold effort the present bank had made to control the government ... are but premonitions of the fate that await the American people should they be deluded into a perpetuation of this institution or the establishment of another like it."*[3]

116

A hundred years later during the great depression president Franklin Roosevelt admitted that the financial sector had successfully gained control of the entire country. In a letter to white house regular, Edward Mandell House, Roosevelt wrote *"The real truth of the matter is, as you and I know that a financial element in the large centers has OWNED the Government of the U.S. since the days of Andrew Jackson."*[4]

This will become even more interesting when we learn in a later chapter that House was actually a front man for the bankers, who was also a mentor to many American presidents, most notably Woodrow Wilson and Franklin Roosevelt. He was more or less the Henry Kissinger of the early 20th century. Understanding the history and looking at the corruption within the financial sector today it is possible to connect the dots and make sense of what's going on with the economy. With just one small piece of hidden information the story seems to come together, and this is just one quick example of how discovering some of this occult history can shed light onto confusing or overwhelming situations.

Even more confusing than the economic situation is the endless cycle of senseless wars taking place all over the world. Again, many people don't have a proper historical reference when it comes to the military industrial complex. What is taking place right now is what has been taking place for the past few thousand years, conquest. Powerful governments and the financial interests that back them are creating empires all around the world, while making a fortune selling weapons and pillaging natural resources. They are invading lands that they are confident they can conquer and once they do so, they set up their companies and start taking any resources of value that they can find, all on stolen property that they then claim as their own. This is what the banking dynasties, the US and the United Nations are doing, and it is nothing new. Since the days of Alexander the Great or the Roman Empire power hungry political and financial groups have set off around the world in conquest.

The similarities between the ancient Roman Empire and the current American society are astonishing. A quick look at the history of the Roman Empire can really clear up a lot of confusion about the radical expansion of the US military. Despite the government generated myth that war is good for the economy, war is in fact the absolute worst financial predicament that a country can get themselves into. There is nothing more costly than a war, especially these days. Looking back at almost every empire that has ever collapsed, including ancient Rome, an excessive wartime policy has always been the downfall of the civilization.

The Roman warmongers had convinced their people that they were spreading "civilization" and that foreign enemies were a threat to their everyday life. Even closer to our own time we can see how the British empire used military force to destroy the lands of millions of native people in the name of "colonization" or "democracy". Even America itself is a British colony where an untold number of native shaman people were murdered and had their land stolen by the government. Sadly, America has followed in the footsteps of the British, spreading a corrupt system of democracy around the world by the barrel of a gun. Regardless of what excuse they give us, they are still doing the same thing that has been done in the past, just because the language involved and excuses given are different doesn't mean that anything has changed.

George Orwell said *"He, who controls the present, controls the past. He who controls the past, controls the future."*[5] What he meant by this statement was that if someone can control how a society sees their history, it would then be easy for them to control the direction that the society would take. This has been the situation throughout western civilization, the elite has been able to get away with the same crimes again and again by distorting our view of history and having a tight control of which historical information reached the masses. As we have been told many times before, *"those who are not aware of their history are doomed to repeat it"*. With a clear view of the past we can make responsible decisions for the future, so we don't have to be faced with an unfortunate history repeating itself.

QUOTE SOURCES AND SUGGESTED READING

[0]Secrets of superstar speakers: wisdom from the greatest motivators of our time - Lillet Walters (2000)

[1]The lies of George W. Bush: mastering the politics of deception - David Corn (2003)

[2]Faith, Certainty and the Presidency of George W. Bush By Ron Suskind October 17, 2004 New York Times

[3] Jackson closed the second Federal Bank (est. 1816) with these comments in 1836, his speech was published in the Annals of Congress, Volume 1, pages 1140-1143.

[4]President Franklin D. Roosevelt in a letter to Col. Edward Mandell House (21 November 1933) Source: F.D.R.: His Personal Letters, 1928-1945 (1970 edition) edited by Elliott Roosevelt

[5] 1984 - George Orwell

[SR1] Secret Societies and Psychological Warfare by Michael A. Hoffman II

[SR2] The Politically Incorrect Guide to American History by Thomas E. Woods Jr.

[SR3] Matrix of Power by Jordan Maxwell

[SR4] Common Sense by Thomas Paine

[SR5] The making of the English working class by E.P. Thompson

"When a well-packaged web of lies has been sold gradually to the masses over generations, the truth will seem utterly preposterous and its speaker a raving lunatic."-Dresden James (Writer) [0]

28. Powerful People Commit Crimes and Lie About It…. This Is No "Theory"

Large scale crimes are complicated and very difficult to carry out, so they require multiple people working together in secret, in order for them to be successful. Something on the scale of a bank heist would require a handful of people, while something like a mass murder or drug trafficking operation requires a much larger network of more well connected and well protected criminals. Whether they are street gangs, mafias, cartels or governments, these crime syndicates all go through great lengths to keep the vital details of their operations a secret and to provide a cover story that justifies their existence and excuses the atrocities that they are unable to hide.

It is not uncommon for criminal groups to present a drastically different picture of themselves to the public, because ultimately the fate of their mission is dependent upon public opinion. When a criminal or criminal group has the support of the public they can go on undetected until they eventually grow arrogant and cross the line, exposing themselves in the process.

The government, the mafia, a banking cartel and a street gang may look like different groups but they behave in very much the same way and use many of the same excuses to justify their violent actions. If you ask any of these groups why they exist and what purpose they serve, the answer will always be protection, security and financial necessity. The only thing that separates these groups in reality is a difference in resources, public image and scale of operations. All of the previously mentioned groups use intimidation, force and manipulation as they battle rival groups over dominance, resources and territory.

It's no secret that big business works so closely with the government that they are arguably the same entity, this fact is highlighted by the revolving door that exists between these two different factions of the state. Most people who find themselves in high level political positions were once CEO's of fortune 100 companies, and those who weren't will likely become a well-connected lobbyist upon leaving office.

Dick Cheney, vice president and top executive at Halliburton, or Goldman Sachs CEO turned treasury secretary Henry Paulson, would be among the most obvious examples of this revolving door. Both of the crooks in question undoubtedly used their political positions to influence events in such a way that would greatly benefit their respective businesses, this is commonplace in Washington.

The relationships between the world's most powerful people are blurred in the public, but behind the scenes many of them work very closely together, went to the same colleges, go to the same social clubs, attend the same meetings and send their children to the same schools. What this tells us is that beyond political parties and campaign rhetoric there are many connections and relationships which are rarely discussed in the public. As I said before, public opinion is basically the only thing that is holding a criminal back from committing their next crime, which is why people who carry out large scale violence or theft are so interested in learning how to control and manipulate public opinion.

Taking this process a step further, the government has been able to develop a forced monopoly on education, while developing an equally damaging monopoly over the media, which is largely run by corporations. Since big business and government both represent different arms of the same ruling class, we can say that together through their control of various social institutions, such as the media and education system, they are able to direct public opinion away from their crimes, and establish a nationalistic folklore in the public consciousness

121

which is favorable to their worldview. This nationalistic folklore is nothing but a collection of cover stories with very little supporting evidence, and sadly these cover stories have been accepted as truth by the general public.

One of the basic defense mechanisms of the criminal establishment is to ridicule and attack anyone who dares to question the false reality which they have meticulously created. The term "conspiracy theorist" developed during the early 20th century and was used to describe people who didn't believe in the "mafia".

That's correct, for a good part of the 20th century, the government completely denied the existence of this organized crime syndicate. This is most likely due to the fact that the mafia was the government's underground army. Later "conspiracy theorist" was used to describe the people who didn't believe the official story of the JFK assassination. This term is intended to automatically discredit a person or their ideas without actually taking a look at the arguments or evidence that they are providing. This is a relatively new shortcut in thinking, but it is similar to terms like "heretic" or "traitor" which were used to discredit truth seekers and dissenters throughout history. It wasn't until 1997 that the term conspiracy theory appeared in the English dictionary, the same year that a Hollywood film was released of the same title.

By definition the word conspiracy means *"a secret agreement between two or more people to perform an unlawful act"*. So we can say that the definition of conspiracy theory would be *"an accusation of a secret agreement between two or more people to perform an unlawful act"*. When a conspiracy theory ends up being true it then turns into a conspiracy case, because conspiracy is considered a crime in most instances.

Every day in our corrupt judicial system people are sent to jail on counts of "conspiracy". Mob bosses, drug dealers, gang members, stock brokers and politicians alike, get charged with conspiracy when they are found to be planning illegal acts in secret. Technically a lawyer who is working to prosecute suspects in a bank robbery could be considered a conspiracy theorist. Yet the term "conspiracy theory" has such a negative stigma attached to it that it is used as an argument ender in the media and political circles. What this implies is that we aren't allowed to make accusations of unlawful acts on the part of the ruling class. It seems the discussion is over once you start making claims about people who have power and wealth.

The term conspiracy theory is often associated with stories like big foot, the loch ness monster or Hollywood gossip found in supermarket tabloids. These fantasies are all designed to create fictitious controversy. This is necessary in order to establish a public bias, so that when real controversy presents itself, the public is reliant on the story which is seen as most popular or easiest to believe. The unfortunate thing about how this works, is that the "official story" is always created and presented by the people who are in question of committing the crimes. This is like allowing a criminal to be their own prosecutor, judge, jury and press.

Much of the stigma surrounding conspiracy theories comes from government intimidation. As I have been discussing, the government is just like one big gang or mafia organization. They use the same tactics to keep their wrong doings secret, including murder and witness intimidation. It is normal for activists to get death threats and be otherwise victimized through government fear tactics.

Nonviolent revolutionary and civil rights hero Martin Luther King JR. had his phone tapped by the CIA, received regular death threats and even had several bombs left at his house. Later, classified documents came to surface showing how many of these threats were actually ordered by the US government as a part of their counter activist program called "COINTELPRO". COINTELPRO waged war against the US population in an attempt to slow down the social progress which threatened the goals of the establishment.

When it comes to political conspiracy theory, whoever is making the accusation is many times on point, and if they're not, it's still possible that the government just did a really good job covering their tracks. Luckily for us, many times they do slip up, or someone on the inside is brave enough to bring information to the surface. As a result of these revelations, some of the incidents that people once considered conspiracy theories are actually now proven to be true.

The Manhattan Project was the military program that developed the atomic bomb. This project was considered by most people to be a conspiracy theory for years, until the bombs eventually dropped. Whole towns were built to test the first nuclear weapons. All of the residents were sworn to secrecy and spread out between one of the 30 testing sites across North America and the UK. The Manhattan project started out as a small testing operation in 1939, but in the few years it was in operation, it grew to employ over 130,000 people, all under strict secrecy.

There is also a very popular misconception in the mainstream consciousness that the weight of evidence is on the side of the establishment, when in reality this is far from the case. The amount of evidence that proves government corruption and conspiracies against the people far outweighs any evidence defending the establishment against the claims of "conspiracy theorists". As an example, I'll start with a controversial issue that continues to divide people all over the world, that being the destruction of the world trade center buildings on 9/11.

There is no hard evidence whatsoever linking CIA asset and patsy Osama Bin Laden to the attacks, yet according to the media, education systems and other arms of the establishment, he has become the "undisputed mastermind" of the attacks. In fact, the only evidence that the establishment rests upon is their "9/11 commission" which has since been exposed as a sham.

124

Most of the people who oversaw this commission have since came forward and admitted that they were forced into presenting a version of events that was scripted by the establishment. One of these commissioners named John Farmer even wrote a book called "*The Ground Truth*", detailing how evidence was intentionally left out of the report and how the blame was intentionally placed on Arabs in order to foment war in the Middle East. The flimsy 9/11 narrative suffered another fatal blow when the US government claimed to have killed Osama Bin Laden in 2011 without offering any evidence and changing the story multiple times. These few circumstances illustrate important cases where there was no evidence to back up the version of events that was handed down by the establishment.

The mainstream culture will lead you to believe that things like mind control, eugenics, depopulation programs, false flag attacks, the establishment of world government and other claims of corruption are unfounded theories with no evidence behind them. However, there is a substantial amount of evidence proving that all of the aforementioned claims are verifiably true. Declassified government documents, admissions of guilt and studies carried out by the members of the establishment in question offer direct insight into these issues. Throughout the rest of this book I will be citing those documents, quoting those confessions and laying out all of the evidence to prove the claims that I am making. I will also discuss the work of propaganda experts and scientists who developed mind control techniques and aristocrats who openly admit their crimes against humanity. If this kind of information was actually brought out in a trial it would prove beyond doubt that the establishment is implicit in subverting public opinion, using nefarious methods and guilty of conspiring with other members of the ruling class to expand their power and wealth.

So what's so hard to believe about powerful corporations and members of our government secretly getting together to plan global events? It seems like it's almost necessary for these parties to have meetings about their future policies. These plans are obviously more effective when carried out in secret, so the culture of lies in politics seems to be a natural result of self-preservation. Yet, when someone brings this point to light they are ridiculed in the media and their observation is labeled as "conspiracy theory", which one immediately associates with big foot type stories.

Many of the accusations that are brought up against the government that are labeled as conspiracy theories are eventually proven to be true way after the fact, just like the Manhattan project. The gulf of Tonkin incident, The Watergate scandal, The Tuskegee experiments, The Iran contra situation and other world changing events have all been exposed as conspiracies. Before the truths of these events were exposed, the government and puppet media organizations labeled all of these stories as "conspiracy theories", that the public should not take seriously. When evidence was finally uncovered that proved otherwise, it became apparent that there were actual conspiracies taking place and that the government and media were lying all along. Our "leaders" tell us to not give any thought to conspiracy theories just as anyone who is hiding something will tell you to not look for it or the wizard of Oz will tell you not to mind the man behind the curtain.

QUOTE SOURCES AND SUGGESTED READING
[0]Liberty Quotes - Christopher Kalabus (2009)
[SR1] American Assassination: The Strange Death of Senator Paul Wellstone by James H. Fetzer
[SR2] JFK: The CIA, Vietnam, and the Plot to Assassinate JFK by L. Fletcher Prouty
[SR3] None Dare Call it Conspiracy by Gary Allen
[SR4] Behold a pale horse – William Cooper

"The Bankers own the earth. Take it away from them, but leave them the power to create deposits, and with the flick of the pen they will create enough deposits to buy it back again. However, take it away from them, and all the great fortunes like mine will disappear and they ought to disappear, for this would be a happier and better world to live in. But, if you wish to remain the slaves of Bankers and pay the cost of your own slavery, let them continue to create deposits." [0] Sir Josiah Stamp (President of the Bank of England in the 1920's)

29. The Banking Backstory of Friday The 13th

The unlucky Friday the 13th is one of the most well recognized superstitions in the western world. This tradition is over 700 years old and has a very interesting origin. During the 12th century there was a massive religious war that consumed most of Europe and Asia. Europeans referred to these times as "the crusades". This war lasted centuries and allowed an elite class of knights to accumulate so much power and wealth that their influence rivaled both the monarchy and the church. The Knights of the Temple of Solomon, or more commonly known as "The Knights Templar" were the most influential political force of their time. They were the world's first international bankers and were the corporate giant of the middle ages.

The Templar Knights were a military force throughout the entire crusades, but didn't become a strong political organization until they were given diplomatic immunity by the church in 1126. Their close relationship with the church was unusual for the time, as the lifestyle of a knight was usually associated more with the monarchy. The Knights Templar represented both the warrior and the priest, and they were often referred to as the "fighting monks". This best of both worlds diplomacy allowed the knights to form their own political dynasty which transcended the established powers of the time. They did not have to abide by the same rules as the church or the monarchy, but instead they had the advantage and privileges of both institutions.

127

During the crusades it was rumored that the Templars studied alchemy and discovered forbidden knowledge on their journeys. This would not be the first time that this has happened in history, it is actually quite common for conquerors to return home with ancient artifacts, just like napoleon did with the Rosetta stone, for example. Some say that instead of offering their discoveries to museums the Templars kept the artifacts and knowledge within their own order. This is all speculation and legend, but what we do know for certain is that the Templars were conniving aristocrats who became the world's most successful multinational bankers.

They had most of the known world caught in a complex pyramid scheme that is eerily similar to the scams that are being run by international bankers today. They collected taxes for protecting trade roads, bankrolled both sides of all the wars and exploited the massive peasant class, using them as workhorses to build their fortunes. Through these shady practices the knights ended up having more money than the monarchy and the church combined. Both the church and the monarchy were deeply in debt to the Templars from loans they had taken out, so one would be able to argue quite easily that the Templars were the most dominant political institution of the time.

Eventually the monarchy grew very threatened by the immense power of the Knights Templar. The person to finally take action against the Templars was King Phillip the 4th of France. Since the Templars were under the protection of the church, King Phillip needed papal permission to overthrow them. In order to get this blessing, Phillip covertly murdered 2 popes in less than a year until a candidate of his choice was in power. With all the necessary steps taken King Phillip made his move. On the morning of Friday, April 13 1307 there was a surprise raid on all the Templar offices. The knights were being arrested on over a hundred different counts of heresy and treason and many confessed after being brutally tortured. After a short, rigged trial the Templars were sentenced to burn at the stake. The grand master of the Knights Templar cursed the king and pope before he was executed, and synchronisticaly both died within the year.

It is said that a fleet of Templar warships managed to escape France the night before the raids, which allowed those remaining members to maintain control of world events from behind the scenes. They apparently did this by changing their names and moving to various different parts of the known world. In fact, it is said by many that the Templars who managed to escape the inquisition fled to Switzerland and reestablished their international banking cartel there.

This theory makes sense considering that the country has been a safe haven for bankers and robber barons for centuries. There are over 500 major banking institutions in Switzerland, the majority of them are owned and controlled by various elite bloodlines and covert organizations that I'll describe in detail later on. It is estimated that around 35% of all the wealth in the world is held in Switzerland. The World Trade Organization or WTO is also based in Switzerland. These banks are among some of the only financial institutions in Europe who aren't subject to audits and investigations from the new European Union government. The financial district in London called "the city", as well as the Vatican in Italy is also given the same kind of protection and secrecy, but they are the only areas in Europe that have those kinds of privileges. It is also rather interesting that the Swiss Guard is responsible for guarding the pope (located in Italy, not Switzerland), a task that was once the job of the Knights Templar.

The flag of Switzerland is actually an inversion of the Templar's shield, the flag being red with a white cross and the shield being white with a red cross. It is important to mention that the banking elite may have ties to the areas government and economy, but they have nothing to do with the people of Switzerland. They do not represent them and their actions should not be held against the people of this country. In fact, Switzerland is one of the best places on earth to live, with very free social policies. They have a low crime rate because everyone in the country is armed and drugs are legal. They also remain neutral in all major wars, but still, when there is smoke there is usually fire. Although I wouldn't mind living in Switzerland myself and imagine it is filled with wonderful people, there are just too many clues pointing to this region as playing a vital role in the many worldwide banking schemes. With this being a very realistic possibility, Templar influence would seem to put the puzzle together nicely, but it's not something that we have been able to prove yet. Switzerland is just one of the many places where the ruling class has established a stronghold to operate from, the same goes with "The City" in London, the Vatican, Washington DC and Zionist Israel. The people that live in these places have nothing to do with the elite's plans, aside from being used as workhorses, cannon fodder and political pawns.

Since the days of their fall from grace, the Templar Knights and their predecessors have learned their lesson, and have continued their work in secret. Even if the official order went underground, their business model and diplomatic strategies are still very much alive today and have a deep impact on our way of life. The Templars became an all-powerful "invisible government" by mastering and manipulating politics and finance, much like the bankers that influence world events today. In fact, today's multinational bankers follow the Templars model precisely and use all of the same age old tactics to exploit the masses.

QUOTE SOURCES AND SUGGESTED READING
[0] The Legalized Crime of Banking - Silas W. Adams (1958)
[SR1] Babylon's Banksters by Joseph P. Farrell
[SR2] The Place of Enchantment by Alex Owen

"Illegal aliens have always been a problem in the United States, ask any Indian" - Robert Orben (Comedian) [0]

30. America Was Not Discovered, It Was Stolen

The shaman people that inhabited North and South America prior to its brutal European takeover built a vast and organized civilization. They lived in structured societies that were very connected with spirituality and nature. There was very little sickness and they had medicinal plants for every condition which were far superior to today's pharmaceuticals. The indigenous people were extremely happy, things like depression, mental illness, crime or greed were not nearly as prevalent in their culture, as is seen in ours.

Now I'm not so naive as to think that all the natives were totally peaceful, but the kind of mass violence seen in the west was certainly not present. There were many different tribes scattered throughout North and South America, some of them peaceful, some of them violent, it was literally a whole new world inhabited by a vast network of societies each with their own unique culture.

One common myth about the native people is that they had no respect for property rights. In reality, native cultures had complex systems of trade which even included various currencies, using anything from shells to animal pelts. They just didn't happen to keep complicated records and write everything down on paper as the westerners did.

There were definitely some tribes that employed slave labor and practiced human sacrifice, but these groups were more hierarchical in structure than the rest of the native populations. This kind of organized violence was also more common in areas of dense population.

To say that there was just one civilization here before colonization began, would be a disservice to the diverse culture of the pre Columbus Americas. Making the generalization that

131

every tribe in that hemisphere was the same would be like saying that Canada, Mexico and the United States had identical cultures today. Contrary to the Europeans claims that the Americas were a vast uninhabited wilderness, there was actually a massive native population that numbered in the hundreds of millions. Traces of this large population seemed easy enough to destroy at first, considering the natives put a great deal of care into making as little an impact on their environment as possible. However, as time passes archeologists are continuing to uncover evidence that the pre Columbus civilizations were much more advanced and populated than the historical record tells us. Even the ship logs of early European explorers show us a much different story than we were told in history class.

That's not the only thing we were lied to about in history class. The ruling class at the time was also well aware that there were unexplored continents on the other side of the Atlantic Ocean. Many early European civilizations took voyages to the other side of the Atlantic over a thousand years ago, it is even believed that early Irish and Norse cultures actually had trade established with some Native American tribes. All of this information was hidden from most of the general public, only the nobility who were literate and had a decent understanding of history knew that the world was twice as big as most people believed. As I discuss many times throughout this book, oppressive warmongering rulers always hide important information from their subjects so they are easier to control and more willing to accept subpar living standards, this situation is no different. The myth that the world was flat was merely propaganda to keep explorers from traveling west and discovering the new world before the monarchy was able to claim it.

Due to lack of resources and the extensive crusades and inquisitions that were raging in Europe for many centuries, it took the elite until 1492 to make their official move across the Atlantic Ocean. Prior to this, only exploratory voyages were taken to the new world in order to prepare and gather information for future colonization. When the elite were ready for conquest they sent an inquisitor and mapmaker by the name of Christopher Columbus to begin the Native American genocide and colonization process. Columbus was not an explorer but one of the few elite members of society that had access to occult information such as the existence of the Americas.

He knew exactly where he was going when he set sail across the Atlantic Ocean. He most likely obtained this knowledge through a secret society he belonged to called "the Knights of Christ" ,which was apparently a surviving order of the Knights Templar. This connection would explain why all of the ships from his famous first voyage were flying the colors of the Knights Templar, the Maltese Red Cross. Regardless of where Columbus got his information his mission was certain, to harvest natural resources using native slave labor and to claim land for the monarchy. This colonization would begin one of the most brutal genocides in known human history.

When Columbus reached the new world he arrived in the Caribbean islands and established his first settlement in what is now Haiti. Upon their arrival, the Europeans immediately started looking for gold and began persecuting the native people. Columbus was under extreme pressure to return to Europe with as much gold as possible, in order to repay the monarchy for funding his voyage. To speed up the process Columbus and his men became even more brutal with the native people. They ordered every man, woman and child they found to collect a certain amount of gold every three months. The natives that reached their quota would receive a copper token that they would wear around their neck. If they were found without these tokens they were brutally tortured and murdered. Because of the trusting nature and disposition of the native people, the barbarian conquerors easily took advantage of them. In old ship logs we can see the ignorant and ruthless attitude that the European invaders had towards the indigenous people.

In his journal Columbus wrote *"they are so naïve and so free with their possessions that no one who has not witnessed them would believe it. When you ask for something they have, they never say no. To the contrary, they offer to share with anyone. They brought us parrots and balls of cotton and spears and many other things, which they exchanged for the glass beads and hawks' bells. They willingly traded everything they owned.... They do not bear arms, and do not know them, for I showed them a sword, they took it by the edge and cut themselves out of ignorance. They have no iron. Their spears are made of cane. They would make fine servants. With fifty men we could subjugate them all and make them do whatever we want".* [1]

The atrocities committed by Columbus and his crew were just the beginning of the American holocaust which eventually destroyed a vast and thriving civilization. Over the half millennia that followed, different European nations set up colonies in lands that did not belong to them and killed hundreds of millions of people to do so. Hundreds of years of murder and displacement have left the native shaman people with a fraction of their population, all of which have been forced onto small concentration camp like reservations. The age of imperialism saw the genocide of many civilizations in Africa, Australia and Asia as well as the Americas.

QUOTE SOURCES AND SUGGESTED READING
[0] Robert Orben - Patterns in prehistory by Robert J. Wenke (p. 587)
[1] A Peoples History of the United States - Howard Zinn
[SR1] 1491: New Revelations of the Americas Before Columbus

"When fascism comes to America, it will be wrapped in the flag and carrying the cross" - Sinclair Lewis (Writer) [0]

31. The Nazi Agenda Reborn

Our whole lives we have been told in school, at home and through the media that America is the greatest country in the world and is a beacon of moral integrity on the planet earth. We were taught that our society is the most humane and free type of civilization that is physically possible. Yet this same story has been told in the most fascist dictatorships, so who's to say that America is any different? History shows that our government has certainly not acted much different from some of the harsh dictators that we have seen throughout the world in the 20th century. In fact, the American government and its major corporations have done business with these regimes, and in many cases even carried out the same oppressive policies themselves.

The most reviled of all fascist regimes in recent history is that of Adolph Hitler and the Nazi party of Germany. Hitler's regime took advantage of the terrible economic situation that Germany was riddled with after World War 1, and used advanced propaganda to generate public support for his insane policies. Many have even deemed this man to be an "antichrist", and rightfully so. If such a thing exists then Hitler is a prime candidate. He is responsible for building concentration camps, committing genocide and creating a totalitarian police state for the German people. It is also important to note that most of the German people were duped by the Nazi propaganda machine and actually believed that these oppressive policies were for their safety and for the good of the country. This was a horrible situation where a savage oligarchy took advantage of millions of people, but all under the guise of safety, security and freedom.

If there ever was a political institution that was a threat to freedom and civil rights it was the Nazi party. But this is not the reason why the Americans decided to fight them in World War 2.

In fact, the Americans and the Germans had extremely good diplomacy before Japan bombed Pearl Harbor.

Many American businesses and politicians worked very closely with the Nazis even after the two countries were at war with each other. The holocaust had already claimed the lives of millions of German people by that point, and a police state had long since been established, so whoever was doing business with the Nazis at that point knew exactly who they were getting involved with.

The war really had nothing to do with ideological differences or "liberating" populations from oppressive rulers, but it was a massive business move for governments and big corporations. There was some level of conquest, with various elites redrawing Europe and the Middle East, but there were also a lot of short term gains for those involved through kickbacks from arms manufactures. War is never a "moral" issue, it is always about the ruling classes of different countries fighting over wealth and power, every single time, and both world wars are no different.

Prior to the Americans getting involved in the war there were corners of the political arena that were actually big supporters of the Nazi party, both for business purposes and common interests such as eugenics. The most prominent American politician to work with the Nazis was actually George W. Bush's grandfather Prescott Bush. There is no doubt that he was funding and working with the Nazis, because his company's assets were seized in 1942 by the United States government under the "trading with the enemy" act. He worked at the head of a financial firm called Brown Brothers Harriman which acted as a US base for the Nazi business interests. Brown Brothers Harriman was one of the biggest international investment firms in the 1930's and they sent millions of dollars in gold overseas to rebuild the German army and fund the Nazi party. This racket was finally exposed on July 30th of 1942 when the New York Herald Tribune posted an article called "*Hitler's Angel Has three million dollars in US Bank*". This article raised suspicion about the bank being a "secret nest" for Nazi elites and eventually sparked the investigation that took down the operation.

Some of America's largest corporations also contributed to the atrocities committed in Germany during the Second World War. They saw the Nazi party as a rising political force in Europe and they wanted a piece of that business. Many of them also had similar political and social interests as well. Among those corporations, IBM was by far the most heavily involved with Hitler. In 1933, the year that Hitler came to power, IBM invested millions of dollars into Nazi Germany and built a factory in Berlin. Once established in Germany, IBM began building the cataloging machines that Hitler would need to organize his genocide.

This technology was used to process and register which citizens would be sent to ghettos or concentration camps. Without the IBM cataloging devices known as the "Hollerith" machines the Nazis would have still carried out the holocaust, but it wouldn't have been nearly as organized, widespread or deadly. IBM was not the only company that helped Hitler and his Nazi regime rise to power. Without the help of companies like General Electric, Standard Oil, I.G Farben and Ford Motors the Nazis would have never had the resources or the technology to build a militarized empire from the ashes of the collapsed Weimar Republic.

There were many minds and organizations behind the Nazi policy of world domination, this brutal regime was not just the work of one lone crazed individual, but was a network of elite powers that have been trying to take over the world for many centuries. Hitler just happened to be the front man of the group. This network includes royal bloodlines and the few elite families that dominate international business, as well as various "think tanks", secret societies, intelligence organizations and other esoteric groups. These groups have no loyalty to the countries that they represent, as they fund and support both sides in every war. Eventually these international groups don't even want these countries to exist anyway, their goal is a global dictatorship that is controlled under one political, economic and military force. This was Hitler's stated goal and the mission of many supporting organizations that outlived the Nazi regime and moved on to implant their fascist ideals into other governments that showed potential for power.

The multinational network behind global policy doesn't "choose sides" like they force the rest of us to do. They try to influence as many "sides" as they possibly can to increase the odds of them completing their mission. For example, in World War 2 they backed the US, the UK, the Soviets, the Nazis, among others, to ensure that no matter the outcome, they would have a strong influence on the winner of the war. All of these aforementioned countries have a strong history of imperialism and racism which is in part due to the influence of the elite nation builders that sit behind their governments. It's important to note that they use racism as a weapon against every single ethnicity, they change the heritage that they vilify depending upon the political climate in order to suit their agenda. Any group or race of people that happens to be in the way of their plans becomes a target for racial discrimination. During the times of colonization it was the native tribes, during the times of slavery it was Africans, in Nazi Germany it was the Jews, and now in the "war on terror" it is the Muslims.

The same forces were behind all of these atrocities, although different regimes may have led the various campaigns. We know that these events have been put into motion by the same groups because of transactions that take place between businesses (i.e. IG Farben, GE, and Standard Oil) and families (i.e. Bush) who all have ruling class backgrounds and connections. These companies are still around today, but have had to change their names various times due to their unscrupulous practices. Standard oil has splintered out into most of the major oil companies, IG Farben is now involved with big pharma, and GE is still causing trouble under the same name.

After the war, the Nazi military power in Germany came to an end, but many key figures in the regime were scouted and recruited by governments and corporations from all over the world. Many of the primary influences, backers and financiers of the Nazi party also went on to coach new world "leaders" on how to handle their military and foreign policy. The Americans rounded up dozens of Nazi scientists, economists and military officers to give them jobs for the U.S government. In many cases the government had Nazis excused from war crimes so they could begin working for America. These Nazi transfers took place under a classified government project called "operation paperclip". Through this project many top ranking members of the Nazi party became integrated into the American government. One notable example is that of Wernher von Braun, a Nazi rocket scientist who was hired by the US government through operation paperclip, and who later worked with NASA as the chief engineer for the Saturn-V launch rocket that sent the Apollo spacecraft to the moon.

America was not the only country to be infected with the Nazi mentality after the end of World War 2. The United Kingdom also maintained contact with the elite circles that financed and encouraged Hitler's rise to power, which makes sense considering the UK had a longer relationship with these groups than the Nazis did, even during and before the war. It could be argued that the whole Nazi party was a creation of Anglo-American interests. This has been confirmed by the research of economics professor Antony C. Sutton in his book "*Wall Street and the rise of Hitler*".

When it was time for peace treaties to be signed and territorial lines to be redrawn at the end of the war, it only makes sense that the ruling class, who had been influencing all sides from the beginning, would have a strong influence in this process, that is one of their main objectives in creating these wars to begin with. The elite pretty much ran the entire diplomatic process and used their influence over the established governments to create the United Nations. I'll get more into the specifics of this later, but the UN would become the groundwork for their next attempt at global domination. Through the UN the aristocracy was able to create the structure and draw the borders for the post war nations, as well as police the world according to their politics. Sadly, this same elite now has a strong influence in the United States, Israel and the whole continent of Europe, with many puppet regimes throughout the Middle East and Africa.

QUOTE SOURCES AND SUGGESTED READING
[0] It Can't Happen Here - Sinclair Lewis (1935)
[SR1] Leanord Piekoff –The Ominous Parallels
[SR2] The Rise of the Fourth Reich   by Jim Marrs
[SR3] Unholy Alliance: A History of Nazi Involvement with the Occult By Peter Levenda
[SR4] Wall Street and the Rise of Hitler - Antony C. Sutton

"If I were reincarnated I would wish to be returned to earth as a killer virus to lower human population levels." - Prince Phillip (Psychopathic Monarch) [0]

32. Darwinism, Eugenics and the Silent Genocide

Charles Darwin is one of the most respected figures in scientific history and his ideological theories have changed the way that we look at the world and how we practice science. Although "Darwinism" consists of more theory and assumption than scientific law, it is still held to be absolute truth in the western world. Charles Darwin did make some incredible observations about the natural world that no one in the west had even approached at the time. However, these natural observations were corrupted by his own ideological assumptions. There is a lot of truth in Darwin's work, but the truth that exists within his research really doesn't do anything to prove his materialistic assumptions.

Darwin's painfully damaging assumptions did not come from his research in the wilderness, but from his upbringing as a white wealthy Englishman under the strict rule of the Catholic Church. Darwin belonged to a popular movement at the time that was fed up with the churches tyrannical rule. The aristocracy also had economic and strategic reasons for wanting to break down the established religious order, as the divine right of kings prevented the nobility from attaining more wealth and power than they already had. Darwin and his colleagues belonged to that privileged class which sought to disprove any kind of spirituality and remove the spirit from serious intellectual discussion. This was an understandable goal considering the extremely repressive nature of the church at the time, but what they did was throw the baby out with the bathwater, for lack of a better term.

It is true that the Anglo Saxon church in its many variations was unrealistic, outdated and oppressive, even at the time of Darwin, but for some reason he didn't draw the line with organized

141

religion, but wanted to rule out the supernatural altogether. Darwin and his colleagues assumed that since spirituality in their culture was represented by an oppressive control system that the idea of spirit was somehow damaging to the human condition. In reality it was just the corrupted mainstream versions of religion which Darwin was exposed to that shaped his whole spiritual view. Even if the idea of spirit was some kind of menace, Darwin's observations have nothing to do with spirituality. Yes, Darwin's observations do disprove many specific points of the King James Bible, which did totally cripple that institution. However, the Christian bible or any other holy book for that matter is not any kind of representation of human spirituality. It is simply a book that was written by rulers and then passed along to the public as the "word of god". Therefore, Darwin's findings only disprove the claims of specific organized religions, but have no implications for spirituality in general.

In Darwin's time, there was an idea among the aristocracy that their genetics were superior to that of the rest of society. Many families including Darwin's took this belief to extreme levels by practicing incest as a tradition. They thought that if adolescents were to marry within their own family then not only would all the wealth stay in the family, but the "good" genes would also. This also ensured that the family fortunes would be retained for many future generations. This practice is very common in aristocratic families, which explains why they are all extremely mentally unstable. Darwin came from a very classist and racist elite level of society and that is reflected in his work, especially "The Descent of Man".

One of the most famous cases of royal incest is found in the Hapsburg dynasty that produced rulers in Spain, Austria, Hungary, Belgium, the Netherlands and the German empire. Around 1700, the Spanish branch of this empire fell apart suddenly and died off. Recent studies of the Hapsburg Family Tree show that sickness and deformity due to incest was responsible for the sudden demise of this "royal bloodline". The most successful political dynasty in America, the Bush family is notorious for inbreeding. In fact, George Bush Sr. and his wife Barbara Bush are actually in the same bloodline, which is the Pierce or Percy bloodline. The British house of this bloodline is named Percy and the American house is named Pierce. The elite's family structures are very complicated, with many "houses" and surnames that are omitted from the public dialogue to avoid scrutiny and cover up their ongoing eugenics experiments. I am only singling out the Bush family because it's an example that those of you in the west will recognize, but in countries all over the world, in every continent there are elitists and monarchs who hold this world view.

The ruling class of every nation is obsessed with breeding and is using the best of our advanced technology and medical science to guarantee that their heirs will be somehow thoroughbred. Since the aristocracy has been practicing selective breeding for centuries, they are under the impression that they are already of a superior stock to the rest of humanity, thanks to the "care" that their ancestors took in breeding. This is of course just an egotistical delusion that justifies their exploitative treatment towards the rest of humanity.

Darwin's other dehumanizing ideology is his "survival of the fittest" mantra. Darwin didn't just come up with this philosophy out of thin air, this was actually an idea that has been traditionally held by families of nobility since before the Middle Ages. It was this philosophy that the aristocracy used to justify their inhumane treatment of the serfs and peons that built their empires and tended to their fields. The saying "survival of the fittest" was actually coined by an aristocrat named Thomas Robert Malthus who was openly brutal and inhumane in his descriptions of the poor, or as he called them "the lower races".

In a 1798 publication called "*An Essay on the Principle of Population*", Malthus suggested that planned food shortages could be used to decrease the population of the poor through starvation. This was the root for the idea of "population control", because a large population is very difficult for the ruling class to

143

manage while retaining their own wealth and power. Malthus suggested that the streets should be made narrower and that more people should be crowded into living quarters to encourage conditions that would bring back the plague. In that same essay, he said that villages should be built next to stagnant pools where germs could fester, and all remedies and cures would only be available to those who could afford it. In his own words *"we are bound in justice and honor formally to disclaim the right of the poor to support. To this end, I should propose a regulation be made declaring that no child born should ever be entitled to parish assistance. This infant is comparatively speaking, of little value to society, as others will immediately supply its place...All children beyond what would be required to keep up the population to this level must perish, unless room be made for them by the deaths of grown persons."* [1]

In so many words, what he was suggesting was establishing a national limit on child births, and executing any child that was born past that limit. In the times of Malthus, many elite circles were publicly speculating that if the world's population were to exceed 3 billion people there would be mass famine and destruction of all the resources on earth. Obviously, they were all very wrong. Malthus was wrong about many things, but nonetheless he was one of Darwin's primary influences and one of the most racist and arrogant aristocrats of the Victorian age. Without the writings of this brutal aristocrat and his predecessor Herbert Spencer it is very possible that population reduction would have played no part in Darwin's philosophy. Their racist and classist tendencies were prevalent even in Darwin's early work. In fact, his most famous work *"Origin of Species"* was originally titled *"Preservation of Favored Races"*.

The true danger of Darwin's philosophy was exposed during the Second World War when "Social Darwinism" took Germany by storm and became the cornerstone of Hitler's most inhumane policies. Social Darwinism applies the survival of the fittest idea to human society and implies that our species would be stronger, if the weaker end of the gene pool were to be eliminated. The pursuit of this "stronger species" would come in the form of an institution called "eugenics" which is still around today. Eugenics is defined in most dictionaries as *"the study of or belief in the possibility of improving the qualities of the human species or a human population, especially by such means as discouraging reproduction by persons having genetic defects or presumed to have inheritable undesirable traits or encouraging reproduction by persons presumed to have inheritable desirable traits."* This sadistic philosophy resulted in the sterilization, institutionalization and genocide of millions of people throughout the world who were marked as subhuman by the ruling class.

Although Darwin's philosophy laid the groundwork for the eugenics movement it was not him who actually coined the term "eugenics", but it was his cousin Francis Galton. Galton's vision for the eugenics movement was to develop it into a science that would influence public policy until it eventually became a kind of religion. Galton defined eugenics as *"the study of agencies under social control that may improve or impair the racial qualities of future generations, whether physically or mentally."*[2]

In the beginning of the 20th century Galton began to introduce his new science to various intellectual circles around the world. He was gaining prominence around the time of Charles Darwin's death, and seeming as if it were planned, Galton was there to carry the torch. Towards the end of Darwin's life his writings became darker and he was much more open about the ultimate social goals of his philosophy. His final book "Descent of Man" is obviously the work of a eugenicist, in it he clearly suggested that the evolution of humanity should be engineered by the Anglo-Saxon aristocracy, which he saw as a superior race.

There are many quotes in that book which illustrate his point of view, but none as clear and concise as this. Darwin published the following words *"With savages, the weak in body or mind are soon eliminated; and those that survive commonly exhibit a vigorous state of health. We civilized men, on the other hand, do our utmost to check the process of elimination; we build asylums*

145

for the imbecile, the maimed, and the sick; we institute poor-laws and our medical men exert their utmost skill to save the life of every one to the last moment, Thus the weak members of civilized societies propagate their kind. No one who has attended to the breeding of domestic animals will doubt that this must be highly injurious to the race of man. It is surprising how soon a want of care, or care wrongly directed, leads to the degeneration of a domestic race; but excepting in the case of man himself, hardly any one is so ignorant as to allow his worst animals to breed." [3]

If Darwin had lived longer his rhetoric would have undoubtedly grown as blatantly racist as that of his cousin. Correspondence between the two shows that Galton was the one who introduced the philosophy of eugenics to Darwin. Just two years after the Descent of Man was published and nearly a decade before Darwin's death, Galton wrote a letter to the Times of London suggesting that the British move Chinese immigrants into Africa as a more stealthy way of carrying out genocide on the native population.

The letter read in part *"My proposal is to make the encouragement of the Chinese settlements at one or more suitable places on the East Coast of Africa a part of our national policy, in the belief that the Chinese immigrants would not only maintain their position, but that they would multiply and their descendants supplant the inferior Negro race. I should expect the large part of the African seaboard, now sparsely occupied by lazy, palavering savages living under the nominal sovereignty of the Zanzibar, or Portugal, might in a few years be tenanted by industrious, order loving Chinese, living either as a semi-detached dependency of China, or else in perfect freedom under their own law."* [4] Sadly, this letter was actually published, as this was the prevailing kind of attitude among the aristocracy at the time, so that was what the papers printed.

The eugenics movement swept across Europe and the US, it was taught in schools, praised in the media and finally pushed through as government policy almost everywhere. The Nazi party was not the only regime during those times that were guilty of forcing harsh eugenics policies on their people. All over the United States during World War 2 people who were depressed, handicap, alcoholic or even children who were as young as 7 years old who happened to score too low on standardized IQ tests were singled out and sterilized. More than 42,000 people were sterilized in America between 1941 and 1943 under the guise of eugenics, so Germany wasn't the only country at the time that had sick master race schemes. In fact, one of the most influential books to Hitler's ideology was a book called "*Passing of the Great Race*" by an American named Madison Grant. Hitler called passing of the great race his "bible" and wrote Grant numerous fan letters.

Madison Grant was another eugenicist disguised as a philanthropist who was very influential in American politics. He was friends with numerous presidents, including Theodore Roosevelt and Herbert Hoover. It is no secret that the American government has an extremely racist track record and subjected the Native American and African population to the same inhumane treatment that the population of Europe received from Hitler. Grant was not alone either, Eugenics was a matter of national policy and still is today, though under various different names and disguises.

The first birth control efforts in America were motivated by Eugenics policies, and were specifically targeted at minorities and the poor working class. A Eugenicist by the name of Margaret Sanger established the countries first birth control bureaucracy "Planned Parenthood". Today this organization enjoys the respect of most progressives because they see it as providing an affordable service to the community. While this may be true for some, the sinister roots and intentions of this organization are not to be ignored. Margaret Sanger was surprisingly profane when discussing her ideas about eugenics in writing or public speeches. It was a stated goal of hers to limit the number of births among minorities, she called this effort "The

Negro Project". It is terribly ironic that Planned Parenthood is seen as a philanthropic organization because Sanger was extremely clear about the fact that she was not a charity worker.

In "The Pivot of Civilization" she writes *"Even if we accept organized charity at its own valuation, and grant that it does the best it can, it is exposed to a more profound criticism. It reveals a fundamental and irremediable defect. Its very success, it's very efficiency, it's very necessity to the social order, are themselves the most unanswerable indictment. Organized charity itself is the symptom of a malignant social disease. Those vast, complex, interrelated organizations aiming to control and to diminish the spread of misery and destitution and all the menacing evils that spring out of this sinisterly fertile soil, are the surest sign that our civilization has bred, is breeding and is perpetuating constantly increasing numbers of defectives, delinquents and dependents. My criticism, therefore, is not directed at the failure of philanthropy, but rather at its success."* [5]

It is true that there is some positive impact that Planned Parenthood has on many individuals, but that is merely an unintended consequence. Again, this was all revealed by Sanger in her writings. In that same book she writes "*Every single case of inherited defect, every malformed child, every congenitally tainted human being brought into this world is of infinite importance to that poor individual; but it is of scarcely less importance to the rest of us and to all of our children who must pay in one way or another for these biological and racial mistakes."* [6]

In these difficult times that we are living in, birth control and abortion are a very real option for most people, and I'm in no way condemning anyone who chooses either. However, that does not change the intentions behind these programs, and it is important that we have all of the right information before we make life changing decisions. These are the only methods of population reduction that operate in the light of day, the darker eugenics programs are carefully disguised and largely unknown to the general public.

The darker goals of eugenics were explored deeper by the works of Bertrand Russell, an author who championed many ideas of the ruling class. In *"The Impact of Science on Society"* Russell writes *"I do not pretend that birth control is the only way in which population can be kept from increasing... War... has hitherto been disappointing in this respect, but perhaps bacteriological war may prove more effective. If a Black Death could be spread throughout the world once in every generation survivors could procreate freely without making the world too full... The state of affairs might be somewhat unpleasant, but what of that? Really high-minded people are indifferent to happiness, especially other people's... There are three ways of securing a society that shall be stable as regards population. The first is that of birth control, the second that of infanticide or really destructive wars, and the third that of general misery except for a powerful minority..."* [7]

When most people hear this kind of talk their first instinct is to ask "why would they do this?" or "what do they have to gain that they don't already have". Russell's next suggestion reveals the dark endgame of eugenics, he writes *"Gradually, by selective breeding, the congenital differences between rulers and ruled will increase until they become almost different species. A revolt of the plebs would become as unthinkable as an organized insurrection of sheep against the practice of eating mutton."*[8]

According to this testimony, the elite have been seeking to branch humanity off into two different species with the most of humanity descending into a slave race, and the Anglo-American aristocracy being the dominant "master race". This is why to this day elite families only breed with each other and in many cases breed within their own families. This is also why they dumbed down public education and are poisoning the general population, in hopes to speed along this process of creating two separate human species, the slaves and the slave drivers.

In that same book, Bertrand Russell reveals how poisons of

149

various kinds would help to speed along the evolutionary divergence and reduce the population. On page 66 he writes *"Diet, injections, and injunctions will combine, from a very early age, to produce the sort of character and the sort of beliefs that the authorities consider desirable, and any serious criticism of the powers that be will become psychologically impossible. Even if all are miserable, all will believe themselves happy, because the government will tell them they are so."*[9]

These are among some of the most complex descriptions of eugenics to date, giving us some insight behind the plan and ultimate goal of this genocidal social movement. As with Darwin, Bertrand Russell is very popular among modern atheists for his criticisms of the church and organized religion, but most aren't aware of his support for oligarchy and political control.

Eugenics was openly a social policy for most of the industrialized nations in the world until the peak of World War 2. At this time, Hitler's extreme implementation of eugenics exposed the true nature of this sick pseudoscience and forced it underground. In the United States, the eugenics movement changed its name and splintered off into various branches including genetics, population control, transhumanism and social biology, among others. The Rockefellers, Rothschild's and Carnegies were some of the primary financiers for eugenics programs in the west and after World War 2 they just renamed their foundations to avoid public scrutiny. The *"American Eugenics Society"* became the *"Population Council"* and the aristocracy began funding their eugenics operations through tax exempt foundations and parading their expenditures to the public as "charitable contributions to society". Today these same organizations force sterilizing vaccinations onto third world populations, all the while acting like they are providing humanitarian aid to the people.

When straight foreword eugenics failed they simply changed the rhetoric to that of population control and the working class was told that they were poor not because of corruption, but because there were just too many of them and not enough resources to

150

go around. This lie is incredibly offensive when you take a look at the vast disparities within our societies where there is literally a ruling class and a serf class. Today the leading causes for hunger and poverty are war, displacement, lack of infrastructure and overexploited resources (usually on the part of large corporations and governments), but nowhere internationally is overpopulation officially recognized as having any part in world hunger. In fact, there is more than enough food produced in today's industrialized agriculture industry to feed the whole world and then some, but unfortunately some people can't afford that food and others live in areas where there isn't even proper infrastructure to transport it. Reducing the global population would still not help the remaining people get food, therefore it would have no effect on world hunger or poverty. Thinning out the population and making it easier to maintain has been a goal of the aristocracy since ancient times and it continues to this day, but would honestly do nothing to improve quality of life for those of us who are suffering.

The new face of eugenics was extremely deceptive and its advocates were more secretive about the true intent of their work. The eugenics movement grew more dangerous at this time, not only because of their disguised approach but also as a result of the growing influence of international bureaucracies. The United Nations is the largest of these, but there are also various other satellite groups that work on the behalf of the UN but under different names. One such organization was UNESCO, an Educational, Scientific, and Cultural establishment with underlying eugenic goals. The first director of this organization was Julian Huxley, a eugenicist from a prominent English family.

His writings had the same kind of master race themes that were expressed by his predecessor's, showing a continuation of the eugenics agenda over the span of many generations. In one published interview he said "*The lowest strata are reproducing too fast. Therefore... they must not have too easy access to relief or hospital treatment lest the removal of the last check on natural selection should make it too easy for children to be produced or to survive; long unemployment should be a ground for sterilization.*"[10] UNESCO is just one of the many international organizations who are working to reduce the world's population.

This is the kind of danger that is embodied in the deceptive ideologies that Darwinism represents. Yes, creatures do evolve over time and adapt to their environment, but that fact should not change how we feel spiritually and it should not alienate us from our fellow human beings by upholding divisive and self-destructive ideals. What Darwin did was point out obvious scientific observations and used those observations as proof to hold up his own political and idealistic agenda. I will agree that Darwin's legitimate findings about evolution logically assassinated the claims of most organized religion. I see this as a very positive and important contribution to the philosophic dialogue, because most organized religions are simply political groups that use our desire for natural spirituality to manipulate our perception of the world, thus influencing our actions. However, this contribution does not mean that everything he said was true and it does not mean that he had benevolent intentions with his work. An enemy of your enemy isn't always your friend. Even the best philosophers in history like Aristotle, and Plato believed in slavery and other forms of subjugation. So while certain philosophers may make meaningful contributions, it's important for us to dissect every word they say and compare it with our own values instead of just accepting every aspect of someone's philosophy without question, just because they happened to do something that we respect.

Today the ideas of Darwin, Galton and other early eugenic scientists are still very much alive among the aristocracy in almost every single part of the world, as it is a philosophy which justifies their authority and allows them to tamper with human evolution. The typical mainstream assumption about eugenics is that it was some misguided, but well-meaning social experiment of the past. However, overpopulation fear mongering and

152

government depopulation programs are very much alive today and are being implemented before our very eyes. Current President Barack Obama picked a man named John Holdren as his "Science Czar" who helped write a book called 'Ecoscience" in the 1970's, that took the social goals of eugenics and gave it the language of the environmental movement, which was starting to grow in popularity. He and other eugenicists at the time sought to hijack the momentum of the environmental movement so they could use it to justify depopulation policies. They knew that if they could convince the public that their policies were for the good of the environment they would be able to advance their eugenics agenda with minimal public resistance.

The book "Ecoscience" discusses forced abortion and mass sterilization as possible "solutions" to the apparent "overpopulation problem". Holdren has backpedaled on some of these statements now that he is in public office, but only because those ideas are becoming more unpopular as the public begins to do their own research. Talk of "master races" and "social engineering" has become taboo in the mainstream culture, so people who advocate these kinds of ideas needed a new way of presenting their social policies. Typically eugenics policies are now sold as environmental protection efforts or charity to the poor, things that everyone would be in support of. Sadly, this is all just the new public relations spin that has been applied to eugenics propaganda. The government and their corporations are responsible for most of the environmental pollution that takes place on this earth, environmental protection can't possibly be a goal for them. It is a traditional role of government and ruling class to tell the working class whatever they want to hear in order to justify new policies that would otherwise be unpopular, this is one of those cases.

Many of today's top eugenicists are actually seen as "philanthropists" or charity workers because their public relations efforts are so persuasive. Bill Gates is a perfect example of this situation, he has established depopulation programs across the world, but disguised them as social programs that are apparently

153

for the "good of the people". If you listened to what the mainstream media had to say, you would believe that Bill Gates was spending his fortune trying to "cure AIDS" or bring "medical care" to third world countries with large vaccination programs. On the other hand if you actually listened to what Bill Gates was saying about these vaccination programs then you would see that his goal is not to improve public health, but actually to stop population growth. This is achieved by adding sterilization chemicals to the vaccinations and then forcing those vaccinations on the population at the barrel of a gun.

At the invite only TED2010 Conference in Long Beach, California, Bill Gates revealed the true intentions of his vaccination programs. In a speech titled "Innovating to Zero!" he said "First we got population. The world today has 6.8 billion people. That's headed up to about 9 billion. Now if we do a really great job on new vaccines, health care, reproductive health services, we lower that by perhaps 10 or 15 percent."[11]

If you look back at what he said you will see that he is suggesting that vaccines will actually work to lower the world's population. This statement makes absolutely no sense if the vaccines were intended to help people and extend their life expectancy. This was a quote that never made it into the headlines because it offers a glimpse into the true nature of modern eugenics, which is very popular among the media tycoons that control the headlines. For example, in a 1996 interview for the Audubon nature magazine, the owner of CNN, Ted Turner said that the population should be reduced by 95%! Since then he has slightly retracted his statement, but not much, saying that a population reduction of 2/3 would be more "reasonable". Ted Turner has also advocated a one child policy, despite having five children himself. These two are simply following in the footsteps of the aristocrats who came before them and are just a few of the many who are still advancing the eugenics agenda today.

Various tax exempt foundations waste billions of dollars every

154

year on untested vaccinations, genetically modified food projects and birth control, instead of spending that money on improving water systems and infrastructure. If a child gets vaccinated and is still forced to survive on contaminated water every day, they really aren't much better off at all, even if the vaccines were safe, which they are not. Sterilizing vaccinations are not just hearsay, in 1995, UNICEF's anti-tetanus vaccinations were contaminated with B-hCG, a pregnancy hormone that can permanently sterilize women. The cost of improving basic public services would actually be much less than the vaccination projects and would greatly improve health, but it wouldn't reduce the population, so that option is not considered. This is especially startling when we remember Bertrand Russell's predictions about using diet, vaccinations and biological agents to cull the population. The people who created some of the first vaccines like the small pox antidote for example, actually refuse to take most modern vaccinations due to the harmful toxins that they now contain.

Today most eugenics projects are filtered through tax exempt foundations and international organizations like the United Nations, Club Of Rome, Rockefeller Foundation, Ford Foundation or the Bill and Melinda Gates Foundation, just to name a few. In the early 1990's, the Club of Rome published a book titled "*The First Global Revolution*", which was the follow up to their fear mongering best seller "*Limits of Growth*" from 1972. The First Global Revolution gave a very up front description of their plan to use the environmental movement as a means to promote depopulation policies. The report read "*It would seem that humans need a common motivation, namely a common adversary, to organize and act together in the vacuum; such a motivation must be found to bring the divided nations together to face an outside enemy, either a real one or else one invented for the purpose. New enemies therefore have to be identified. New strategies imagined, new weapons devised. The common enemy of humanity is man. In searching for a new enemy to unite us, we came up with the idea that pollution, the threat of global warming, water shortages, famine and the like would fit the bill. All these dangers are caused by human intervention, and it is only through changed attitudes and behavior that they can be overcome. The real enemy then, is humanity itself. The old democracies have functioned reasonably well over the last 200 years, but they appear now to be in a phase of complacent stagnation with little evidence of real leadership and innovation Democracy is not a panacea. It cannot organize everything and it is unaware of its own limits. These facts must be faced squarely. Sacrilegious though this may sound, democracy is no longer well suited for the tasks ahead. The complexity and the technical nature of many of today's problems do not always allow elected representatives to make competent decisions at the right time."*[12]

What is being discussed here by one of the most influential think tanks in the world is forced population reduction justified by "real or invented" environmental concerns. In some areas of the world, where there already is very little social freedom, these policies are already beginning to take effect. Even today in China there is a "one child policy" in which families are forced to have abortions if they get pregnant and already have a child. This policy has led to a crisis where the males greatly outweigh the females and created a situation that many have called "gendercide". Despite the dangers of the one child policy it has been embraced by the UN and major tax exempt foundations, as they are both determined to stifle the human population.

In many oppressive societies throughout history the ruling class has sought to control every aspect of the citizen's life, even breeding. This was suggested by Plato in "The Republic", so we know that selective breeding and controlling the population growth of the underclass has been an obsession of elites since at least the time of ancient Greece. Through the centuries the idea of selective breeding has grown into a silent method of warfare, waged over centuries against the working class and third world populations. Many of the major contributors to the eugenics movement are praised as great progressives by the education system, media and pop culture. Despite their popular status these people have introduced some very negative and destructive ideas into the human consciousness, ideas that have been unquestioned and uninvestigated by mainstream culture.

According to Professor Steven W Mosher of the international Population Research Institute the populations in Europe and North America would actually be in decline if it were not for people migrating into the country. The number of births taking place worldwide has been in sharp decline over the past 20 years. If this trend continues then the world's population will quickly peak and then begin a mysterious and dangerous decline. Furthermore, to suggest that reducing the global population will actually improve the quality of life for the people here is resting upon the misconception that poverty is a result of overpopulation. To improve life for people on earth we need to find ways to get people what they need, reducing the amount of people will not help the ones left get what they need. There is more than enough room and resources for all of the people on earth and then some, but unfortunately small numbers of people control these resources using criminal gangs called governments and cartels.

QUOTE SOURCES AND SUGGESTED READING
[0] Trashing the Planet, by Dixy Lee Ray with Lou Guzzo,
[1] An Essay on the Principle of Population - Robert Malthus
[2] The Eugenics Review, a journal published by the Eugenics Education Society (1909)
[3] The Descent of Man – Charles Darwin
[4] Francis Galton to the Times of London, June 6th, 1873
[5] The Pivot of Civilization - Margaret Sanger (1922) Chapter 5
[6] The Pivot of Civilization - Margaret Sanger (1922), p. 274.
[7] The Impact of science on society - Bertrand Russell
[8] The Impact of science on society - Bertrand Russell
[9] The Impact of science on society - Bertrand Russell
[10] Huxley J.S. 1947. Man in the modern world.
[11] http://www.voltairenet.org/Bill-Gates-talks-about-vaccines-to

"In a society that tries to standardize thinking, individuality is not highly prized." -Alex Grey

Section 6

Social Engineering & Psychological Warfare

"You assist an evil system most effectively by obeying its orders and decrees. An evil system never deserves such allegiance. Allegiance to it means partaking of the evil. A good person will resist an evil system with his or her whole soul." -Mahatma Gandhi (Philosopher)

33. 5 Vital Strategies for Peacefully Underthrowing the Status Quo

One of the main reasons why the general population is so attached to the status quo is because many people are looking for a step by step process for how we can peacefully neutralize the power structure and achieve peace on this planet.

This step by step process is not a possibility, because human actions and the advancement of technology are both totally unpredictable. Sadly, it seems that people are waiting for a list of instructions that could never exist.

However, there is definitely hope, because although we cannot precisely chart the course to freedom, we can develop workable solutions that will lead us in the right direction and help us achieve greater levels of peace in our own lives. In this chapter, I am going to list the 5 strategies that I am most supportive of right now, and offer a brief description of how they work and why I believe they are effective approaches to meeting this goal.

(1) – Finding personal freedom – This should definitely be the first step, because when we find peace in our own hearts we are much better prepared and equipped to bring peace into the hearts of others. When you are able to find freedom in your own personal life, you will set a positive example for your peers to follow and you will be contributing to the paradigm shift by "being the change that you want to see in the world" as Gandhi said.

(2) -Practicing Agorism – Agorism is a strategy of noncompliance that uses counter economics and underground markets as a way of keeping power in the hands of the average people, thus slowly diminishing the power and relevance of the control structure. Growing food, using bitcoin, homeschooling, running a small business without licenses, bartering and starting community currencies are all examples of agorist activities. Some agorists are even so bold as to create businesses that will challenge existing state monopolies, like we saw earlier this year when Detroit residents created their own community protection agencies because the police were no longer responding to 911 calls. It is as simple as finding a need in your community for a particular good or service, and attempting to provide that value without any sort of interaction with the government or any other unchosen 3rd parties. In other words, the basic idea is to try solving the problem yourself, with your community instead of waiting around for a politician to make the problem worse.

(3) – Reinventing oldspeak – When it comes to the power of words, the general population is far outmatched by the ruling class. There have been generations of work among the aristocracy completely dedicated to mastering the art of verbal manipulation and deception. They have their newspeak, which cloaks their transgressions in an air of false legitimacy, so we in turn, need to develop an oldspeak that describes reality as it is, but we need to be just as innovative and creative as those working against us. Specific solutions for this step are included in the earlier chapter "An Error in Communication"

(4) – Peaceful parenting – The kind of society that we want to create, is eventually going to be the society that our children will be responsible for. When they become adults, they will interact with each other based on the example that was set for them by their elders. The more children who have lives that are filled with peace, negotiation and tranquility, the better chance there is of that kind of society existing when those children grow up.

Parenting is probably the most important responsibility that any of us will take on in our entire lives, and it is actually our greatest avenue of affecting real change in the world. It is very possible that the fight for freedom will be either won or lost by the next

160

generation, which means that it is up to us to make sure that our children are free to create their own path in learning, without being subjected to the oppressive indoctrination processes that are so prevalent in government schools.

Likewise, it is important that we are not authoritarian with our children, if we truly want the next generation to live in freedom. This does not mean letting children do whatever they want, but it means treating them with the same respect that you would treat an adult that was bigger than you.

(5) -Philosophy and education – As a society we have all been completely betrayed by the public education system and the mainstream media. We have been given false values, irrational principles, and have been led completely astray to the point where it is difficult to make sense of the world, which ultimately results in unfavorable and dangerous behavior. A good many people in the world have fallen victim to this deception, but most people snap out of it quickly when they are able to make sense of reality. This is where philosophy and education come in, because the damage that propaganda has inflicted on our minds is actually fairly easy to reverse, and today with the internet people are now able to teach themselves any subject, any time, at any age and usually for free. So we do have that ability to advance philosophy and have widespread education even in this world today where we are still limited by the current system and its failures.

"If I was educated I would be a damn fool" - Bob Marley *(Reggae Musician)* [0]

34. Education as Indoctrination

The education system in America and most of the rest of the world is a corrupt establishment that does a lot more harm than it does good. The main focus of public education is to mold young minds into accepting authority and to teach them the very basic skills that they will need to be a part of the work force. Schools do not teach people how to think, but only what to think, or more accurately how to remember and regurgitate information which has been fed to them. The useful information that is taught in schools would realistically only take a few months per year to go over, but passing along this information is not what's important to the public school system. What is important to them is the day to day structure of how the school is run which "socializes" and indoctrinates the children. This structure is designed to break the child's spirit and teach them to be submissive to authority figures. It is also specifically designed to groom working class children for their future jobs, which will be at a corporation or bureaucracy of their choosing.

The first public education system was developed in 1819 in Prussia, which is now Germany. This country was very much under authoritarian rule and it is obvious to see that their education system was developed to refine social control. The public education system was separated into 3 different levels, where students were divided based on which class of society they were born into. The nobility would receive the highest level of education where they had an advanced curriculum including the arts and various critical thinking exercises. They were actually arrogant enough to call this level "Real Schulen", which is actually German for "Real School", you just can't make this stuff up! The middle tier, which didn't teach critical thinking, was reserved for the assistants and professionals that served the elite. Then finally the public education system was for the majority of the population. This was the least advanced tier in

162

the education system where creative thinking was completely eliminated. The lower classes were taught how to be obedient and were only given the information that was needed to do their mundane jobs.

The public indoctrination system grew ever more complicated with the industrial revolution and the need for factory laborers. America at the time was at the forefront of manufacturing and the owners of the country's largest factories felt it would be in their best interest to redesign the public education system so that they could mold their future workforce from their youngest and most impressionable years. The usual suspects were involved in this infiltration of the schooling system. Between 1900 and 1920 Andrew Carnegie and John D. Rockefeller alone pumped more money into the education system than the federal government did.

The ruling class also created foundations to fund the educators and the academics that would push this new ideology forward. One of these foundations, John D. Rockefeller's General Education Board had this to say in their opening mission statement *"In our dreams, people yield themselves with perfect docility to our molding hands. The present education conventions of intellectual and character education fade from their minds and unhampered by tradition we work our own good will upon a grateful and responsive folk. We shall not try to make these people or any of their children into men of learning or philosophers, or men of science. We have not to raise up from them authors, educators, poets or men of letters, great artists, painters, musicians, nor lawyers, doctors, statesmen, politicians, creatures of whom we have ample supply. The task is simple. We will organize children and teach them in an perfect way the things their fathers and mothers are doing in an imperfect way"*. [1]

Again, you can feel the elitist bigotry seething in those words, they are describing their wishes to "mold" their servant class into the perfect slaves. Remember, the ruling class looks at us as a different, inferior race that is only here for their personal use and exploitation. There is no doubt that their eugenics based philosophies are deeply woven into the fabric of our education system.

The connection between eugenicists and early educators is well documented. One of these early scholars was a man named Edward Thorndike, he was a strong proponent for introducing dehumanizing eugenics projects and social engineering efforts. These projects included population control, sterilization and other age old practices that have been adopted by the most brutal dictators in history. He is the man responsible for "educational psychology", a school of psychology which established that certain areas of history, logic and philosophy made students resistant to manipulation because it encouraged the children to develop their own independent intellect and made their minds less pliable. This was seen as a problem as the whole point of the public education system was to mold the minds of the working class for the assembly lines and the battlefield.

In an essay for Columbia's Teacher College in 1911 Thorndike suggested that schools should have a role in "selective breeding". In the essay Thorndike talks of how schools should be "*instruments of managed evolution, establishing conditions for selective breeding before the masses take things into their own hands*"[2]. Thorndike was not the only educator to adopt these eugenics based philosophies, this was in fact the dominant attitude within the many government bureaucracies that were developing at the time. Although the rhetoric is toned down these days, the basic result of public education remains the same. Another one of these phony intellectual puppets was Edward Ross, a sociologist who published a mind control manifesto in 1906 called "social control". In it he says "*plans are underway to replace family, community and church with propaganda, mass-media and education...people are only little plastic lumps of dough*" [3]. These were people who were promoting Hitler's ideas when Hitler was a teenager!

In Nazi Germany standardized testing was at the very center of the indoctrination process, and the same tradition continues today in schools throughout America and Europe. If schools were truly designed to educate then standardized testing would have never been introduced. Testing and grading are techniques that are used to TRAIN, CONDITION and CATEGORIZE, not to teach or educate. The propagandized ideologies of the establishment tell us that rigid structure and standardized testing is necessary "for the children" to succeed. That is because the approach they're suggesting is the only way to create the society that they wish to create, so they will accept no other way of doing business and will do their best to downplay the advantages of any alternatives.

Standardized testing was championed by yet another front man for the elite named H. H. Cadard, who was chairman for the Psychology Department at Princeton. He was another eugenicist who saw public education as a tool for creating a worker class hive. In his writings he openly shared his views as if they were not a grossly offensive, he once said *"standardized testing would cause the lower classes to confront their biological inferiority, sort of like wearing a dunce cap. In time that would discourage reproduction of the ants on the anthill"*[4].

Many people believe that the current public education system is something that we have chosen as a society because we want to teach our children about the world, but sadly like many government institutions it is not something we have asked for, but something that has been forced on us by the ruling class. When public schooling started being discussed in the United States, the majority of the public was opposed to it and saw it as an attack on their civil liberties. This is why specific curriculum is required by law, contradictory curriculum is banned by law and children are forced to go to school by law. When something is required by law you can tell that it is a top priority for the establishment and will specifically serve the ruling class, this is because the needs of the ruling class are the government's main concern. When the working class needs something to survive there is a mountain of red tape and endless debate, but when the elite throw a temper tantrum about their cartels losing money, they get a multi trillion dollar blank check in the form of a bailout or subsidy.

America's public indoctrination system has gotten progressively worse as time has passed, and as the ruling class has better mastered the art of social engineering. In 1967 "the behavioral teacher educational project" was launched, which outlined in detail the true goals of the schooling system. This programs self-stated mission was to achieve "*the impersonal manipulation through schooling of a future America in which few will be able to maintain control over their own opinions*" [5]. It also stated that "*each individual receives at birth, a multipurpose identification number which enables employers and other controllers to keep track of them*". [6]

According to the language of their own programs they are grooming the youth of the country for a tightly controlled "worker bee" lifestyle. This system was being designed specifically to create factory workers and crush creativity. This all makes sense when you notice that awards are not given out in school for creativity and self-expression, but for perfect attendance and obedience. This is the same reason why the school bells between classes are reminiscent of the early factory bells and whistles that would separate shifts in the sweatshops of the industrial age.

More recently during the Clinton administration the government made a move to take over the education system so it was under even more extreme control. This attempt is well documented because On Sept. 25, 1998, Rep. Bob Schaffer submitted an 18 page letter to the congressional record outlining the Clinton administration's plans for the education system. It came to be known as "Marc Tucker's Dear Hillary letter", named after Marc Tucker, president of the National Center on Education and the Economy. This letter was from Marc Tucker to the Clintons on November 11th, 1992, just a week after Bill Clinton was "elected"

166

president.

In the letter he talks of "training" and "human resources" and asks for the implementation of three different laws. In the following years Clinton passed these laws, they were the "Goals 2000 Act", the "School-to-Work Act", and the "Elementary and Secondary Education Act". These acts made standardized testing nationally required and set up a nationwide database for keeping track of students. Tucker said the plan was designed to *"remold the entire American system into a seamless web that literally extends from cradle to grave"*. [7] As usual, this plan was to be implemented over an extended period of time as to avoid public resistance to any sudden change. The system would be built to eventually use "job matching" programs that would place students in certain job categories depending upon their standardized test scores.

The Clinton education policy was not specific to just his administration, like many efforts in Washington this has been a bi-partisan effort slowly built over many different presidential terms. It has long been the goal of the establishment to put these measures into place, but they work incrementally so small steps are made one by one over long periods of time, in order to make the moves seem unrelated and to keep a relatively low profile. When these politicians and self-appointed "experts" speak of "human resources" and "social engineering" that is exactly what they mean, they see us as a "resource" to be "engineered" or controlled. Their motives and goals are hidden in plain sight in the very language of the laws that they pass and the philosophies they endorse.

The overall curriculum and structure in public schools has remained the same from the original Prussian model, all the way to present day. Critical thinking is not only suppressed but it is almost completely condemned within school walls. Students that exhibit signs of creativity are often times singled out by teachers as trouble makers because they are typically more resistant to authority and more independent. Sometimes when a student's

167

creativity cannot be broken they are forced to take mind numbing psychoactive drugs like Ritalin or Adderall.

Repetitious training exercises are also hidden within the basic structure of a school day. In America children are forced to "pledge allegiance" to the flag every single day, this exercise is designed to implant nationalistic tendencies into the conscious mind of the student. Demanding students to walk in a straight line or ask before going to the bathroom is a more subtle form of training, however it also sets them up to "fall in line" when they graduate school and move on with their lives. Homework is given so students are so consumed with the mandated material that they have no time to learn anything on their own. Later, when they get out of school their curiosity is totally destroyed and they no longer have any desire to learn anything at all because they associate learning with the forced repetitious bore that public schooling is. Students leave school thinking that they have already learned everything of importance in the world, and they look forward to being relieved of the stress that they now associate with learning.

The authoritarian nature of the public education system also works to further polarize the class structure by rewarding conformists who are willing to obey, and punishing nonconformists who wish to seek their own answers and form their own opinions. Eventually when these children grow up, those who were willing to conform to the teachings of the system often find themselves with better jobs and more money, which results in an easier, less stressful lifestyle and a higher position in society. People of high positions in society, so called experts often receive more respect for their opinions whether that respect is deserved or not, while the rest of us struggle to have our voices heard. The people who are able to shut up and do as they're told are rewarded, thus encouraging them to reinforce the status quo and project the teachings of the establishment onto the rest of society. This is how propaganda becomes philosophy and the ideas of the elite are assimilated into culture and turn into the norms that are worshiped by society.

168

Along with the indoctrinating structure of the public school system, the curriculum is also distorted to fit a political agenda. In 2010, in the state of Texas there was a lot of controversy surrounding a textbook company that was trying to rewrite history in order to advance a neo-con agenda. The NAACP was completely infuriated by a few textbook changes in particular regarding slavery and the celebration of Jim Crow laws. Since most textbooks printed in America come from Texas this was a very serious issue that affected the minds of millions of impressionable children.

Generally the historical curriculum in government school is skewed to portray the establishment in a positive light. History lessons make warmongers look like martyrs because the warmongers have control over the formation of these lessons. Many of the harsh realities involving the civil war, the great depression and the civil rights movements were completely left out, along with the real history of slave owning aristocratic presidents and robber barons. These are pivotal points in history that one must have a clear picture of in order to make sense of what is going on in the world today. Without a proper understanding of the injustice that our species has overcome in the past, we will not be able to overcome the injustices that we are experiencing in the present.

The most vital lesson that has been removed from our education system is not made up of a list of facts like one may believe, but is actually a step by step process in critical thinking called the "trivium". The trivium allows one to become autodidactic, which simply means "self-taught". This process was removed from the public education system because as I mentioned, the people who were in charge of the curriculum were not interested in teaching our children how to think, but rather what to think. Prior to the Prussian schooling model, the classical education was comprised of two parts, the trivium and the quadrivium. The trivium consisted of grammar, logic and rhetoric while the quadrivium was arithmetic, geometry, music, and astronomy, together they make up the 7 liberal arts.

One of the main proponents of modern "education" was President Woodrow Wilson. He admitted very plainly that *"We want one class of persons to have a liberal education, and we want another class of persons, a very much larger class, of necessity, in every society, to forego the privileges of a liberal education and fit themselves to perform specific difficult manual tasks."* [8]

When he mentioned a "liberal education" he was most definitely referring to the trivium and quadrivium, most specifically the trivium. Logic and critical thinking were considered to be useless or dangerous skills for the working class to be developing, so these studies were occulted from the mainstream and reserved for the ruling class. Without learning the proper critical thinking skills the general population is left vulnerable to psychological attack and manipulation. This is especially apparent when one class of people is given these tools and everyone else is not, it allows those who have the information to easily prey on those who do not.

Good, honest people that want to educate and make a positive impact on people's lives are naturally drawn to becoming a teacher. Unfortunately, when they eventually get into that position they realize that their hands are tied in a lot of ways in regards to what can be taught to the students. Teachers are more or less forced to uphold the status quo and pass the establishments propaganda onto the students. Most of the people that end up being teachers are great people with the best intentions, but they are simply being used as a spokesperson for the state mandated curriculum. When a teacher steps out of those narrow boundaries they risk losing their job and tarnishing their reputation, this is because those boundaries are in place to "mold the minds" of the students. This isn't to say that a legitimate community school system is impossible, but it certainly isn't going to happen with the kind of subversive culture and corrupt establishment that we are faced with today. These laws and the overall way we look at education needs to be challenged.

The truth is that government schooling is not designed to help children in any way, it is intended to train them. This training process is actually very damaging to children, as many educators have noticed. John Taylor Gatto was New York City Teacher of the Year in 1989, 1990, and 1991, and New York State Teacher of the Year in 1991. After years of struggling with the state mandated curriculum, he eventually decided to quit teaching in government schools. He quit at the height of his teaching career by posting an article in the Wall Street Journal OP Ed pages entitled "I quit, I think". In his resignation he admitted that he could no longer continue a career where he was forced to hurt children and ruin their minds year after year. The harm that he felt he was inflicting on children was not directly physical, but was a kind of subliminal brainwashing that took place through what Gatto referred to as "the hidden curriculum". Gatto recognized that the structure of modern schooling was designed in such a way to discourage creativity, independence and individuality while reinforcing obedience to authority. His Wall Street journal article started with the following:

"I've taught public school for 26 years but I just can't do it anymore. For years I asked the local school board and superintendent to let me teach a curriculum that doesn't hurt kids, but they had other fish to fry. So I'm going to quit, I think. I've come slowly to understand what it is I really teach: A curriculum of confusion, class position, arbitrary justice, vulgarity, rudeness, disrespect for privacy, indifference to quality, and utter dependency. I teach how to fit into a world I don't want to live in. I just can't do it anymore. I can't train children to wait to be told what to do; I can't train people to drop what they are doing when a bell sounds; I can't persuade children to feel some justice in their class placement when there isn't any, and I can't persuade children to believe teachers have valuable secrets they can acquire by becoming our disciples. That isn't true. Government schooling is the most radical adventure in history. It kills the

family by monopolizing the best times of childhood and by teaching disrespect for home and parents. An exaggeration? Hardly. Parents aren't meant to participate in our form of schooling, rhetoric to the contrary. My orders as schoolteacher are to make children fit an animal training system, not to help each find his or her personal path."[9]

Proper education is a necessary part of our advancement on this earth. If we are not able to create a better learning environment for our children then they will be doomed to repeat the same madness that came before them. The whole structure of our education system is completely unnecessary, and never was relevant to begin with.

Given the right conditions to grow, a child's mind would be able to do incredible things, but they will become thoughtless drones if they are forced into a strict regimen where they are not able to think creatively and freely.

We must develop an education paradigm which celebrates creativity and individuality and actually works to educate, instead of indoctrinate. This is why now more than ever parents are choosing to take matters into their own hands and homeschool their children or use alternative education centers. In 2010 the number of children being homeschooled was 2 million and rapidly climbing as the public is becoming more aware of the faults in the government education system.

Homeschooling is still frightening to a lot of people because the idea of sending children off to a state institution for 12 years has become so deeply ingrained in western culture, even though the government is obviously a horrible candidate for a babysitter. However, this is actually a relatively new practice and literacy rates have actually plummeted since the government got involved in education and forced parents to send their children to specific schools by law. That's not to say that organized group learning isn't a valuable thing, but there's no need for government involvement for organized group learning to take place.

Many of the alternative learning centers popping up worldwide have adopted the Montessori Method of education which to some extent allows children to direct their own path in learning. This method is named after and was developed by an Italian educator and physician by the name of Maria Montessori. Her work rested upon the idea that when given freedom and independence children will grow into far more responsible adults and will have a continued interest in learning. Montessori took what she knew about developmental psychology and applied that to her work with children and had great success with improving the outlook and learning abilities of her students. There are many affordable options available for parents who don't want to put their children through government schools and even more options will develop as more people begin to understand the disadvantages of state education.

QUOTE SOURCES AND SUGGESTED READING
[0]As recorded in Time Will Tell (1992) by Declan Lowney
[1] The Underground History of American Education (2001) - John Taylor Gatto
[2]The Underground History of American Education (2001) - John Taylor Gatto
[3] Social Control (1901) - Edward Roth
[4] Dumbing Us Down: The Hidden Curriculum of Compulsory Schooling (1992). - John Taylor Gatto
[5][6] The Underground History of American Education (2001) -
[7] None dare call it education, John A. Stormer
[8] The Papers of Woodrow Wilson: 1908-1909
[9] The Wall Street Journal, July 25, 1991

"Technological progress is like an axe in the hands of a pathological criminal." -Albert Einstein (Scientist) [0]

35. Social Engineering and the Scientific Dictatorship

Since the first power hungry tyrant took the throne, the establishment has always used the most advanced technology of its time as a weapon against anyone who threatened their authority. The most powerful tools and deepest knowledge have always been hoarded by the ruling class because they fear that if they were to lose the technological advantage then they will also lose their social dominance as well. Since technological advancement itself has been pushed along primarily by warmongers, most of the tools and techniques that have been developed throughout history have been designed to help a small group of people to dominate a larger group of people. This goes for all weapons like the atomic bomb as well as neutral devices like the printing press, modern computers or the Hollerith machine that IBM made for Hitler. The neutral devices that I mentioned can be used for both good and evil depending on how they are applied. Unfortunately, for most of the people on earth, the ruling class has always used any technology they could get their hands on to advance their totalitarian agenda. Likewise, they are usually able to weaponize any kind of peaceful technology that comes about, and then subsequently hoard that technology for themselves.

Technological advancement and scientific progress are among the primary sources for human power on the planet earth, this is not inherently good or evil, but it depends on how that science or technology is applied in the world. Using the Einstein quote from the beginning of the chapter as an example, an axe is a tool that can be applied positively if in the correct hands, but could also be used as a weapon if it falls into the wrong hands. As Einstein recognized, science and technology have been monopolized and controlled by different psychopathic rulers for a very long time. An unbelievable amount of time, human energy and resources are poured into scientific research that was requested by the

174

government or the ruling oligarchy that sits behind it. Most of this research is applied to military technology as well as a myriad of social control mechanisms, psychological warfare techniques and other means of maintaining power.

In addition to disseminating propaganda and developing new methods of controlling people, the social planners were also responsible for steering the direction of technological progress. This was achieved by strictly controlling the process by which one joins the scientific establishment, and then monopolizing their time with military or eugenics projects once they were finally certified. This is how the militarization of technology and scientific progress has accelerated in the past hundred years.

In the 20th century, weapons of war and systems of control were able to grow more threatening than ever before with the help of electricity, air travel, quantum physics, industrial manufacturing and other breakthroughs. For the first time in history, the tools that were available to power hungry tyrants had the ability to destroy entire civilizations and severely damage the environment. Warfare and despotism were horrific in previous centuries, but now with the ability to instantly spy on anyone or attack anywhere in the world, at any time, an unprecedented level of power has been achieved by our illegitimate rulers.

Today we are certainly dealing with a different breed of authoritarianism, one that many have rightfully described as a "scientific dictatorship". Aldous Huxley was mainly responsible for popularizing this term. He is the author who wrote Brave New World, a dystopian novel in which a scientific dictatorship ruled over humanity. However, his interests in these topics were much deeper than just science fiction, as his family was actually heavily involved in the scientific industrial complex. Aldous may have been the black sheep of the family because in his writings he always seemed to portray the scientific dictatorship in a negative light while his family openly praised eugenics and psychological manipulation techniques. How Aldous truly felt on these subjects is not known for sure, but in his books and his speeches he condemned these oppressive applications of science. It is a personal theory of mine that Aldous may have been more humane than the rest of his family due to his psychedelic experience that was documented in the book "The Doors of Perception".

Brave New World depicted a society where citizens were subject to constant state propaganda and were coaxed into taking mood stabilizing drugs which kept them apathetic. On March 20, 1962 Aldous Huxley gave a speech at Berkley University and revealed that his book was based on actual research that was taking place within the scientific industrial complex, by order of the government and ruling class.

During the Speech Huxley said "*It seems to me that the nature of the ultimate revolution with which we are now faced is precisely this: That we are in process of developing a whole series of techniques which will enable the controlling oligarchy who have always existed and presumably will always exist to get people to love their servitude. This is the, it seems to me, the ultimate in malevolent revolutions shall we say, and this is a problem which has interested me many years and about which I wrote thirty years ago, a fable, Brave New World, which is an account of society making use of all the devices available and some of the devices which I imagined to be possible making use of them in order to, first of all, to standardize the population, to iron out inconvenient human differences, to create, to say, mass produced models of human beings arranged in some sort of scientific caste system. Since then, I have continued to be extremely interested in this problem and I have noticed with increasing dismay a number of the predictions which were purely fantastic when I made them thirty years ago have come true or seem in process of coming true.*

A number of techniques about which I talked seem to be here already. And there seems to be a general movement in the direction of this kind of ultimate revolution, a method of control by which a people can be made to enjoy a state of affairs by which any decent standard they ought not to enjoy. This, the enjoyment of servitude, Well this process is, as I say, has gone on for over the years, and I have become more and more interested in what is happening." [1]

This knowledge was coming from a well-respected scientist and multi-generational insider of the establishment, he was one of the brightest minds of his time. Huxley's credibility and experience behind the scenes made this speech a stunning revelation that shed new light on the darkest corners of scientific research. His brother Julian was a biologist, as well as the first Director of UNESCO and a founder of the World Wildlife Fund. As I described earlier, these particular organizations, especially UNESCO have been slowly working to create a scientific dictatorship since well before Aldous spoke at Berkley, which makes his speech even more interesting.

The Huxley's ran in the same circles as another prominent Eugenicist Bertrand Russell, who was also extremely open about his elitist views. In his book *"The Impact of Science on Society"* Russell discussed social engineering and a scientific dictatorship.

Russell writes, *"I think the subject which will be of most importance politically is mass psychology. Mass psychology is, scientifically speaking, not a very advanced study... This study is immensely useful to practical men, whether they wish to become rich or to acquire the government. It is, of course, as a science, founded upon individual psychology, but hitherto it has employed rule-of-thumb methods which were based upon a kind of intuitive common sense. Its importance has been enormously increased by the growth of modern methods of propaganda. Of these the most influential is what is called 'education'. Religion plays a part, though a diminishing one; the Press, the cinema and the radio play an increasing part. What is essential in mass psychology is the art of persuasion. If you compare a speech of Hitler's with a speech of (say) Edmund Burke, you will see what strides have been made in the art since the eighteenth century.*

177

What went wrong formerly was that people had read in books that man is a rational animal, and framed their arguments on this hypothesis. We now know that limelight and a brass band do more to persuade than can be done by the most elegant train of syllogisms. It may be hoped that in time anybody will be able to persuade anybody of anything if he can catch the patient young and is provided by the State with money and equipment. This subject will make great strides when it is taken up by scientists under a scientific dictatorship."[2]

A few pages later he continues *"Apart from the danger of war, I see no reason why such a regime should be unstable. After all, most civilized and semi-civilized countries known to history have had a large class of slaves or serfs completely subordinate to their owners. There is nothing in human nature that makes the persistence of such a system impossible. And the whole development of scientific technique has made it easier than it used to be to maintain a despotic rule of a minority. When the government controls the distribution of food, its power is absolute so long as it can count on the police and the armed forces. And their loyalty can be secured by giving them some of the privileges of the governing class. I do not see how any internal movement of revolt can ever bring freedom to the oppressed in a modern scientific dictatorship"*[3]

Bertrand Russell advocated the idea of a scientific dictatorship because as a member of the oligarchy he stood to gain a lot of power through becoming a social engineer. He belonged to a privileged group of intellectuals who would ultimately become the new priest class in western culture, molding public opinion according to their personal philosophies. This new expert class was filling the philosophical void that was created when the ideas of the church fell out of favor, leaving the aristocracy with very little influence over the minds of their subjects. Instead of being encouraged to apply the methods of science to their own lives, people were asked to depend on statements from the "experts" to dictate their opinions. This kind of mentality has consumed today's culture to the point where no one trusts their own judgment about anything, but will trust every word that comes from an establishment "expert" without doing any background research of their own. Despite the impressive intellectual credentials held by the so called 'experts", many of them are on the establishments payroll and wouldn't dare speak out against the status quo even if they know in their hearts that it is the right thing to do.

The "expert" classes of scientists, educators, politicians, and other prominent intellectuals have been working to deceive the general population for almost an entire century. That's not to say that every single member of the scientific community is a part of this plan, but the people at the very top, at the heads of foundations, those who control the bureaucracies, they are the ones who I am referring to. One such social engineer is Zbigniew Brzezinski, a tyrant who is still a major influence in geopolitics. In 1970 he wrote of a scientific dictatorship, laying out his goals for the 21st century by saying "*society would be dominated by an elite whose claim to political power would rest on allegedly superior scientific know-how. Unhindered by the restraints of traditional liberal values, this elite would not hesitate to achieve its political ends by using the latest modern techniques for influencing public behavior and keeping society under close surveillance and control. Under such circumstances, the scientific and technological momentum of the country would not be reversed but would actually feed on the situation it exploits*".[4]

As I have pointed out many times so far, the ruling class has no problem revealing their goals, and some have stated on the record that they wish to establish a worldwide scientific dictatorship. It only makes sense that they will take advantage of their incredible wealth to develop technology that will assist them in achieving their goals. This is not mere speculation either, but has been documented by various members of the scientific establishment over many generations. The fact that scientific advancement is presently monopolized by the most corrupt element of our society should not push us to vilify science itself,

179

but the lessons of this unfortunate predicament should teach us to be much more careful with such an important responsibility and to not allow this kind of power to be centralized in a few hands. The vast knowledge and ever growing technology that humans take for granted is an extremely powerful gift that seems to be specific to our species, at least as far as this planet is concerned. This power and responsibility has been greatly disrespected by those who maintain control. The most expensive and time consuming technological projects undertaken by humankind have not been for the betterment of society, but were designed to kill, control and otherwise dehumanize innocent people.

When children grow up dreaming of becoming scientists they have the purest of aspirations and if they were left to pursue their own studies they would be able to accomplish the unimaginable. Unfortunately, to become a member of the scientific community one has to jump through many bureaucratic hoops until they are eventually inducted into an establishment which is tightly regulated and directed by warmongers and control freak aristocrats. People spend half of their lives taking classes, passing tests and filling out applications in hopes that one day they can become a scientist and cure a disease. After years of struggling to make the cut they realize that there is no funding for their charitable projects, and that if they dare step outside of the established guidelines they will be exiled from the scientific community.

In order to send scientific progress in a more positive direction it is necessary to develop a more open, transparent and decentralized scientific establishment. Influence from the government and military industrial complex is the primary reason for our dismal technological outlook, and like many things science would flourish in the absence of the state. Think about the resources that are used for war and social control, now imagine if those resources, and that energy were applied to curing diseases, space travel, free and clean energy solutions, food production and sustainable agriculture. Amazing things would be able to take place if only human beings were allowed to use their intellect and the resources of the earth to achieve positive goals instead of destruction. This is not a radical concept, it was understood by President Eisenhower as he revealed in his 1961 farewell address before leaving office, when he said:

"Today, the solitary inventor, tinkering in his shop, has been overshadowed by task forces of scientists in laboratories and testing fields. In the same fashion, the free university, historically the fountainhead of free ideas and scientific discovery, has experienced a revolution in the conduct of research. Partly because of the huge costs involved, a government contract becomes virtually a substitute for intellectual curiosity. For every old blackboard there are now hundreds of new electronic computers. The prospect of domination of the nation's scholars by Federal employment, project allocations, and the power of money is ever present – and is gravely to be regarded. Yet, in holding scientific research and discovery in respect, as we should, we must also be alert to the equal and opposite danger that public policy could itself become the captive of a scientific-technological elite."[5]

QUOTE SOURCES AND SUGGESTED READING
[0] The handbook of conflict resolution: theory and practice - Morton Deutsch, Peter T. Coleman, Eric Colton Marcus (2006)
[1] Aldous Huxley, March 20, 1962 Berkeley Language Center - Speech Archive SA 0269
[2] Bertrand Russell, The Impact of Science on Society, (Routledge, 1985), page 40
[3] Bertrand Russell, The Impact of Science on Society, (Routledge, 1985), page 66
[4] Zbigniew Brzezinski, Between Two Ages: America's Role in the Technetronic Era. (Viking Press, New York, 1970), page 97
[5] Dwight D. Eisenhower, Eisenhower's Farewell Address to the Nation. January 17, 1961

"Today the tyrant rules not by club or fist, but disguised as a market researcher, he shepherds his flocks in the ways of utility and comfort" - Marshall McLuhan (Writer) [0]

36. Propaganda, Public Relations and Psychological Warfare

Public Relations, better known as advertising, is one of the most important industries to reinvent itself in the 20th century and most people actually know very little about it. It has changed the way we are governed and has laid the foundation for our materialistic consumer culture, as well as opened the floodgate for advanced psychological warfare. From propaganda to deceptive marketing, the field of public relations has allowed politicians and corporations to manipulate the desires and opinions of the working class. These practices were put in place so the ruling class could have better control over the much larger serf population.

In the early 20th century there was growing discontent among the general public, who had finally become tired of being treated like second class citizens. The people began to hold strikes, boycotts and take any action they could to weaken the establishment, in hopes to bring about a more humane society and working environment. This was bad news for those in control because they need the cooperation of the working class to build their empires and fill the ranks in their armies. The government and corporations needed a more respectable image, and that need gave rise to the public relations movement.

There were many minds that made this movement possible, but the field itself is most typically associated with a man named Edward Bernays. Bernays is known as the father of public relations not because he was the first or only person to study propaganda, but rather because he was the first person to explain its practical use in a published work. He was also the first person to use the term "public relations" to describe the work of the propagandist. In his famous book bluntly titled

"Propaganda", Bernays highlighted his own work and the works of many other prominent figures in the public relations industry.

It is important to mention that Edward Bernays came from a very prominent family in the field of psychology, as he was the nephew of Sigmund Freud, the "father of psychology". Freud's discoveries about the human unconscious were the basis of his nephews work. Bernays used what he knew about the inner workings of the mind as a tool of persuasion to control the masses through their subconscious. In "Propaganda" Bernays doesn't even attempt to sugarcoat his sinister plan when he makes statements like this one:

"The conscious and intelligent manipulation of the organized habits and opinions of the masses is an important element in democratic society. Those who manipulate this unseen mechanism of society constitute an invisible government which is the true ruling power of our country. We are governed, our minds are molded, our tastes formed, our ideas suggested, largely by men we have never heard of...in almost every act of our daily lives, whether in the sphere of politics or business, in our social conduct or our ethical thinking we are dominated by the relatively small number of persons...who understand the mental processes and social patterns of the masses. It is they who pull the wires that control the public mind." [1]

Before Bernays published "propaganda" in 1928, advertisements were far less complicated than the ones that were seen after. While advertisements in the past would just describe a product and its uses, now they would appeal to the viewer's subconscious fears and desires in order to make a mental connection between product and consumer. Do you ever wonder why commercials often times have absolutely nothing to do with the product they are trying to sell? It is because they are trying to sell an image that you can relate to, not just a product. An unbelievable amount of thought, time and energy is put into every advertisement. Just think about how much money a 30 second commercial spot during the super bowl costs. These

183

corporations know exactly what they are doing. They are playing on your emotions and subconscious through their advertisements so you buy their product, whether you want to or not.

Edward Bernays clients were some of the most successful businesses of the time, thanks to Bernays cunning advertisements. Betty Crocker approached him when they were having trouble selling their instant cake mix. Bernays instructed them to change the recipe by adding an egg, which would make the consumer feel that they weren't just using an "instant mix". Bernays trick worked, and sales soared. His next client though, was far less innocent. A short time later Bernays was approached by the American Tobacco Company who was trying to figure out how to convince females to smoke cigarettes. Apparently at the time there was a stigma attached to females smoking as it was not "lady like". Bernays and the ATC wanted to end this taboo and open up the tobacco market to the feminine half of the human population, which would double sales. Bernays exploited the women's civil right struggle by making advertisements that claimed it was liberating and empowering for women to smoke cigarettes. In his advertisements, Bernays called cigarettes "torches of freedom" and encouraged young feminists to "light up". Again his deceptive marketing worked and the American Tobacco Company got incredibly rich.

One of the other PR masterminds that Edward Bernays mentions in his book is none other than Ivy Lee who was also working to build the propaganda industry at the time, but from a slightly different angle. Where Bernays was focused on creating the psychology of consumerism, Lee was more interested in "crisis management" or in other words getting his billionaire clients out of trouble and restoring their public image. Today both trains of thought have converged to create a well-rounded system of deception and public perception management, where an underclass of consumers is almost entirely convinced that their corrupt masters are wonderful people.

Ivy Lee's most infamous clients were the Rockefellers, and his first order of business for them was to repair their tarnished reputation. The Rockefellers were America's first billionaires who acquired their wealth by exploiting their workers, exploiting natural resources and operating cartels within the railroad, banking and oil industries. Their reputation took a turn for the worse after Colorado's "Bloody Ludlow" massacre in 1914 in which the ruthless aristocrats ordered the national guard to attack striking workers who were protesting outside the factories. When the battle was over, 20 people were dead, only one of them was a soldier and many of them were children. Historian Howard Zinn called the massacre "*the culminating act of perhaps the most violent struggle between corporate power and laboring men in American history*". After this incident it became apparent to the Rockefellers and other titans of industry that they needed help with perception management and damage control.

There was rightfully a growing distrust for the corporations and the ruling class among the majority of Americans at the time and the ruling class knew they had to do something to change it. The Rockefellers acted by hiring Ivy Lee to manage and improve their public image. Lee was probably chosen for the job because years earlier he came up with an idea that would revolutionize how corporations and governments communicated with the peasant class. In 1906 when a horrible train accident happened in Atlantic City, Lee suggested that the company issue a statement presenting their side of the story to the press, this was to be the first "press release".

The disaster was caused by negligence on the part of the railroad company and was witnessed by hundreds of people, so the press release was a special measure taken in hopes to get their side of the story out first. The press release scheme was a success and two days later the New York Times just printed the company's statement word for word! This kind of insanity continues to this day where "news" reporters simply regurgitate the statement from the white house or from Exxon about what they're doing, instead of making any attempt at investigative journalism.

Lee certainly had his hands full with the Rockefeller family because unlike an isolated train wreck, this aristocratic dynasty was hurting and exploiting the people on a daily basis, and have been for generations. Starting with the Ludlow Massacre, Lee began to change the public image of the family and their businesses even if it meant telling blatant lies. Lee sent out mass bulletins claiming that the people who had been killed in the Colorado protests were the victims of a house fire caused by an "overturned stove". He also accused a popular union worker named "Mother Jones" of being a prostitute and running a brothel.

In addition to lying, Lee suggested that the families make high profile donations to various charities and have photographs taken of them handing out money to the commoners to make the public think that they were good hearted and generous people. Again the plan worked and the application of public relations was able to resurrect Rockefeller's reputation and then build it to the point where it is today. At the time of his death Lee was being investigated by congress for his work with the Nazis through the company IG Farben and a proxy firm called the German Dye Trust, he was also a founding member of the Council on Foreign Relations, which I will explain in detail later on.

It was common for the public relations tycoons to be involved in various competing political organizations as well as competing corporations, and that same tradition continues today. Even non-government organized crime syndicates have used public relations techniques to keep themselves in the good graces of the public. For example, famous gangster Al Capone was loved by his community because he ran soup kitchens and made sure he was seen as a generous and upstanding citizen. Public relations for a government sponsored crime syndicate is far more complicated, of course.

186

One early public relations expert Walter Lippmann worked closely with Edward Bernays and was specifically interested in the use of propaganda to push the public into a war or to agree with other unpopular political policies. In his work, Lippmann was explicit in defending the ruling classes "need" to control the behavior of the working class, in his thinking this kind of control was "necessary in a democracy". Lippmann's book, "*Public Opinion*" opens with Plato's "*Allegory of the Cave*", which is very revealing if you're familiar with the story.

For those of you who are not familiar with the Allegory of the Cave, I'll take a minute to summarize this wonderful parable. The story describes a group of people who have been held prisoner in a cave for their entire lives. In the cave, the prisoners are chained to the floor in such a way that they can only face a blank wall and cannot move or look in any other direction. All day they are forced to watch shadow figures that are projected onto a wall by puppets parading in front of a fire, which is positioned at the back of the cave. In simpler terms, this would be like a modern day television or projector screen. The prisoners actually believe the shadows in front of them are the only thing that is real, as it is the only thing they have been exposed to for their entire lives. They have given the shadows names and have a whole system of beliefs built around them. The philosopher is represented by the person who is freed from his chains and escapes the cave to see the outside world for what it is. When the philosopher returns and attempts to explain the outside world to his cellmates, he is met with disbelief and hostility. Even if the philosopher were to unchain another prisoner and show him the outside world, it would be too difficult to describe and so far outside of their frame of reality that they would still insist on remaining in the comforts of their familiar cave. The released prisoners would be hurt and confused by their new discovery and may even become angry with the philosopher for showing him the outside world.

When the philosopher returns to the cave after being exposed to the true nature of reality, Plato concludes that "*Wouldn't he

remember his first home, what passed for wisdom there, and his
fellow prisoners, and consider himself happy and them pitiable?
And wouldn't he disdain whatever honors, praises, and prizes
were awarded there to the ones who guessed best which
shadows followed which? Moreover, if he to return there,
wouldn't he be rather bad at their game, no longer being
accustomed to the darkness? Wouldn't it be said of him that he
went up and came back with his eyes corrupted, and that it's not
even worth trying to go up? And if they were somehow able to
get their hands on and kill the man who attempts to release them
and show them the outside world, wouldn't they kill him?" [2]

The Allegory of the Cave shows us that our thoughts and beliefs
can be shaped and molded according to someone else's will, if
that person (or group of people) has the ability to control all of
the information we receive from a very young age. Furthermore,
it shows us that when the prisoners are conditioned enough to a
specific way of life and specific frame of reality, then they
themselves will act as a guard or warden for themselves, and
any fellow prisoners who might dare to question the status quo.

The fact that Lippmann opens his book with this parable shows
us that he feels its teachings are extremely important to his
whole philosophy, otherwise he would have started the book out
some other way. In relation to the Allegory of the Cave,
Lippmann's goal is to be the force manipulating the "shadows on
the wall" thus controlling the minds of those in the "cave", or
world. The term public opinion was meant to describe the false
version of reality that is created by the propagandists on behalf
of the ruling class.

This is not merely speculation, but was described by Lippmann
himself when he wrote that *"We have learned to call this*
propaganda. A group of men, who can prevent independent
access to the event, can arrange the news to suit their
purpose... ...In order to conduct a propaganda campaign; there
must be some barrier between the public and the event. Access
to the real environment must be limited, before anyone can

create a pseudo-environment he thinks wise or desirable."[3] This "pseudo-environment" is similar to what I referred to earlier as "nationalistic folklore", or what is known in the military as psychological operations or "psy-ops", for short.

Lippmann was interested in shaping public opinion in such a way that the general population could be easily forced into doing whatever was asked of them, or in his words he was trying to "manufacture consent". If you are familiar with the activist and scholar Noam Chomsky then you will recognize the term "Manufacturing Consent", as it is one of his most popular books, but the term was actually originally coined by Lippmann.

In his own words Lippmann discusses the process of manufacturing consent, in public opinion he writes "*That the manufacture of consent is capable of great refinements no one, I think, denies. The process by which public opinions arise is certainly no less intricate than it has appeared in these pages, and the opportunities for manipulation open to anyone who understands the process are plain enough. . . . As a result of psychological research, coupled with the modern means of communication, the practice of democracy has turned a corner. A revolution is taking place, infinitely more significant than any shifting of economic power. . . . Under the impact of propaganda, not necessarily in the sinister meaning of the word alone, the old constants of our thinking have become variables. It is no longer possible, for example, to believe in the original dogma of democracy; that the knowledge needed for the management of human affairs comes up spontaneously from the human heart. Where we act on that theory we expose ourselves to self-deception, and to forms of persuasion that we cannot verify. It has been demonstrated that we cannot rely upon intuition, conscience, or the accidents of casual opinion if we are to deal with the world beyond our reach.*" [4]

These sentiments are echoed in Bernays work as well, In Propaganda he writes "*In theory, every citizen makes up his mind on public questions and matters of private conduct. In*

189

practice, if all men had to study for themselves the abstruse economic, political, and ethical data involved in every question, they would find it impossible to come to a conclusion about anything......It might be better to have, instead of propaganda and special pleading, committees of wise men who would choose our rulers, dictate our conduct, private and public, and decide upon the best types of clothes for us to wear and the best kinds of food for us to eat. But we have chosen the opposite method, that of open competition. We must find a way to make free competition function with reasonable smoothness. To achieve this society has consented to permit free competition to be organized by leadership and propaganda. Some of the phenomena of this process are criticized—the manipulation of news, the inflation of personality, and the general ballyhoo by which politicians and commercial products and social ideas are brought to the consciousness of the masses. The instruments by which public opinion is organized and focused may be misused. But such organization and focusing are necessary to orderly life." [5]

This twisted world view was common among the intellectual elite at the time and still resonates today through their teachings. "Propaganda" actually wasn't a bad word until it was picked up and used by Hitler, who was an avid reader of the work coming from western PR experts. Prior to Hitler, propaganda was a totally acceptable word that was used by politicians and advertisers frequently.

In the work of both Lippmann and Bernays, they suggested that advanced psychological techniques had already been applied to propaganda since prior to World War 1, and they knew first hand. It was these two professors who convinced President Woodrow Wilson to establish the Tavistock Institute of Human Relations, an organization that was designed to use psychological techniques against the American people in order to get them to comply with unpopular policies.

The first main objective of the Tavistock Institute and its team of

190

professional con men was to convince the American people that it was a good idea to get into World War 1. This was quite an undertaking considering that most Americans were opposed to any war, especially one that was halfway around the world and didn't concern them. President Wilson was also "elected" on an antiwar platform so Tavistock really had their work cut out for them. This foundation was funded by American tax dollars, the British royal family, the Rothschild's, the Milner Group and the Rockefeller family trusts.

The propaganda created at the Tavistock Institute was so effective that the organization would continue to get support and funding until eventually growing to become an integral part of the military industrial complex, as it is to this day. The research that took place here has shaped our lives and our society more than anyone can imagine. Things that are often taken for granted were actually a direct result of this research, like the opinion poll for example. The opinion poll was a creation of the Tavistock Institute, and was developed with the intention of molding public opinion, not measuring it. Today the Tavistock Institute still exists, but now it is only one of many psychological warfare interests that have extensive geopolitical influence.

While the Tavistock camp focused on the group mind and the nature of public opinion, there was a similar group of psychologists performing lab experiments with animals and human beings in order to develop future methods of controlling the mind. These lab studies provided research on human behavior that would later be used by public relations firms when they developed new techniques for social manipulation. The psychologists that specialized in these studies became known as "behaviorists", a term that was coined by wannabe Dr. Frankenstein, John B. Watson.

In the very opening paragraph of one of his famous articles Watson summarizes his studies. He writes "*Psychology as the behaviorist views it is a purely objective experimental branch of natural science. Its theoretical goal is the prediction and control*

191

of behavior. Introspection forms no essential part of its methods, nor is the scientific value of its data dependent upon the readiness with which they lend themselves to interpretation in terms of consciousness. The behaviorist, in his efforts to get a unitary scheme of animal response, recognizes no dividing line between man and brute. The behavior of man, with all of its refinement and complexity, forms only a part of the behaviorist's total scheme of investigation." [6]

So the stated goal of behaviorism is more or less to predict and control the behavior of human beings. To meet this goal Watson would conduct experiments on animals and even human beings. He obsessed over the idea of one day being able to create and study a "baby farm" in which he would train groups of infant children from birth. Watson is famous for saying *"Give me a dozen healthy infants, well-formed, and my own specified world to bring them up in and I'll guarantee to take any one at random and train him to become any type of specialist I might select – doctor, lawyer, artist, merchant-chief and, yes, even beggar-man and thief, regardless of his talents, penchants, tendencies, abilities, vocations, and race of his ancestors. I am going beyond my facts and I admit it, but so have the advocates of the contrary and they have been doing it for many thousands of years."* [7] Watson and other establishment scientists even used their own children for experimentation to avoid public attention. It was the controversial work of the behaviorists that laid the foundation for a whole new realm of experimental psychology, which would then be taken advantage of by the largest governments and corporations in the world.

By the time that Watson retired from psychology and advertising, an equally twisted individual named B.F Skinner was ready to carry the torch and continue behaviorism research. Skinner is known best for his development of "operant conditioning", which is based on the idea of psychological training and conditioning by reinforcement. Skinner believed that all learned behavior is rooted in either a positive or negative response to certain actions which could be both predicted and conditioned. In other words, a behavior will increase if it is followed by positive reinforcement and will decrease if it is followed by negative reinforcement. He demonstrated this with his "operant conditioning chamber" which is now popularly known as the "skinner box". He would place animals in a chamber which contained a lever that the animal could press in order to obtain food or water as a type of reinforcement. It was also possible to deliver punishments like electric shocks through the floor of the chamber.

Skinner openly admitted that his research was going to be used to manipulate and condition human beings, but he argued that this was always going to happen in societies anyway, he just wanted to make sure that people were "manipulated correctly", and that him and his friends were the ones doing it. Skinner had picked up where Watson left off, and brought a whole new dynamic to the development of psychological warfare and mass mind control. Their unethical studies have joined the works of Bernays and Lippmann to become the dogma for the new generation of public relations consultants. Together their studies have delved so deep into the human consciousness that they seem to know more about the rest of society than we know about ourselves. These propagandists are among the most influential people of the past hundred years, even though their names have remained under the radar. This is by no mistake, the education system and the media are vital in keeping these historical figures and their impact on society a tightly guarded secret.

Public relations is now one of the most profitable and ruthless industries in the world and ethics have not improved at all since the mid-20th century, if anything they have progressively deteriorated. To find examples of these unethical practices one need look no further than today's leading PR firms. Among those firms is Burson-Marsteller a group that specializes in playing damage control for the world's worst corporations, torturers and dictators. A 2002 article by John Vidal in the UK's Guardian newspaper paints a fairly accurate picture of the company's activities.

The article states that *"Burson-Marsteller is the company that governments with poor human rights records and corporations in trouble with environmentalists have turned to when in crisis. The world's biggest PR company was employed by the Nigerian government to discredit reports of genocide during the Biafran war, the Argentinean junta after the disappearance of 35,000 civilians, and the Indonesian government after the massacres in East Timor. It also worked to improve the image of the late Romanian president Nicolae Ceausescu and the Saudi royal family. Its corporate clients have included the Three Mile Island nuclear plant, which suffered a partial meltdown in 1979, Union Carbide after the Bhopal gas leak killed up to 15,000 people in India, BP after the sinking of the Torrey Canyon oil tanker in 1967 and the British government after BSE emerged. In the past few years it has acted for big tobacco companies and the European biotechnology industry to challenge the green lobby and counter Greenpeace arguments on GM food."* [8] These kinds of activities are the rule for today's PR firms, not the exception. The most violent governments and corporations on the earth seem to have infinite resources, which allows them to pay off the witnesses and then hire expert propagandists to clean up their public image afterwards.

Some of the most hyped up news images of our time surrounding war were not actually real, but were simply public relations stunts, designed as psychological warfare operations. No one in America can forget the image of Saddam Hussein's statue being toppled and covered with an American flag, yet few people realize that this was a hoax, a staged psychological operation coordinated between the military and the media. In July of 2004 journalist Jon Elmer exposed an internal army study of the war showing that this whole statue scenario was indeed a set up. In the article, Elmer writes *"the infamous toppling of the statue of Saddam Hussein in Firdos Square in central Baghdad on April 9, 2003 was stage-managed by American troops and not a spontaneous reaction by Iraqis. According to the study, a Marine colonel first decided to topple the statue, and an Army psychological operations unit turned the event into a propaganda moment... The Marines brought in cheering Iraqi children in order to make the scene appear authentic, the study said. Allegations that the event was staged were made in April of last year, mostly by opponents of the war, but were ignored or ridiculed by the US government and most visible media outlets.* "[9]

The statue hoax was just one example in a long list of lies and psychological operations surrounding the multiple wars in Iraq. At the onset of Operation Desert Storm, in 1990, a public relations firm by the name of Hill and Knowlton spent millions of dollars on the government's behalf, constructing news pieces that would sell the war to the American public. One of the most moving pranks to come from this push to war was the testimony of a 15-year-old Kuwaiti girl, known only by her first name of Nayirah. In a videotaped testimony that was later distributed to the media she said "*I volunteered at the al-Addan hospital, While I was there, I saw the Iraqi soldiers come into the hospital with guns, and go into the room where . . . babies were in incubators. They took the babies out of the incubators, took the incubators, and left the babies on the cold floor to die.*"[10]

Sounds horrible huh? Well, luckily it never happened, this too was a fabricated event designed to dehumanize the Iraqi people. The whole thing was exposed when the journalists discovered that the witness, Nayirah was actually the daughter of a US ambassador, who was being coaxed by military psychological operations specialists. If the government and media cooperate to deceive the American public during times of war then there should be no doubt in your mind that the same techniques are used during times of peace, and especially elections.

Psychological warfare and mass manipulation have surely been taking place since Plato's time, as his Allegory of the Cave provides a clear analogy to describe how the few have controlled the many for thousands of years. Our whole modern society is a replica of the early Greek and Roman empires, so it should come as no surprise that Plato's stories are just as relevant today as

195

they were in ancient times. In many ancient societies the elite owned slaves and the vast majority of the population was also in servitude to the ruling class, though they may have had a bit more freedom than slaves. Despite this inhumane class structure and relentless conquest the "leaders" of these civilizations proclaimed to be champions of freedom and democracy.

To maintain the illusion of a free and open society the elites retained a high level of education while at the same time suppressing the knowledge that was exposed to the indentured public. As with many feudal systems, the commoners were mostly illiterate, and although they weren't forbidden from learning, most of them were always working so hard that they had no time to study. This created a situation in which the ruling few used their superior education to manipulate the masses who unknowingly had their intellect subverted by the establishment.

The practice of using the intellect to rule by mental coercion became known in ancient times as "sophism". The sophists of the ancient world were expert deceivers and that tradition has carried on today within almost every government on the planet. The term sophist has roots in the Greek word sophisma which means "I am wise". Today we use the word "sophisticated" to describe people who are more affluent and cultured than the rest of society, this word is also derived from the same place. After time sophism became closely associated with politics because the ruling class took advantage of their superior knowledge and used it to manipulate the commoners into accepting high taxes, war and unfair living conditions. This was no accident, the elite knew exactly what they were doing. It is even said that the great philosopher Aristotle was harshly reprimanded by Alexander the great for sharing too much of his powerful information with the commoners. Aristotle was actually Alexander's teacher, but the young conqueror knew that the lessons he received were more valuable to him if he and his court were the only people who had access to them. Today's ruling class is no different from Alexander the great, they are still suppressing and manipulating

196

information with the intent of dominating the minds of others.

Now in the 21st century, psychological warfare invades every aspect of modern life. It has made its way into every form of media and even into our education system, it is now deeply embedded in our culture. It has also extended deep into the political arena and has helped politicians further master the art of deception. Our thoughts are constantly being manipulated using these techniques. Many of us have trouble separating our own thoughts from those that have been implanted into our consciousness by the many subversive external stimuli that we encounter on a day to day basis. How do you protect yourself from this invasion of the mind? The best place to start is to turn off the TV, resist having a materialistic attitude and do your own research into the history and practices of the advertisement and PR Industries. Their propaganda has no effect on an informed and self-aware human being.

QUOTE SOURCES AND SUGGESTED READING
[0] The Mechanical Bride: Folklore Of Industrial Man - Marshall McLuhan (1967)
[1] Propaganda - Edward Bernays
[2] The Republic – Plato
[3] Public Opinion - Walter Lippmann
[4] Public Opinion - Walter Lippmann
[5] Propaganda - Edward Bernays
[6] Psychology as the Behaviorist Views It - John B Watson
[7] Psychology as the Behaviorist Views It - John B Watson
[8] http://www.guardian.co.uk/science/2002/jan/08/gm.activists
[9] http://newstandardnews.net/content/index.cfm/items/641
[10] Second Front: Censorship and Propaganda in the Gulf War (1993) - John R. MacArthur

"The Matrix is everywhere. It is all around us. Even now, in this very room. You can see it when you look out your window or when you turn on your television. You can feel it when you go to work... when you go to church... when you pay your taxes. It is the wool that has been pulled over your eyes to blind you from the truth. That you are a slave, Neo. Like everyone else you were born into bondage. Born into a prison that you cannot smell or taste or touch. A prison for your mind." – Morpheus *(The Matrix - Film)* [0]

37. Advertising and the Subliminal Culture

Today the teachings of the modern propagandists have taken on a life of their own and become the number one secret weapon used by corporations against their customers as well as governments against their subjects. As a result of the culture that was created by public relations pioneers, the western world greatly underestimates the power of the subconscious mind. Many believe that they have total control over everything they think and do. However, if this were a fact then addiction would not be such a problem in our society, tobacco use would not be the leading cause of death. This kind of situation illustrates how our willpower is not stronger than our subconscious minds in many cases, and it goes a lot deeper than that too.

We are being constantly bombarded with a swarm of images every single hour! Whether it is from the TV or billboards, magazines, internet or even clothing, you are being spoken to through what we call the media. The people who are assembling these messages are doing so in hopes to make you act in a certain way, or to buy in a certain way. So if these stimuli can trigger buying impulses, then what's to say they aren't triggering other impulses to?

It seems foolish to think that if someone watches a horror movie that they're going to go on a murder rampage, but that's not exactly what I'm suggesting here. What I am suggesting is that these images do have some effect on our opinions, desires and actions. This is a known clinical fact and is taken advantage of by PR firms, politicians, newscasters and anyone else who wishes to control your subconscious mind. If these powerful people spend this much time and energy discovering how to manipulate your subconscious through market research, which they do, then there must be some truth to all this.

Someone who surrounds themselves with violent or materialistic media may be more predisposed to violent or materialistic thoughts. Maybe they have some self-control; maybe they don't act on these thoughts, but the information is still there, stored in the subconscious mind of the consumer, only to surface later in the form of stress, illness or bad mood. People don't want to hear this, though; they like their slasher movies and violent video games. Vicariously living through an on-screen character playing out a dramatic war scene gives them a rush, setting off triggers in their brains that are naturally designed to react to threatening or surprising situations.

There is a complex public relations effort behind every powerful industry. In fact, advertising is a huge and secretive industry all in itself. Most good salesmen know more about the art of persuasion then they do about the product they're selling, most times they actually know very little about the product they're selling. There are literally volumes of books, filled with deceptive maneuvers and sneaky persuasive tricks for advertisers to use. A handful of these books have been revealed to the public, but the contents of most of them remain a mystery to most of us, because the courses that one must go through to become a certified salesman are very private and not offered in any college. To learn the tricks of this trade one must apply and be accepted before taking any courses. The art of persuasion is used by advertisers, politicians and bankers alike to ensure that the public accepts their worldview.

In the past few years since the western occupation of the Middle East, there has been a barrage of military propaganda in every corner of American culture. Children are a primary target for this

199

propaganda, mainly through the use of "combat simulator" video games. Combat simulators are commonplace at the top of the sales charts, and oftentimes bring in more money than big Hollywood blockbusters. These Video games glorify the military and have helped the rest of the media to desensitize a whole generation from the horrors of war. In late 2010, a videogame by the name of "Call of Duty Black Ops" made headlines as one of the top grossing games of all time. This game was a hypnotic gore fest that millions of young people became obsessed with, many of whom didn't even agree with America's imperialistic wars in the Middle East, but were just caught up in the flashy advertising and the mob frenzy surrounding the game.

The reason why these games are able to take hold of people and transcend their political barriers is because the consumers are grossly underestimating the power of their unconscious minds. People are caught up in the mentality that "it's just a game" and think that they have the good sense to separate fiction from reality. The only reason why they feel such a connection to this kind of media in the first place is because they are familiar with the rush that they get when a fight or flight situation on the screen sets off brain triggers to release endorphins into their bloodstream. That doesn't sound much like a conscious decision to me. Just because you're not going on a shooting spree in a shopping mall like you saw on the videogame doesn't mean that you won't be more likely to get road rage, depression or generally have unsettling thoughts because you have surrounded yourself with violent media.

People will argue that this violence has been with us for centuries and say that it is natural for humans to seek out violence for entertainment, but this is not the case. While it is true that violence is deeply entrenched in history, violent media tends to only become popular in a violent militaristic culture where the population is already predisposed to aggression because they are exposed to so much of it, and trained to embrace it from an early age. In a society where aggression isn't encouraged and the military doesn't have a strong presence

200

in the pop culture there is very little interest in violent media among the population. It should come as no surprise that civilizations without strong central governments and frequent war have very little violence to deal with in their everyday lives. While imperialistic empires such as America are flooded with violent media and struggle with high violent crime rates, which are all a direct result of the aggressive culture that is created by a wartime atmosphere.

QUOTE SOURCES AND SUGGESTED READING
[0] Morpheus – The Matrix
[SR1] Mind programming by Eldon Taylor
[SR2] Subliminal adventures in erotic art by Wilson Bryan key
[SR3] The secret sales pitch by August Bullock

"If you're not careful the newspapers will have you hating the people who are oppressed and loving the people who are doing the oppressing." – Malcolm X (Activist) [0]

38. Mainstream Media is Mass Mind Control

Most people form their opinions about world events based on the information that they get from television, newspapers and other mainstream media sources. This situation is very dangerous considering the bias and corruption that exists within that industry. The media holds an incredible power to manipulate the direction of world events through their control of public opinion. This power naturally draws the attention of groups that wish to sway public opinion in order to promote their agenda or whitewash their crimes.

The media has now become one of the biggest businesses in the world due to their influence of public opinion. Over the last century, many large companies have been battling over media dominance, attempting to have total control over what is said in the public arena. These companies are almost always heavily involved in politics and international business affairs, many times even depending on the government for funding. Through controlling the dialogue in the media they are able to portray their business practices and political allies in a positive light, even if this is accomplished by telling blatant lies. It is even generally accepted fact that all of the corporate news outlets have their own political agendas. What is not realized is that even though they may have different party affiliations, the major media sources are all on the same team and advertise the same general worldview.

In the early 1980s there were over 50 corporations which controlled all of the news media in America. This is a small number considering that it accounted for television, movies, magazines, books and music all combined. Before the First World War there were actually hundreds of corporations that made up the US media. This corporate monopolization is largely due to government regulation that prevents independent journalists from reaching the masses. In 1983 a man by the name of Ben Bagdikian published a book called "The Media Monopoly" which pointed out the consolidation going on in the media at the time. In his book, Bagdikian predicted that the meager number of 50 corporations would dwindle very quickly to less than a dozen companies in coming decades. His predictions were met with a great deal of criticism in the mainstream circuit, and that was to be expected considering they were the target of his accusations. Sure enough though, over the next 25 years the media would be consolidated into fewer and fewer hands. Now in 2010 the media is completely dominated by only 6 companies! Time Warner, Disney, Rupert Murdoch's News Corporation, Bertelsmann, Viacom and General Electric are in complete control of the media in the western world.

The corporate takeover of the US media is verified in the Congressional Record for 1917, when Congressman Callaway said "*In March, 1915, the J.P. Morgan interests, the steel, shipbuilding, and powder interest, and their subsidiary organizations, got together 12 men high up in the newspaper world and employed them to select the most influential newspapers in the United States and sufficient number of them to control generally the policy of the daily press ...They found it was only necessary to purchase the control of 25 of the greatest papers. An agreement was reached; the policy of the papers was bought, to be paid for by the month; an editor was furnished for each paper to properly supervise and edit information regarding the questions of preparedness, militarism, financial policies, and other things of national and international nature considered vital to the interests of the purchasers.*" [1]

Today's mainstream media is merely an avenue for the elite to distribute their propaganda, it works in the same way as the political system with two sides that are pushing the same agenda. They attack each other on trivial issues, but still more or less push the government agenda on major policies. A key example of this charade is seen with the three primary television news networks, FOX, MSNBC, and CNN. FOX is owned by Rupert Murdoch's "News Corp", this is the least trusted source for news in America, but still has a great deal of influence on many people's opinions. This has been known to be a "right-wing" or "conservative" news source. MSNBC is on the other side, apparently. MSNBC is considered the more "liberal" or "left-wing" news source, while CNN is said to reside in the middle of the road. The way that their programming is structured appeals to different demographics, but overall they are promoting the same general ideas, just with minor differences to suit their target audiences.

This is the same way that MTV appeals to a different demographic than Nickelodeon but still has the same kind of political agenda and overtones, why you ask? Because they're owned by the same company, Viacom. The news channels may not be this blatantly obvious, because they are owned by different companies. However, it should come as no surprise that all of these different companies have the same agendas considering how centralized our media is. So let's take a look at who owns CNN, FOX, and MSNBC to see what they may have in common politically. Which seems kind of important considering this is the primary place where Americans seem to get their political information from.

CNN is owned by AOL/Time Warner, MSNBC is owned by Microsoft and General Electric and FOX is owned by Billionaire news tycoon Rupert Murdoch. General Electric is owned and controlled mostly by the infamous Rockefeller banking & railroad dynasty who history has shown to be tyrants and robber barons. The News headquarters for General Electric's NBC studios are actually in a 70 story skyscraper called, The Rockefeller Center. This is of course, owned by the Rockefellers. This same building is also home to the offices of Time Warner. Time Warner also has close ties to the Rockefellers, but is mostly controlled by the J.P Morgan dynasty. Both of these families have worked together to rob the public blind for generations. It's also

204

important to mention that the US government worked with the Rockefellers, General Electric and Westinghouse to finance and engineer the first hydrogen bomb.

So what does this information tell us? It tells us that most of the world's mainstream media sources are owned by multinational corporations and international bankers, and then regulated by governments on top of that. This is extremely important considering that most of the problems in the world are being caused by these very interests.

Think about it this way, on MSNBC you are seeing the views that would benefit Microsoft and General Electric, on FOX you are seeing views that would benefit News Corp and on CNN you are seeing views that would benefit Time Warner.

Additionally, you have more multinational corporations with their own agendas advertising on their network, providing a source of income that the broadcasters come to depend on. For example, major military contractors like Northrop Grumman or Boeing have tons of commercials all over the mainstream news, but what average citizen has any interest in the products that these companies have to offer? Are rocket launchers and aircraft carriers on the average American's shopping list? Of course not!

Well, then why do these military contractors spend so much money on television advertisements? So they can use those advertising dollars as leverage against the broadcaster, in order to control how their corporation is presented in the news. If a broadcaster is being paid millions of dollars per month by Boeing to run their commercials then they aren't going to be able to say anything negative about the war, it's that simple.

You won't be able to find information that is critical of multinational corporations, governments or the banking industry through sources that are owned, regulated and funded by multinational corporations, governments and banks, its common sense. Sadly, these interests are the biggest enemies of freedom, yet it is them who are responsible for molding the opinions of people all over the world. It should come as no surprise that there is so much confusion!

If you think the print media might be better, think again. Most of the major print sources are also owned by these same companies. The two largest print news sources in the world, the Associated Press and Reuters are both owned by the Rothschild banking dynasty. These sources pass down information to subsidiaries that are owned by companies like Time Warner, General Electric and News Corp. Rupert Murdoch, the same media tycoon who catches so much criticism for his slanted programming on FOX news actually owns almost 200 newspapers, including The Times of London, The Wall Street Journal and the New York Post. He also owns 100 cable TV channels including Fox and 19 sports channels, 9 satellite and 40 regular TV networks, 40 publishing houses, and a movie studio. His opinions are directly influenced by banking families, multinational corporations and political donors.

So in short, control over publishing, recording and top cable companies belongs to GE, Time Warner, Viacom, Disney and Newscorp. These are directly or indirectly owned by the Rockefellers, Rothschilds, and Morgans, all of which own multinational corporations and international financial institutions. These are the richest people in the world who live lives of luxury on the backs of the working class and the third world. Don't think for a minute that these same figures don't also have a hidden hand in politics, because they do.

It costs such an incredible amount of money to run for president, the kind of money that only multinational corporations and foundations have access to. So all would-be Presidential candidates, be it democrat or republican, are forced to rely on multinational corporations for their campaign funding. This means when they get into office they are more or less indebted to multinational corporations and then they must make sure that their policies are in line with the wishes of those who funded their rise to power.

It has become apparent that the media is a big public relations tool for the big corporations and the politicians that they put into power. Digging deeper, most of these corporations have direct ownership connections to powerful industry and banking dynasties such as the Rockefellers, Morgans, and Rothschild's to name a few. David Rockefeller said it all in his 1991 Trilateral Commission meeting speech *"We are grateful to The Washington Post, the New York Times, Time Magazine and other great publications whose directors have attended our meetings and respected their promises of discretion for almost forty years. It would have been impossible for us to develop our plan for the world if we had been subject to the bright lights of publicity during those years."*[2] Statements like this show how the ruling class is deliberately keeping crimes against humanity away from public view by maintaining control of what is covered in the media.

This problem may seem overwhelming, but there are a lot of solutions that are well within our reach. The internet allows anyone with some time and dedication to present their point of view to the rest of the world. Everyday independent media sources are popping up that aren't afraid to question authority or the ruling class that runs the media. Until the average person is given fair representation in the mainstream media we must use the internet as a tool to get our suppressed message to the masses. We must also continue to fight corporate control and government regulation of the media. Most importantly we need to become the media ourselves, with cheap video cameras and the internet we can do this research for ourselves and bring the information to other people, just as I do on a very low budget.

QUOTE SOURCES AND SUGGESTED READING
[0] Malcolm X speaks By Malcolm X, George Breitman
[1] The Congressional Record, February 9, 1917, Vol. 54
[2] Matrix of Power By Jordan Maxwell
[SR1] The Mechanical Bride: Marshall McLuhan (1967)

39. Television Programming is Programming Your Mind

Television has only been around for about 100 years and in that short amount of time it has drastically changed how human beings think and behave. Television's impact on society has been far more negative than positive, because of how it disconnects humanity from nature and promotes materialistic values through its programming. Everything that is shown on TV today has been selected by the government and multinational corporations that own the broadcasters. Everything that is put out by these broadcasters must be approved by the government boards that oversee the industry, namely the FCC. If a program is not approved by the FCC then it is not allowed to be aired. This conflict usually doesn't occur though because the FCC and the multinational media corporations generally have the same interests. What this basically means is that the only thing that is on television are things that the government or large multinational corporations want you to see, just as I explained with the news earlier. This is one of the establishment's best tools of social control, which they use to distract and manipulate the minds of the masses.

Many people are very naive in thinking that the things they see on TV have absolutely no effect on their mental processes. The human subconscious is much stronger than most people are willing to admit. This means that there is a very good possibility that the situations and imagery seen on television will have an impact on how they think and react to everyday life. What a lot of people don't know is that after watching TV for just a few seconds, the viewer goes into a suggestive state of hypnosis. A recent study conducted by a Dr. Aric Sigman looked into the effect that television has on the brain chemistry and critical thinking skills. He published his findings in a book called "*Remotely Controlled*" which reconfirmed many points that were first brought up in 1971 by a Professor Herbert Krugman in his studies on television and the subconscious.

Their research shows that it only takes 30 seconds of watching TV to be put in a highly suggestible hypnotic state. This hypnotic state has been proven in studies by reading alpha waves that have been emitted from viewers. Alpha waves are an uncommon brain wave pattern also present in the state of "light hypnosis" that hypnotists use for suggestion therapy. Have you ever tried to get someone's attention while they were watching TV? Usually it is pretty difficult to detach someone from their fixed gaze because of the light hypnotic state that their brain is in. When considering the highly suggestible state of mind that television creates in people, it becomes alarming that an average American sees over 20,000 commercials and 33,000 murders per year on TV. This fact is especially scary considering the biggest consumers of television are children, who have even less ability than adults to differentiate between reality and fiction.

Television induced hypnosis also disables the neo-cortex or "higher brain" and increases activity in the limbic system or "lower brain". The limbic system is the region of the brain that triggers desires and sexual arousal, it has often been referred to as the "reptile brain". This region is unable to differentiate between what is real and what is an act, it sees everything that it can visualize as being real. If you are watching something frightening on the television, your heart will beat faster and you will begin to tremble, this is because the parts of your brain that are actually active are not the parts that can tell the difference between reality and fiction. So while you may consciously realize that what you're watching is not real, your mind is not able to reasonably assess the information because the logical parts of your brain are in a state of sleep.

The vulnerable hypnotic state that television creates has been designed purposely by the politicians and advertisers that put their message out over the airwaves. These messages have been carefully crafted to play on your subconscious fears and desires in order to persuade you to buy their product or go along with their social policy. If you pay attention, you will notice that news, shows and commercials are even more hypnotic and entrancing than regular programming, this is no accident. If you think about it, the whole point of a news program or commercial isn't to inform or entertain you, but to persuade you. There are all kinds of complicated techniques that are used to help with this persuasion, some involve dialogue while others are related to the visual set up of the program. These subliminal influences are largely responsible for the materialistic, nihilistic and violent culture that is so prevalent in most of the world today.

The subliminal threat that television poses on our consciousness is very real, but even on a more surface level it is easy to see how this device has impacted society negatively. Most people generally spend over 24 hours a week in front of the TV, that's over one whole day of every week wasted consuming pop culture that has been created by the establishment. In the past our ancestors would use that time to enjoy the company of the people they cared about, appreciate nature, or use their imagination to create something, while now we sit in a hypnotic state watching violent and materialistic programming. This kind of activity is very unnatural for humans to be taking part in and is not healthy for our mind and soul. That day a week can be spent a lot better if it wasn't in front of the TV. Start by cancelling your cable subscription and minimizing the time you spend in front of the TV, you will feel an immediate difference in consciousness. TV has become an invisible government shackle for the psyche of millions and your mind is better off without it.

"Art is moral passion married to entertainment. Moral passion without entertainment is propaganda, and entertainment without moral passion is television."-Rita Mae Brown (Writer)[0]

40. Bread and Circuses in Hollywood

For the past several centuries, the ruling class has struggled in finding a system of government that allows them to carry out their imperialistic wishes, while maintaining public support at the same time. If they had things their way, every society that was under their control would be a feudal fascist dictatorship. The only reason this isn't the case is because they have seen in the past that this kind of government does not last long, as the people become agitated by the obvious disparities and injustice that exist within their civilization.

Sports, entertainment and overbearing work schedules are used to distract the public from what is going on in their government. This mind control tactic has been used since the time of Ancient Rome, but has gotten more complex and powerful as technology progressed. The ancient Roman "leaders" had an imperialistic policy quite similar to that of modern America. In order to keep their subjects ignorant of the political details of their military programs, the Romans built a powerful entertainment industry. This industry consisted of huge coliseums which hosted brutal sporting events as well as elaborate bathhouses and country clubs for the more timid citizens. These events kept the general public occupied while their corrupt "leaders" ran the country into the ground with poor economic policy and over militarization.

Today's entertainment industry has come a very long way due to technology, but it still serves the same purpose as it did in Ancient Rome. As our political and financial institutions have slowly advanced their world empire over the past few generations, most Americans have been distracted by various forms of media, all of which are filled with pro establishment propaganda. Most major record companies, television broadcasters and media outlets are owned by the ruling class and any of the performers that are featured through those channels are on their payroll. So the scripts, lyrics and even press releases from major artists are often times written by corporations that are owned by the aristocracy. The capital of the modern entertainment world is a place called Hollywood. Interestingly enough, magicians' wands are made of wood from a holly bush. This is no coincidence as everything that comes out of Hollywood is designed to cast a spell, just like a magician's wand. Furthermore, the word entertainment itself means "a diversion for the mind", which is exactly what it is and what it's used for.

It is very common for celebrities to buy into this game and just project whatever kind of ideas they are told to without thinking twice. While it is very rare for celebrities to speak out against the establishment, if this does happen then they are vilified in the media and will face many obstacles in their career as a result of their dissent. One of the most successful celebrities in recent memory to take a stand was Dave Chappelle. His years in the entertainment industry had shown him the corruption that exists behind the scenes and how entertainers are used as pawns to advance the establishment's agenda. When leaving his show and turning down a 20 million dollar deal he said "*I was doing sketches that were funny but socially irresponsible. I felt I was deliberately being encouraged and I was overwhelmed*" and "*I felt in a lot of instances I was deliberately being put through stress because when you're a guy who generates money, people have a vested interest in controlling you.*"[1]

I cannot speak for Chappelle, but from an outsiders perspective it seems that he came to realize that the ideas which are put forth through the mainstream media are intended to make the population more disorderly, materialistic and obedient. It is possible that he began to see these kinds of degrading ideas in the scripts that he was getting from comedy central and wanted no parts in it, regardless of how much money they were offering him. Dave Chappelle is a remarkable human being for refusing to put a price on his artistic integrity and his protest should be a

212

lesson to everyone in the entertainment industry.

Music is not free from propaganda either. While there are many independent rock and hip hop artists who are actually making creative revolutionary music, the mainstream circuit is a direct representation of the ruling elite. Hip hop pioneer Professor Griff of Public Enemy has recently exposed the infiltration of the industry that he helped create. His research shows how some of the biggest names in hip hop are just puppets who are being paid to socially engineer their listeners. His research makes a lot of sense considering that hip hop originated from peaceful gatherings with break dancers, graffiti artists and MCs spreading a message of freedom and equality. That was a message that the establishment couldn't allow, so slowly as a generation or two progressed, they used their vast financial resources to send hip hop in a different direction. This is how in less than 20 years a culture went from being about good times, peace, and empowerment to materialism, violence and misogyny. The same thing has happened with rock music as well, its frontrunners were transformed from antiwar hippies into materialistic, heroin addict Satanists in just a decade.

Major league sporting events are also a part of the propaganda machine, just as the gladiator battles were in ancient Rome. It is not the sports themselves that are detrimental to free thought, but it is simply the over-commercialization of the organized leagues. Getting together with some friends and playing a sport every now and then can be fun and very good for your health. However, sitting in front of a television watching hours of commercials in between millionaires playing a game is not good for your mental or physical health. If you have interest in sports, call up some friends or join a local league and actually play the game yourself instead of sitting at home in front of the TV consuming pop culture. If watching sports is your thing though and that's what you enjoy, more power to you, but if you have ever asked yourself why athletes and entertainers make so much money, all this should clear up some of that confusion.

Billions of dollars pour into these industries on a monthly basis because it has become one of the most effective tools of social control for the ruling class. The mainstream media is the primary mechanism that is perpetuating aggression and fear in our society, which is why people who are aware of this situation should support independent media and underground culture. Surround yourself with the ideas and expressions of everyday people instead of the propaganda that is so apparent in popular culture. If possible find a way to express yourself and create something to bring entertainment to other people.

QUOTE SOURCES AND SUGGESTED READING
[0] Women know everything! By Karen Weekes (page 340)
[1]"The Oprah Winfrey Show" with Dave Chappelle February 3rd 2006

"The most loving parents and relatives commit murder with smiles on their faces. They force us to destroy the person we really are: a subtle kind of murder." - Jim Morrison (Rock Musician) [0]

41. Parental Propaganda

The bond between a parent and a child is one of the strongest human relationships, and since the beginning of time children would learn valuable life lessons from their families. It is for this reason that many authoritarian societies have guided the structure of the family to mold future generations, even before they enter the indoctrination centers that we call schools. The most effective form of propaganda that the establishment has is the ability to impose their values on young impressionable children through their parents.

Using the methods of propaganda that are already in place via the media, education systems and religious institutions, the establishment has created a society where authoritarianism and domination is a part of everyday life. When parents are raising their children they are drawing on a lifetime of propaganda and they feel a great sense of guilt when their child naturally doesn't accept the established norms in society. Children are free and full of spirit, and it has been so long since many parents have felt that way that they simply don't understand. Their oppressive culture and its abhorrent values have brought them so far away from their spirit that they feel that something is wrong if their child does not conform to the establishment's ideals.

This causes parents to be authoritative with their children to encourage conformity. What they are really doing is breaking their child's spirit and preparing them to live in an oppressive world and accept authority. Parents take this aggressive route because of the example that has been set by the established control systems. In our society it is commonplace for people in power or authority to be controlling and close minded, so when someone puts their trust in that kind of society they are going to behave in that same fashion when they fall into a position of authority themselves.

Many good people that only want the best for their family actually end up putting themselves and their children through a lot of pain and turmoil because they are under the impression that their child has to be a certain way. All of this stress and oppression is many times all carried out under the best of intentions.

Today, Parents aren't passing earthly knowledge and wisdom to their children, but instead they are passing down a long list of cultural assumptions, idiosyncrasies and misconceptions. They are passing along the aggressive, materialistic message of the aristocracy which has been instilled in them through years of propaganda and indoctrination. Even worse is the fact that these false values are instilled through constant abuse, sometimes physical, but usually emotional. This has resulted in a situation where in almost every household throughout time children have been psychologically abused. If almost everyone's childhood is like this, is it any surprise that most of the adults in our society behave in such an irrational way?

Now as the empire is crumbling and the middle class is disappearing it is obvious to everyone that the ideals of our society are corrupt. It is important that we don't instill that same set of ideals in future generations or we will be doomed to repeat this cycle of dominance and propaganda yet again. We should be protecting our children from the toxic culture that surrounds us instead of forcing them to conform to it. The values that drive our culture are the reason for a great deal of suffering across the world. So when these values enter a family they will not only have a detrimental personal impact, but they will cause another human being to project the same oppressive energy that is destroying our planet and our species.

The popular spiritual philosopher "Osho" has really summed up this issue of aggressive parenting better than I would ever be able to. Osho says that "The whole idea that children are your *possession is wrong. They are born through you, but they do not belong to you. You have a past, they have only a future. They are not going to live according to you. To live according to you will be almost equivalent to not living at all. They have to live according to themselves — in freedom, in responsibility, in danger, in challenge."* [1]

This is the kind of approach that we should take when raising our children in these confusing and troubled times. If our children are able to think with their own minds, uncorrupted by the cultural programming that our generation was subject to, then they will be able to have a clear vision for a brighter future.

This is not a change that is happening overnight, but is simply a part of a progression that has been evolving for centuries. For the most part, every generation treats their children with just a little bit more respect then they saw from their parents, with that trend speeding up in the 20th century. Physical child abuse, infanticide and child slavery were extremely common throughout history, but in the past century as society has become more conscious about the value of human life, those horrors are thankfully much less common. Physical child abuse still takes place today, but it is much more isolated due to the fear of legal punishment and its recent taboo nature. However, there is still a great deal of emotional and psychological abuse that is dished out to children, even by the most well intentioned adults.

Children are a minority group who remain second class citizens in the eyes of most of the world, their actions scrutinized, their opinions ignored, and their existence is seen as a burden. Most adults fear and envy children, even if they don't realize it. This is because the child is a free spirit that represents change, which the adult has been trained to fear. That fear is then suppressed by attempting to tame the children and train them, just as the parent was trained. This "taming" process is extremely confusing and traumatizing for the child, but unfortunately most parents feel that it is their duty to mold their child to be obedient to authority. Not many have questioned the morality or efficiency of this parenting strategy, but it is still a question of extreme importance. Our children are the future of this world and if they are not treated with respect and given freedom, then there will never be freedom or respect in our societies. That's not to say that children should be allowed to do whatever they want, but it means that they should not be treated like animals to be trained and controlled.

My Goal here is not to criticize anyone who used a mainstream parenting strategy, as that would probably be most of the planet. However, it's important for us to know that the way that we treat children as a species is directly related to the kind of adults that we see in our society. There is an old saying that goes "the hand that rocks the cradle rules the world", and this is very true, which is why it is so important to reevaluate how we treat young people. Our children are the future of this world and if they are not treated with respect and given freedom, then there will never be freedom or respect in our civilization.

QUOTE SOURCES AND SUGGESTED READING
[0]The Doors companion: four decades of commentary - John M. Rocco (1997)
[1]The Art Of Parenting – Osho
[SR1] Raising children compassionately by Marshall B Rosenberg
[SR2] The History of Childhood by Lloyd deMause
[SR3] Punished by Rewards: by Alfie Kohn
[SR 4] Unconditional Parenting By Alfie Kohn

"When you were young, you took on the world, remember how you'd laugh and sing? You've replaced it all with an IRA, internet porn, and a job you hate"- Misery Index (Heavy Metal Band) [0]

42. Inner Child

Throughout the course of our lives we develop a lot of baggage from the various environments that we encounter. We come into this world as pure souls with a clean slate and as we grow we adopt various beliefs and idiosyncrasies from our culture, which eventually manifest as our personal identities. Whether it is race, class, occupation or belief structure, people identify with cultural labels and use those labels to build their personal model of reality. A child sees the natural world with a clearer perspective because their perception is not clouded with cultural conventions and other prejudices. This is why concepts like money, time and authority make no sense at all to children and rightfully so, these are all manmade cultural abstractions that really don't make any sense if you actually think about it from a human perspective.

It is typical for authoritarian societies to condemn their youth because they have not yet been corrupted and molded into an obedient, mechanized citizen. If the youth of any oppressive nation were able to freely grow without being indoctrinated into the cultural control system, then the whole system would be radically changed within one single generation. The establishment knows that their stranglehold on the human race is unnatural, immoral and insane, which is why their ideals are always met with resistance by the youth culture. The ruling class knows that their only hope to maintain political dominance is to vilify their citizens until they have been indoctrinated into the system, or in other words until they "grow up".

However, the human mind is resilient and many of us are able to slip into adulthood with minimal psychological corruption. This growing portion of society may not be popular, but they are very often the source of most of the positive progress that has taken place throughout history. Some of the greatest minds to have walked the earth have recognized that the idea of "growing up" and "fitting in" places people in invisible cultural prisons and corrupts their natural personal philosophies. One of the most brilliant thinkers of the last century, Albert Einstein was one of these people. He himself said that imagination is way more important than knowledge and that *"Common sense is the collection of prejudices acquired by age eighteen."* [1]

He was well aware of the cultural games that were being played with people's minds. When he was 16 years old, one of his schoolteachers told him that he would never amount to anything because of his rebellious, unorthodox attitude. So he did what any free thinking revolutionary would do, he dropped out of school and pursued his education on his own. He went on to become one of the greatest scientists ever, and maintained his rebellious attitude all throughout his entire life. Einstein was against war, elitism and any kind of authority whatsoever. If it was not for his incredible contributions to science he surely would have been considered insane or an enemy of the state by the establishment.

When someone makes it out of childhood without being corrupted they are usually called naive and told that their unorthodox point of view isn't welcome in their society. Many creative and rebellious people who are in touch with their inner child typically receive such negative feedback from family and peers that they actually knowingly submit to a culture which makes no sense to them. This is exactly why you have to be a certain age in order to vote or run for political office. The system makes sure to give people enough time to submit to the established cultural model of reality before they are able to have any impact at all on the direction of the society.

There are many cases where we do have much to learn from our elders and it is true that skills which we depend upon for survival have been passed down through the generations. However, when it comes to a government setting cultural norms, there is

220

always an ulterior motive when information is passed down. That motive is always the same, to maintain control of the population and to defend the power of the established institutions, so they endure the next generation. It is very important to learn and mature and it is possible to do so without "growing up" and limiting yourself with cultural prejudices. Being responsible, respectful and peaceful is what makes you a mature adult, it has nothing to do with fitting in to the established culture.

QUOTE SOURCES AND SUGGESTED READING
[0] Misery Index – Spectator - "Heirs to Thievery" (2010)
[1] The Oxford dictionary of American quotations - Hugh Rawson, Margaret Miner (2006)
[SR1] Emotional Life Of Nations by Lloyd DeMause
[SR2] The Case Against Adolescenceby Robert Epstein PhD

"You have owners. They own you. They own everything. They own all the important land. They own and control the corporations, They've long since bought the senate, the congress, the state houses, the city halls, they've got the judges in their back pockets and they own all the big media companies so they control just about all of the news and information you get to hear. They got you by the balls." –
George Carlin

Section 7

Empire

43. -Feudalism: From the Dark Ages to the New World
44. -Who's The Man
45. -Fabian Socialism and the New World Order
46. –Controlled Conflict in the Middle East
47. -The Birth of the Corporate Beast in America
48. -The Sweatshop Economy
49. -Third World By Design
50. -Royal Landlords
51. -Cursed Dinosaur Blood
52. –The Broken Window Fallacy

"I freed a thousand slaves, I could have freed a thousand more if only they knew they were slaves." - Harriet Tubman (Civil War Hero) [0]

43. Feudalism: From the Dark Ages to the New World

History is the long story of our past, a story that is told in many different ways, with different information depending on where the story is being told. If one does enough research they will find that our past is a cycle of dominance and revolution, of civilizations rising up against authoritarian "leaders" that control their lives and manipulate them into servitude. Though some forms of government are more oppressive than others, the citizens are always duped into believing that their ruler is doing the right thing, otherwise they would join together and overthrow the established dictatorship. A brilliant philosopher by the name of Johann Wolfgang von Goethe is known to have said *"None are more hopelessly enslaved than those who falsely believe they are free."*[1].

Goethe was one of the most famous writers of German history, but his ideas were so radical that they were often met with resistance from tyrants. When the Nazi regime was burning books prior to the Second World War, many of Goethe's writings were targeted and destroyed. His words are as true today for your average person as they were for the serfs in the middle ages who lived their whole life to serve a master that wouldn't allow them to read.

In the Middle Ages, Europe consisted of large pieces of land that were owned by wealthy royal knights called "lords". The lords basically used slave labor to acquire great wealth, but instead of putting their subjects in bars and chains, the lords manipulated the "serfs" into servitude using fear and debt. Most average people living during this time led lives of slavery without even realizing it and yet they still feared and respected the oppressive rulers that were responsible for their difficult lives. The lords would achieve this social dominance through letting people build

223

houses on their land and live there in exchange for their servitude. Once the subject entered the agreement he would be indebted for labor and military purposes. Shockingly, this property actually belonged to the serfs to begin with, but was stolen and hoarded by the aristocracy through using intimidation and mind games.

In most cases the lords were far more educated than their subjects and would prevent them from reading or learning anything that would make it possible for them to achieve social independence. This is very similar to the sharecropping system that wealthy slave owners in early America used to manipulate people into slave labor. In the Middle Ages, the plots of land that the lords ruled over were called "fiefdoms", in the times of slavery they were called "plantations", same idea. This kind of feudal economic set up still takes place today almost everywhere, but of course the language to describe it has evolved in order to make the public believe that "serfs", "slaves", "lords" and "masters" are all things of the past. Sadly, they are just as much of a reality today as they were centuries ago.

Today's complicated economic & legal systems were devised by the "lords" as a method of maintaining their wealth. These systems were sold to the population as a means of developing personal financial freedom and protection when in reality they created a very complicated and deceptive form of slavery. The fact that there are a few subclasses among the "working class" or "serf's" seems to make the public believe that everyone has some level of opportunity, but all of these subclasses are peons compared to the people who print the money and control the economy. This works the same in both capitalist and communist societies around the world, a wealthy few live in luxury on the backs of their struggling citizens. With both systems the middle class is nonexistent and the upper class has a total stranglehold on the lives of the lower class. This financial enslavement has been achieved like it always has, through debt and fear. Evidence of these tactics are all around us, as I will explain later in this book.

The upper class still manipulates average people into working for them for their entire lives, receiving pathetic compensation that makes it impossible to maintain a comfortable life. Also, just as the lords of the middle ages controlled the information that their subjects had access to, the upper class in today's world own all the major media outlets and control the curriculum in the education system. They do their best to make sure it's their side of the story that is presented to the general population and they use the many organizations that they are connected with to condemn anyone who offers another side to the story.

Some fiefdoms were better than others and some lords less ruthless than others. While the "leaders" would bicker over their petty differences, their societies were all pyramid schemes that served an oligarchy at the expense of the majority of the population. Centuries later nothing has changed, almost every single nation in the world is controlled by a power hungry oligarchy that allows millions of citizens to live in poverty. The many "countries" across the planet today are controlled by an aristocracy who apparently keep their people "free" and "safe" while at the same time enslaving them with debt and sending them to war. Some countries are better than others, some governments more oppressive than others. While the various "leaders" may bicker over their petty differences, every single one of them are facilitating and benefiting from their own feudal society.

The big secret is that nothing about the relationship between lord and serf has changed since the days when feudalism was openly accepted as a political and economic system. Technological advancements over the last millennia have provided todays serfs with a far more comfortable lifestyle than that of their ancestors. However the relationship between the working class and the ruling class has changed very little. Today it is possible for someone to have wall to wall carpeting, running water, electronic trinkets and home appliances, but that doesn't change the fact that they have to hand over a majority of their earnings to someone who has an obscene amount of control over their personal lives. The people are still unjustly taxed, sent to war for no purpose and subjected to a life of fear and confusion just as they were in the dark ages.

Thanks to human ingenuity and the steady advance of technology, most of us in the west are not subject to living in straw huts scavenging for food, but again this does not mean that we are free or financially independent, it simply means we just happen to be slightly more comfortable than those who came before us. The tiny group of aristocrats that have ruled over Europe and its colonies for centuries have been continuously looting resources from the working class and developing a stranglehold on the private lives of everyday citizens in order to protect their wealth and positions of power. Nothing about the social structure or role of authority in everyday life has changed, so while technological advancement has given us immediate comfort and the illusion of wealth, we remain under the financial and legal control of a few powerful psychopaths.

When you take a close look at how global events have progressed over the ages you will find that many of the families who dominate politics and economics today have bloodlines that actually trace back to the feudal lords of the Middle Ages. In Middle Eastern and third world countries this is painfully obvious because there are still royal dynasties who openly claim that it is their birthright to rule over their country, while in the west the aristocrats are a bit less open.

However, the aristocrats in the United States and Great Brittan have blood as royal as a Saudi king. For example, let's take a look at the past few presidential candidates in America. Bush, Cheney and Bill Clinton are all distant cousins and descendants of Charlemagne, a French monarch who ruled most of Europe during his lifetime (742-814). 35 US presidents have genes that trace back to this Charlemagne, while the other 10 or so trace back to Alfred the Great who was king of England in the 9th century. Many of the most prominent banking families also come from these bloodlines, so the royalty dominates the business world as well as the political world.

In the election of 2004 George Bush and John Kerry were the options for US president, but both candidates were distant cousins to the Queen of England and even belonged to the same secret society at Yale University, the morbidly named Skull and Bones fraternity! If that isn't creepy enough for you, I'd also like to mention that all descendants of Charlemagne are also great, great, great etc. Grandchildren of Prince Vlad III Dracula of Wallachia (modern Romania). This was the sick and depraved ruler who was known as a butcher and who eventually became the inspiration for the most famous vampire stories in history. Dracula may have had an extra knack for theatrics, but his kind of sadistic inhumane behavior is the norm not the exception within these royal bloodlines.

A genealogist at the New England Historic Genealogical Society in Boston by the name of Gary Boyd Roberts is one of the top experts on the royal ancestry of American presidents. His research links every American president's lineage to different bloodlines of royalty throughout Europe. His findings are also backed up by Burkes Peerage which is the world encyclopedia of royal genealogy. In fact, according to both of these sources, in every election the candidate with the most royal genes has won. The jury on President Barack Obama's lineage is still out because all records of his early life are shrouded in secrecy. Due to the many forged documents and name changes that we have seen from Obama, it is difficult to determine if he has royal blood.

Throughout the rest of the world the story is the same, people that are born into a place of privilege because of the wealth of their ancestors are the new aristocrats who dominate politics and international business. Over the centuries those in power have learned that they can't quickly and forcefully push their way into dominating a large group of people, they need to trick the population into begging for their own enslavement. Countless hours are spent by rulers around the world to find new ways of conning their citizens into giving up their rights and handing their lives over to the state.

Each and every flag waving citizen of any random country throughout the world will tell you that corruption doesn't happen in their country and that their "leader" has their best interests in mind. Almost every government throughout the world is an oligarchy, even within the western countries that claim to conduct their business "democratically". The fact remains that from superpowers like the UK, US, Russia or China to monarchies like Saudi Arabia, there is a small privileged class who makes all of the decisions and exploits the work and ingenuity of the majority of the unknowing population. Many of the actions taken by government are unpopular among the majority of the population, but the plan stays on course despite the backlash.

There are a few rare cases when a new face steps into an important role in the aristocracy, but this is rare and limited to people who make groundbreaking discoveries, inventors, lucky entrepreneurs and other wild cards that happen to find themselves in the company of the elite. This ruling class makes up a very small portion of the population, they account for less than 1% of the world's population. Despite their small size, this elite class has managed to amass most of the world's attainable wealth and land through centuries of conquest and social domination. The families at the very top of this class structure are richer than many of the world's governments combined and their wealth is incalculable in terms that would relate to almost anyone in the world.

The modern feudal lords who work for these families get a smaller slice of the global financial pie, which is still much larger than your average person could imagine. Meanwhile, BILLIONS of people who account for around 99% of the world's population are left to struggle for the remaining scraps that haven't been wasted and hidden away by the feudal dictators. Under these circumstances the vast majority of the population is divided and pitted against each other to battle over the small amount of remaining resources. The feudal masters would much rather see billions of people suffer and die then change the way they do business and risk losing their immense power over the world's population.

Now as has happened many times before, things are beginning to fall apart due to corruption and inequality. The cracks in the system are exposing the true nature of what has been happening all along. We have been used as workhorses and human shields for centuries, our rights taken away and given back with the cycles of revolutions and changes in public opinion. Regardless of our nationality or what country we call home, we have been the pawns of the ruling class for centuries without even realizing it. Even in countries like the U.S and the U.K we are only given the illusion of freedom and we still have very little say in what actually goes on in the government.

Most people have a hard time dealing with these topics and refuse to believe that their lives are being controlled, but in order to free ourselves we need to recognize what's going on and start educating ourselves. The most powerful tool we have in this battle is information, which is why they work so hard to control the information that we have access to. Progress is already being made to stop this vicious cycle of economic control and unnecessary war, because people are finally starting to educate themselves and others. In the rest of this section I will dig deeper and name some of the specific organizations and families who facilitate this global feudal system that I have just described.

QUOTE SOURCES AND SUGGESTED READING
[0]Voices of Hope: Timeless Expressions of Faith from African Americans - Honor Books, Niral R. Burnett (2005)
[1] Goethe: The History of a Man by Emil Ludwig
[SR1] Fire in the Minds of Men: Origins of the Revolutionary Faith by James Billington

"I care not what puppet is placed on the throne of England to rule the Empire, The man that controls Britain's money supply controls the British Empire. And I control the money supply." - Baron Nathan Mayer Rothschild (Aristocrat) [0]

44. Who's "The Man"

Now that we have established that the world is controlled by a global feudal system, it's time to take a look at the specific family lines and political organizations that are responsible for establishing and maintaining that system. Within this Control structure the world consists of two classes, the exploiters and the exploited. The influence and loyalties of the exploiters transcend national borders, ethnic or racial backgrounds as well as religious and political affiliations. Through the ages many empires have fallen, many political regimes came and went, but for the most part, the power and wealth has remained in the same bloodlines and the centralized systems of control are still in place.

Even in times of revolution where kings have been taken from their thrones and removed from power, the wealth and influence of the banking elite has not been threatened for nearly a millennium. Many researchers believe that these lines date back to the time of Rome or even Babylon and I wouldn't doubt that to be the case. If they have managed to stay in power for the past thousand years then I see no reason why they couldn't have for the thousand before it, or a thousand years before that. Although, that would be getting a bit too deep down the rabbit hole for now, so I'm just going to focus on the past few centuries.

The last time anyone has stood up against a ruling banking cartel was when the Knights of Templar were outlawed in the 14th Century, and even then it was an envious king not the citizens who removed the Templars from power. The citizens had very little understanding of just how powerful and influential the Templars were, just as today many people are unaware of who their masters really are. Most of us know that our governments and financial institutions are corrupt, but many people aren't aware that there are specific families and organizations that have been controlling these institutions from behind the scenes for many generations.

Our idea of "the man" or "big brother" has remained limited to the authority figures we have to deal with in everyday life, the police and the politicians. These authority figures are in reality only scapegoats and puppets for a group sometimes known as "the illuminati" or "black nobility" just to name a few on the long list of nicknames this group has been given. This elite network of wealthy families has managed to slip under the radar for many generations through the various different wars and revolutions that have taken place. Who are these ruthless exploiters? Who do our so called "leaders" answer to? Who do our authority figures take orders from?

We know who these tyrants are, they have been hiding in plain sight, in the tallest buildings in every city, at the heads of the largest companies and political organizations in the world. These families did not get their power strictly through brute force, but also by fraudulently acquiring control of different countries' financial and political systems. The people that play a conscious role in facilitating this global feudal system make up less than 1% of the world's population. Together they are the global oligarchy who even the harshest dictators dare not cross, they are the kings of kings. Their global control network is spearheaded by various financial and political organizations which are held in high regard, thanks only to their billion dollar public relations efforts.

Today there are many organizations that work over top of our government which have been put into place by the modern day feudal oligarchy. Many times these organizations are called "think tanks" or "policy institutes". Policy institute is the more appropriate term, because these are the organizations that set the political policy and hand it down to the politicians. This is where the politicians get all their wonderful ideas from! Bush didn't come up with the 300 page patriot act all by himself, but it was actually the work of a think tank called "the project for a new American century". Obama's infamous health plan wasn't something that good ol Barack spent half of law school working on, but that too was the work of a thank tank.

The foreign and economic policy is set by these organizations as well, so that means the government's stance on wars, tax plans or welfare is all decided upon by these groups. Memos and reports created at these organizations make their way through the pentagon and the white house where they eventually land on the president's desk. At this point the president signs to authorize the plan, and reads over the policy so he is prepared to explain it when asked by reporters.

The most powerful of these organizations are the committee of 300, the Bilderberg Group, The Council on Foreign Relations and the Trilateral Commission. There are plenty of other diabolical think tanks, but these are the most influential. The people who belong to these specific groups are the wealthiest people in the world who own and operate the world's largest multinational corporations. The families that sit at the head of these organizations belong to the royal bloodlines that I have been discussing. There are well over a dozen bloodlines who have been secretly working together to exploit the rest of humanity for many centuries.

Sometimes these families have rifts and disagreements about specific policies and sometimes they do get competitive with each other about who will get the bigger piece of the pie, but overall they have shared the same goal for generations. That goal is to establish a worldwide government and connected feudal economic system which will give them complete control of the planet. It's also important to mention that there are millions of people in the world that happen to share these last names, but all of those people obviously aren't within these bloodlines and don't play a role in this exploitation. The commanding bloodlines of the global elite are as follows, Merovingian, Rothschild,

Rockefeller, Astor, Bundy, Collins, DuPont, Freeman, Li, Reynolds, Morgan, Onassis, Oppenheimer, Russel, Van Duyn. In different places all throughout the world these bloodlines are in charge of the most influential political organizations and the wealthiest multinational corporations.

In the west, the Merovingian, Rothschilds, Rockefellers, Morgans are the most influential of these bloodlines. The Merovingian Bloodline is the line of the royal families in Great Brittan and other parts of Europe, this line is also shared by nearly 80% of American presidents. This is the bloodline that descended from Charlemagne and Count Dracula. The Rothschilds, Rockefellers and Morgans should need no introduction, these are the infamous robber barons that have dominated western business culture for centuries and picked up where the Knights Templar left off. Many of the other families I have mentioned played a similar role, but have recently stayed more in the background compared to the Rothschilds, Merovingians, Morgans and Rockefellers. The Rothschilds are by far the wealthiest of these bloodlines and share the biggest piece of the global pie with the Merovingian bloodline, with the Rockefellers following close behind.

These family lines can be traced back to the feudal nobility of the Middle Ages and they are still in control of the majority of the world's attainable wealth, they own most of earth's land surface and they continue to influence global policy in every detail. So what has changed about the relationship between these families and the rest of society since the dark ages? The technology that we have developed has made our lives somewhat less difficult, but all in all we are still a serf class who is controlled by descendants of the tyrants that our ancestors served on the fiefdoms of early Europe.

To carry out covert operations and secretly pass down information through generations the elite uses a vast network of secret societies and so called fraternities as underground training centers. These are organizations where members must take vows of secrecy in order to join and once initiated they plan out global policies that will eventually be presented through the think tanks that they are closely related to.

Many people doubt the influence of secret societies and write them off as harmless "conspiracy theories", but history has shown us that secret societies play a major role in some of the world's most pivotal events. For example, the First World War had a direct impact on the entire world and set in motion a chain of events that would bring the earth's population under tighter control of the global elite. This war was started in 1914 when Archduke Franz Ferdinand of Hungary was assassinated by a secret society called "The Black Hand". The Black Hand had many ties to different ruling class families and its stated goal was to "unify" different nations and city states throughout Serbia and the rest of Europe. It was also said that this secret society was in cahoots with the British intelligence office MI6, this is highly possible considering that intelligence organizations often work with secret societies without the knowledge of the public or government officials.

Secret societies are used to carry out missions that can span over several generations. In the mid 1800's the Rothschilds hired a man by the name of Albert Pike to counter the abolition movement in the United States. The Rothschilds had a heavy hand in the US slave trade and stood to lose a lot of money if slavery was abolished. With Rothschild money, Albert Pike created a secret society called the Klu Klux Klan, a horribly racist group that should need no introduction. Despite the fact that the KKK is one of the most rightfully vilified organizations in the world, there is a statue in Washington DC dedicated to Albert Pike. The statue stands on a pedestal near the foot of Capitol Hill, between the Department of Labor building and the Municipal Building, between 3rd and 4th Streets, on D Street, NW. During his life this racist pawn was known as a humanitarian and philanthropist. What a joke! Although many of the people that call themselves humanitarians and philanthropists these days are also depraved individuals who live lives that are drastically out of line with their public image.

Pike was also very close to a man named Giusseppe Mazzini who would form the Mafia in 1860, another infamous secret society that works closely with the ruling class. These organizations are just the tip of the iceberg when it comes to secret societies established by elite bloodlines. Both Mazzini and Albert Pike belonged to a fraternity known as "Scottish Rite Freemasonry" this is not to be confused with the American Masonic "Blue Lodge's" which are used as social clubs in communities and that almost anyone can join. Scottish Rite Freemasonry is far more exclusive and they actually use the blue lodges as a diversion to hide the true purpose of their secret societies.

The influential freemasonry that most major politicians and aristocrats are involved with is very much a secret society within a secret society. On January 22, 1870 Giusseppe Mazzini wrote a letter to Albert Pike concerning freemasonry, the letter said *"We must allow all the federations to continue just as they are, with their systems, their central authorities and their diverse modes of correspondence between high grades of the same rite, organized as they are at the present, but we must create a super rite, which will remain unknown, to which we will call those Masons of high degree whom we shall select. With regard to our brothers in Masonry, these men must be pledges to the strictest secrecy. Through this supreme rite, we will govern all Freemasonry which will become the one international center, the more powerful because its direction will be unknown."*[1]

Albert Pike was known to study the occult and talk frequently of Satanism. This may sound crazy but as I will outline many times throughout this book Satanism is actually the most popular religion among those in power. This is because Satanism is essentially ego worship that holds power as a key value. Remember that when politicians and aristocrats claim to be of a certain religion it's highly possible that their words are simply political rhetoric just like everything else that comes out of their mouths. Satanism is also deeply intertwined with freemasonry despite the organizations claim that they are non-denominational. Some researchers say this was due to Pikes influence while others believe Satanism has been a part of the elite circles for much longer. Manly P. Hall is one of the best sources on the occult secrets of freemasonry as he himself was a 33rd degree mason, which is the highest possible level. Pike, Mazzini, George Washington, George Bush, Karl Marx and various other powerful establishment figures in recent history are also 33rd degree masons.

In one of his books, Hall writes about the satanic nature of freemasonry, he writes "*The day has come when Fellow Craftsman must know and apply their knowledge. The lost key to their grade is the mastery of emotion, which places the energy of the universe at their disposal. Man can only expect to be entrusted with great power by proving his ability to use it constructively and selflessly. When the Mason learns that the key to the warrior on the block is the proper application of the dynamo of living power, he has learned the mystery of his Craft. The seething energies of Lucifer are in his hands, and before he may step onward and upward, he must prove his ability to properly apply energy. He must follow in the footsteps of his forefather, Tubal-Cain, who with the mighty strength of the war god hammered his sword into a plowsha*re." [2] Manly P. Hall was most likely not a Satanist as he was a bit more of a humanitarian than many of his fellow masons and he actually spoke out about the injustices of authority.

The secretive and politically influential aristocracy has been popularly known as the "Illuminati" for hundreds of years. The secret society began in Bavaria, in 1776 and was originally called "Order of Perfectibilists" until they changed their name to the Illuminati just soon after. The goal of this order was to defend the existing class structure from the approaching revolt of the peasants. The long oppressed and manipulated masses were becoming literate and educated, so the aristocracy knew a revolution was imminent. The once illiterate and indoctrinated working class was starting to demand a better way of life, a more free and equal society. The establishment was seeking to subvert this popular uprising and ensure that things stayed as they were, even in the wake of revolution.

The first order of business for the Illuminati was to build a structured education system so they could influence what the public was learning and guarantee that future generations would be less resistant to authority. They were aware that they could not prevent people from learning altogether, but if they could have control of the specific information that was established as "fact" through a structured education system, they would still be able to complete their goal and carry on business as usual. This idea resulted in the "Prussian Education Model" that I mentioned earlier, which makes sense considering that the Illuminati was formed in Bavaria, and Prussia and Bavaria were in the same general area on maps of 18th century Germany.

As planned, the popular revolutions of the 18th and 19th centuries may have made the working class feel a bit better about themselves, but little had honestly changed about the existing class structure. There were no reparations of wealth, land or power whatsoever, but the elite covered this up using politics and propaganda to obscure the true class structure. Divisions were created in the social structure to splinter the peasants into different classes so just enough people were comfortable enough to uphold the traditional order and convince the rest of society that the status quo was acceptable. Charters and declarations were drawn up by the nobility proclaiming that the popular revolutions succeeded and that equal rights were now guaranteed to the common people, but again these are only pieces of paper. Documents like the Magna Charta and the Constitution are seen by many as milestones, but while they may be useful for court cases they are rarely enforced when it is important and they do nothing to prevent or correct the perils of feudalism.

The Illuminati and its relation to the darker side of freemasonry was even recognized by America's first president George Washington. On October 24, 1798 he wrote a letter to a contact named George Washington Snyder (no relation apparently) where he revealed his knowledge of the Illuminati and its infiltration of the freemasonic lodges across America and Europe. In the letter he says *"It is not my intention to doubt that the doctrine of the Illuminati and the principles of Jacobinism had not spread in the United States. On the contrary, no one is more satisfied of this fact than I am. The idea that I meant to convey, was, that I did not believe that the Lodges of Free Masons in this Country had, as Societies, endeavored to propagate the diabolical tenets of the first, or pernicious principles of the latter (if they are susceptible of separation). That Individuals of them may have done it, or that the founder, or instrument employed to found, the Democratic Societies in the United States, may have had these objects; and actually had a separation of the People from their Government in view, is too evident to be questioned."*[3]

There is no doubt that freemasonry has played a major role behind the scenes in American politics, this fact is made especially clear by the formation of the "Anti Masonic" political party in 1828. This political movement was set off by an incident known as the "Morgan affair" in which a man named William Morgan was preparing to print a book detailing the secrets of the freemasons before he mysteriously disappeared under suspicious circumstances. Like many 3rd parties in American politics, the Anti-Masonic party withered away in a short amount of time because they could not keep up financially with the two dominant parties, but the fact that this party existed shows us that the public has always had a suspicion of secret societies.

There are countless books and articles on the specifics of the many secret societies, and I will recommend some of them at the end of the chapter in the suggested reading section. Due to the overwhelming amount of information that is available on freemasonry I'm just going to cover the basics. Other secret societies that have been known to be used by the elite are Skull

238

and Bones, Hidden Hand, The Round Table, and Bohemian Grove among various other groups that are well documented and fairly easy to find information on. Many of the same people belong to all these different groups and many of them are working towards the same end, a feudal world government ruled by a small group of elites.

With more wealth than any of us could possibly imagine, the ruling class is looking towards World Empire just as so many tyrants have throughout history. Their goal is to gain even more control over the world's population, and create a one world government through trade deals and the United Nations, exactly as they already have with the European Union. This is not a matter of speculation, these goals are openly admitted by the ruling elite almost every time they are interviewed.

In 2002 David Rockefeller published his memoirs where he made this confession *"For more than a century, ideological extremists at either end of the political spectrum have seized upon well-publicized incidents to attack the Rockefeller family for the inordinate influence they claim we wield over American political and economic institutions. Some even believe we are part of a secret cabal working against the best interests of the United States, characterizing my family and me as 'internationalists' and of conspiring with others around the world to build a more integrated global political and economic structure - one world, if you will. If that's the charge, I stand guilty, and I am proud of it."*[4] The New World Order is no longer a "theory" but is in fact an openly admitted goal held by the aristocracy.

The largest and most threatening organizations to the wellbeing of humanity are without a doubt, NATO & the United Nations. I agree with having a safe place for diplomacy between nations, but the United Nations is not the way to do it because it is directly influenced and controlled by the aristocracy of each nation. To give the illusion of an unbiased, fair and equal organization, some 3rd parties and smaller independent countries are given a seat, but their power is limited in comparison to that of the industrial superpowers. This was made quite clear when every nation in the UN approved of a measure that would condemn illegal settlements on Palestinian land, that is, every nation except for the US who used their veto power to cancel the action. This is a privilege that is only awarded to America, China, Russia, France and England, but none of the African or Middle Eastern countries in the UN have the ability to veto any action.

This shows that for the most part the larger superpowers have more influence in the UN than the weaker countries. In other words, the UN is just another place where the more powerful countries can bully the less powerful. The UN also serves as a foundation for world government by linking all the smaller countries together to be pushed around and investigated by the larger superpowers. Through the stronger nations, the global aristocrats use their puppet regimes to advance their feudal agenda. The Council on Foreign Relations (which David Rockefeller is chairmen of) is also heavily involved in influencing the policy at the United Nations. In fact, The United Nations headquarters sits on 18 acres of prime Manhattan land which was donated by the Rockefeller family.

I want to remind you that these accusations are not unfounded and in no means a "theory", this is well documented fact that is constantly being covered up by the establishment and its institutions. Even some rogue politicians are now speaking out against this global fascist agenda. Congressman Ron Paul of Texas was asked in May of 2007 about the New World Order and its relation to the United Nations. Ron Paul responded, *"The first President Bush said the New World Order was in tune-- and that's what they were working for. The U.N. is part of that government. They're working right now very significantly towards a North American Union. That's why there's a lot of people in Washington right now who don't care too much about our borders. They have a philosophical belief that national sovereignty is not important. It's also the reason I've made the very strong suggestion the U.S. need not be in the U.N. for national security reasons.*"[5]

If we were really being honest about things the ruling class would have their own seat at the UN, right next to the US, the UK, China and Russia, because they are in fact just in themselves a superpower to be compared with other nations instead of other families. They are the superpower that has the smallest population yet the largest net worth. If the 7 billion other people in the world would realize what was going on, there would be outrage and widespread revolt.

This is why the elite disguise their influence and their goals while spending billions of dollars cleaning up their public image. When I speak of the global elite, the establishment, the west, the globalists, the Illuminati or any like terms, I am referring to the feudal bloodlines that control governments. This may sound fantastical, but these are simply ominous names that have been given to those who sit behind the throne.

Rarely people that don't come from these bloodlines are able to attain wealth and power that rivals that of the elite, be it through either a stroke of luck, genius or trickery. Surely people like Bill Gates who have amassed unbelievable wealth within a lifetime are approached to join the ranks of the global elite, or else. Bill Gates is just one of the many modern day "philanthropist" types who will aid the current aristocracy in their mission of globalization and eventually pass that mission onto his children in hopes they will continue this legacy.

This is what the already established bloodlines have been doing for centuries, some are more powerful than others and some are more relevant than others during different times in history, but they are all working toward the same goal. Bill Gates has already revealed his true colors through his funding of various eugenics and depopulation efforts. What happens when a new recruit is offered an ultimatum to join the global elite and refuses? They are eliminated.

A historical example of this kind of "elimination" is found with the deaths of the Russian Imperial Romonov family. This entire bloodline was progressively destroyed by the Rothschild dynasty because the Tsar Alexander I of Russia thwarted their attempt to establish a world government in 1814. At this point many of the European governments were in debt to the Rothschilds so they were using that debt as an excuse to set up a world government through interlinked financial systems.

Kind of sounds exactly like what's happening today with the European Union, huh? Well unfortunately for the globalists, Tsar Alexander I of Russia managed to retain his own wealth and was not at the mercy of the Rothschild banking cartel. Due to Alexander's refusal to participate in the economic system and his outspokenness against the Rothschild's plan, his whole bloodline was attacked and systematically killed. With the Romonov bloodline eliminated, the Rothschilds were then able to establish their own puppet regime and gain control of the Russian government.

Most of us could not even begin to imagine the wealth that these families hold because it is beyond what most of us see as "money", currency actually has no value to them. They are the ones who create the currency and collect the taxes, their wealth is measured in continents and people not dollars and cents. Everyone is a slave to these people, even the politicians, and this generation of the banking elite is growing impatient.

They are advancing their plan even more quickly than in previous eras due to technological advancement and unquenchable greed. The seamless implementation of the European Union has given them more confidence that they can consolidate the whole world's economy within their lifetime. Economic consolidation would allow them to create a shadow government that will rule the entire planet from behind the scenes. This process has already begun and these families already wield incredible power over the world's population, but creating a global economic empire will give them supremacy that will be nearly impossible to challenge. Now that you know the people involved in the exploitation it's time we get a bit more into the specifics of their plan, the global dictatorship which has been referred to as the new world order.

QUOTE SOURCES AND SUGGESTED READING
[0] Vile Acts of Evil - Volume 1 - Banking in America - Michael A. Kirchubel (2009)
[1] Occult Theocracy by Lady Queensborough pages 208-209
[2] The Lost Keys of Freemasonry by Manly P. Hall
[3] The Writings of George Washington, vol. 20, p. 518
[4] David Rockefeller: Memoirs p.405
[5]http://www.infowars.com/articles/nwo/ron_paul_first_bush_wa s_working_towards_nwo.htm
[SR1] Pawns in the Game by William Guy Carr
[SR2] Morals and Dogma of the Ancient and Accepted Scottish Rite of Freemasonry - Albert Pike
[SR3] Bloodlines of the Illuminati by Fritz Springmeier
[SR4] Memoirs by David Rockefeller
[SR5] The Anglo American establishment by Dr. Carroll Quigley
[SR6] The Crisis of Democracy By Michel Crozier, Samuel P. Huntington, Joji Watanuki
[SR7] The Grand Chessboard: American Primacy And Its Geostrategic Imperatives by Zbigniew Brzezinski
[SR8] The Last Will and Testament of Cecil J. Rhodes
[SR9] The Lost Keys of Freemasonry by Manly P. Hall
[SR10] The World's Banker: The History of the House of Rothschild by Niall Ferguson
[SR11] America's Secret Establishment by Antony C. Sutton
[SR12] The Lost Keys of Freemasonry by Manly P. Hall
[SR13] The True Story of the Bilderberg Group by Daniel Estulin
[SR14] Tragedy & Hope: A History of the World in Our Time by Carroll Quigley

"We shall have world government whether or not you like it, by conquest or consent." - James Warburg (CFR Member) [0]

45. Fabian Socialism and the New World Order

Ruling the world is something that bloodthirsty tyrants and ruthless aristocrats have been trying to do since ancient times. When people are born into nobility and have every single thing they can ask for, they become unsatisfied with their riches and set their sights on the ultimate prize, world conquest. This is how empire was born.

The bloodlines of the aristocracy believe that they are of a superior race than the rest of humanity and have been inbreeding for centuries to keep their wealth and "royal genes" in the family. This twisted world view has allowed them to build their empires while committing countless human rights violations, in the form of war, slavery and human sacrifice. All along the way the majority of humanity has been carelessly exploited and manipulated without their knowledge. And for what? They have told us it is the work of god, that "civilization" is being cultivated, that an evil menacing enemy is being defeated, or simply that "progress" is being made. The nation builders have given many different excuses for their conquest over the centuries, but the motive has remained the same, to control every person and resource on the planet.

After all this time the ruling elite has gotten mass manipulation and exploitation down to a well mastered science. Behind closed doors these families pass on their goals of world domination and teach their children how to extort and deceive the serf class. Since ancient times their agenda has been to use their wealth and power to influence politicians from behind the scenes. This way, when the public disapproved of how the society was being run, the politicians would act as scapegoats, and the true rulers would retain their wealth and power without criticism.

For many centuries rulers have attempted to build their empires through bloody conquests, and for most of the human population it's gotten extremely old. After many cycles of revolutions the elite began to realize that brute force was not enough to keep down the human spirit. If they wanted to be successful they knew that they would have to take a less obvious, more secretive approach to world conquest. This approach involves gaining control of every economy in the world, which will in turn give them control of both the politicians and the public.

Now that's not to say that the ruling class has given up on using force all together, they are still prepared to rule with an iron fist if someone doesn't comply "diplomatically" with their plans. When they are brought to use force, the aristocracy often hides behind their puppet governments and rationalizes the conquest by claiming that someone is being "liberated" or "protected".

These excuses lead the public to believe that the many military actions that are taking place around the world are merely isolated incidents as opposed to a planned conquest. These conquests are spread out over long periods of time because if everything were to take place in a short amount of time then the public would surely catch on. So they take small steps and incrementally advance their goal of global economic and political dominance, through "diplomacy" when they can and through unrelenting force when all else fails. This political strategy is known as "Incremental Socialism" or "Fabian Socialism", which is basically the establishment of an authoritarian welfare/warfare state through long term deception and diplomacy, as opposed to carrying out just one massive, swift military action. Instead of waging high profile wars to take control of an area's population, business deals and political policies are established behind closed doors that will slowly but surely result in a stealthy conquest. This conquest takes place over the course of many generations and is handed down to the children of the elite, this way everything happens over such a long period of time to make the events seem unrelated and the agenda goes unnoticed.

To articulate this thought, many researches have used the analogy of the boiling frog, which I hope will better illustrate the point I am trying to make. If you try to put a frog into a boiling pot of water it will immediately jump out, but if you put the frog into a pot of water that is room temperature and heat it slowly then the frog will stay in the pot and eventually boil without realizing that the water is getting any hotter. This is exactly the situation we find ourselves in, where slowly but surely over various administrations we are pushed closer and closer towards complete tyranny.

This is definitely no new plot, and was actually recognized by various early American presidents. James Madison, for example once said "*I believe there are more instances of the abridgement of freedom of the people by gradual and silent encroachments of those in power than by violent and sudden usurpations.*"[1] The idea of carrying out plots over multiple generations sounds irrational to most people, but how else would societies be built? Empires are very large projects that could not be built successfully in just one generation. In our history, large architectural projects such as bridges, temples and city infrastructure would take many generations to build. This is how things work when someone is managing a civilization, plans are long term even though they have many short term problems and motivations.

There is a think tank based in the UK called "the Fabian society", which includes many members of the western aristocracy, and works towards consolidating their wealth and expanding their influence. The logo of this secret society is ironically enough a wolf, wearing a sheepskin on its back….a wolf in sheep's clothing. This ideology and political approach has extended far beyond the Fabian society and has reached almost every government in the world. The word "Fabian" comes to us from the name of an ancient Roman dictator named Fabius Maximus Cunctator. He came to power by defeating an overpowering enemy by slowly wearing them down and blocking them off from the resources that they needed to flourish. This brilliant strategy made Fabius a legend and left behind a template for future "leaders" to use in battle and in politics.

The goal of the modern Fabian Socialist is the same ultimate conquest which has been sought after by control freaks for centuries, to create a one world dictatorship under their control. This one world dictatorship is often referred to as the "New World Order". The term New World Order has been used by various western elites in public for at least a hundred years, to describe the global civilization that they were working towards. This goal has been advancing over the course of many generations, through various organizations with a handful of different actors making contributions along the way.

One person who was instrumental in laying much of the foundation for this plan was a British aristocrat and Rothschild agent by the name of Cecil Rhodes. Rhodes was a staunch imperialist and spent his life sending mercenaries around the world plundering developing countries in the name of the British Empire. One of his most profitable ventures came through the conquest of Africa and the creation of the diamond market.

Cecil Rhodes founded the world's most powerful diamond company DeBeers, a cartel that maintains a tight monopoly over the entire industry to this day. To provide stability and slave labor for his diamond mines, Rhodes used the British military to establish apartheid states that were filled with concentration camps and widespread chaos. South Africa and surrounding areas were the base of his operations. In the past they were even blatant enough to call a territory "Rhodesia" (named after Cecil Rhodes), although eventually the name was changed to Zimbabwe to present the illusion that it wasn't a British colony. After Rhodes died he left a great majority of his wealth to the Rothschild dynasty and established The Round Table secret society and the Rhodes scholarship, both of which were intended as a means to bring about world government.

Georgetown Professor Carroll Quigley has some of the best

research on these groups as he had direct access to some archives of the Round Table groups through the Council on Foreign Relations. His epic book Tragedy and Hope is over 1000 pages and chronicles the history of these organizations. In Tragedy and hope he says *"In the middle 1890's Rhodes had a personal income of at least a million pounds sterling a year which he spent so freely for mysterious purposes that he was usually overdrawn on his account ... Cecil Rhodes' commitment to a conspiracy to establish World Government was set down in a series of wills described by Frank Aydelotte in his book American Rhodes Scholarships."*[2]

Quigley reveals his sources in the following passage *"The Rhodes Scholarships... are known to everyone. What is not so widely known is that Rhodes in five previous wills left his fortune to form a secret society, which was to devote itself to the preservation and expansion of the British Empire. And what does not seem to be known to anyone is that this secret society ... continues to exist to this day ...There does exist, and has existed for a generation, an international anglophile network which operates, to some extent, in the way the radical Right believes the communists act. In fact, this network, which we may identify as the Round Table Groups, has no aversion to cooperating with the Communists, or any other groups and frequently does so. I know of the operations of this network because I have studied it for twenty years and was permitted for two years, in the early 1960's, to examine its papers and secret records. I have no aversion to it or to most of its aims and have, for much of my life, been close to it and too many of its instruments. I have objected, both in the past and recently, to a few of its policies ... but in general my chief difference of opinion is that it wishes to remain unknown, and I believe its role in history is significant enough to be known."*[3] I'll remind you that Carroll Quigley is no fringe source, he was a very prominent educator and even taught Rhodes Scholar Bill Clinton. Clinton even mentioned Quigley in his inaugural address, and frequently referred to him as his "mentor".

The original round table groups eventually branched out into larger think tanks such as the Council on Foreign Relations and the Bilderberg Group. For years the very existence of these groups were denied, but recently they have been forced to reveal their associations, thanks to the hard work of activists and the independent media. The CFR membership is now almost completely public and consists of a long list of influential politicians, business tycoons, military leaders and media moguls. The Bilderberg Group is an even more exclusive group which has members in various aristocratic circles worldwide, including the Rothschilds, Rockefellers and multiple royal families. Every year their annual meeting gets even more and more negative attention as the world begins to understand how they have been deceived and manipulated by the people involved with this organization. In 2011 when they met in Switzerland they encountered resistance like they had never seen before, in addition to the scores of activists there were also various politicians from the European Union there to protest the meeting.

Italian politician Mario Borghezio attempted to enter the hotel where the conference was being held and had his nose broken by the paramilitary security staff hired for the event. Interestingly, the security company's logo was the occult symbol of the all seeing eye that appears on our money and has long been the unofficial logo for the "Illuminati". As to what goes on inside, that has been revealed by many moles and investigators. Even former NATO Secretary-General and Bilderberg member Willy Claes has admitted that the group sets global policy. This was revealed by Claes in a June 4, 2010 radio interview with Belgian news website zonnewind.be. The influence of the Bilderberg Group is now mainstream knowledge, and it is becoming obvious that their agenda is not in our best interest.

For the ruling class, global politics is a game for power and the planet is their giant chessboard, on which all of humanity are expendable pieces to be used and sacrificed for the sake of advancing the game. In this game they plan many moves ahead in order to deceive their opponents and always remain on top of everyone else. Many people have a hard time believing that this is going on, but the globalization plot is already in visible motion.

The European Union gives us a glimpse into what the bankers want to do with the rest of the world. Many Americans still may think that the New World Order is just a "theory", but there aren't a whole lot of skeptics left in Europe. Just decades ago, nearly every single nation in Europe had their economy and government taken over by the banking elite. For all ceremonial purposes the countries still have their own governments and borders, but the real power lies in the international banking cartel which centrally controls the European Union. In fact, since the consolidation of Europe, the governments of every European country included are now subservient to the banking elite. This is what they want to do in every single continent across the globe, which I'll remind you is not a farfetched goal for international bankers to have.

This kind of economic and political union has already taken shape in Africa and they are constantly making steps to establish similar super states in both North America and Asia. The process has already begun, through seemingly harmless "trade agreements" and "alliances", which are the same steps that set the European Union into motion. The plan in North America is called "The Security and Prosperity Partnership" and although it has been vehemently denied by most politicians, declassified documents show that this plan is definitely in the works.

All of the predominant political organizations, the education systems and the media are all put into place by the ruling class, so globalized government is obviously going to be portrayed in a positive light within those sources. That doesn't mean that the propaganda and public relations efforts are at all correct. Their sales pitch for global fascism is that it will "end wars", "end economic depression" and so on and so forth. However, the very people that are offering this sales pitch are the ones who are instigating the wars and creating the economic depressions. This is a scam, a set up that has been carefully planned to mold public opinion into accepting a worldwide dictatorship. Public opinion is extremely important, the will of the public is really the only force that has ever been able to subdue power hungry tyrants.

The aristocracy may have all the financial, military and political power in the world, but they are outnumbered to such a degree that they can only continue to build their plan as long as we are willing to go along with it. This is why every single move that they make is designed to win us over and convince us that things are being done in our best interest, when in reality we are being exploited and played for fools. Globalized government will not bring peace and prosperity as promised, it will only lead to more poverty, less freedom and a complete abandon of human rights altogether.

In this section I have discussed many different organizations and groups that play part in facilitating this global feudal system, and each of them play their own specific role in the advancement of authoritarianism. To draw a comparison, I will refer to an old mystery novel by Agatha Christie titled Murder on the Orient Express, released in 1934. This is an analogy that has been used by many great researchers in the past. In the story a detective is faced with the task of finding out who killed one of the passengers onboard a train. There were multiple stab wounds in the victim's body and multiple suspects who appeared to have nothing to do with each other, there were too many clues to make any kind of logical sense of the situation at a glance. Throughout the story, the detective investigates and discovers that all of the seemingly unconnected suspects had ties to the victim, to one another, and they all shared the same motive. In the end they were all guilty and each played an integral part in the homicide.

This story is relevant because it provides the perfect analogy to represent the many different families and organizations that work together to bring about a common end. The ruling class have close ties to one another through their international foundations, and they share the same goal in the sense that they are working to keep their long established feudal systems in power. At this point in time the Council on Foreign Relations and the Bilderberg group are the most publicly active of these organizations, so if you pay attention to what they are doing you can easily decipher the establishment's agenda.

In the democracies of the west, we are taught to take a "pragmatic" approach to the political and economic aspects of our world. The philosophy of pragmatism is a subtle form of surrender in which we are told to accept the status quo despite its many imperfections and sacrifice our ideals for more "practical" solutions that don't "rock the boat", so to speak. Meanwhile, the elite practice a contrasting approach which is relentless and uncompromising. Under these circumstances they are always on the offensive and we are always on the defensive, which is why they have continued to influence global politics for centuries with minimal opposition.

To work within the system and the boundaries laid out by the establishment is to take part in a rat race, but at the same time even to attack these interests head on would play right into their hands as well. The world will never change until the very concept of power and authority is abandoned by the masses, so intellectually challenging the legitimacy of the system itself is the true path to freedom. It is this false authority which they hold over people that allows them to dictate our lives, and has given them a free pass to steal from us until there is nothing left. When that authority disappears they no longer have the entire world to back them up, and they can be judged as individuals.

QUOTE SOURCES AND SUGGESTED READING
[0] Statement by CFR member James Warburg on February 17th, l950
[1] James Madison - Virginia convention of 1788
[2] [3] -Dr. Carroll Quigley, "Tragedy and Hope"

"All war must be just the killing of strangers against whom you feel no personal animosity; strangers whom, in other circumstances, you would help if you found them in trouble, and who would help you if you needed it" - Mark Twain (Writer) [0]

46. Controlled Conflict in the Middle East

The war in the Middle East between Israel and Palestine is by far one of the most serious issues of our time, it is also one of the most controversial and misunderstood. Most any place on earth has a history of conflict, and the Middle East is no different. There were many crusades fought in those areas mainly carried out by invading European Christians in the name of religion, but for the sake of empire. Prior to World War 2, Jewish and Muslim people lived in relative peace in the territory which is now Israel, at the time it was just known as Syria. These were all remnants of the once unified Ottoman Empire that was divided and split apart by British imperialism. Most of the people that lived in Syria at this time were of Arab descent, but there was also a much smaller portion of society who was Jewish. Regardless of this discrepancy there was very little hostility among the different religions until British influence and western intervention brought a whole new dynamic to the situation.

The state of Israel developed during a very important time in world history, between the first and second world wars. The end of the First World War brought with it the League of Nations who rewrote borders and territory lines all over the world. The League of Nations was an organization that was proposed by the international banking interests that funded and instigated the war. This institution was designed so the ruling class could have more control over world events. Many of the policies established by the League of Nations after the First World War were specifically designed to cause future conflict in Europe. For example, the harsh penalties enacted on the German people caused years of economic turmoil that eventually left them vulnerable enough to be exploited by the tyrant Adolph Hitler. The aristocracy planned to profit off of future wars by selling weapons, making loans and expanding their world dominance using the puppet regimes that they had in place in the British and United States governments. The territory lines and policies set up after World War 1 in Europe established the conditions that would eventually lead to World War 2, and perhaps even World War 3.

When the Second World War became even more profitable than the first, the ruling class decided to once again set a pretense for future wars. Once again they used the League of Nations which at this point had changed its name to the United Nations, to escalate hostilities in areas they wished to dominate. This is how the great rivalry between communism and capitalism, and the resulting cold war developed. The cold war resulted in a massive arms race that sold a lot of weapons for the ruling class and it allowed them to further divide the most powerful nations, in turn making them easier to influence and take control of. This also gave them an excuse to use military action on self-sustaining rebel nations that were not compliant with western policies.

One of the main areas that they wished to instigate trouble in was the Middle East, due to its abundance in oil, a natural resource that became extremely important on the global stage during the First World War.

Through diplomatic maneuvers following World War 2, the Rothschilds and the rest of the western oligarchy were able to establish an avenue for their future conquest in the region.

There was a massive Jewish refugee population in the years following the holocaust and the ruling class has very little sympathy for people in these kinds of situations. Refugees of any creed, color or nationality are treated by all governments as if they were lepers, and despite the hardships that the strong Jewish people had just been put through, they were seen as nothing more than a "problem" to the United Nations. At the same time another "problem" being discussed behind the scenes

254

at the UN was how to maintain a stronghold in the oil rich Middle East. The western powers were having a difficult time exploiting the predominantly Arab region, and many "leaders" in the area were also being "uncooperative" with western companies who sought to move in and plunder the regions natural resources.

Nothing makes the aristocracy happier than "solving" two or more of their "problems" at the same time, in a single action. The creation of the state of Israel did just that. Seeing that Jewish people had a biblical connection to the area, the UN claimed that their motivation was to establish a Jewish homeland. However, what they actually did was set up an imperial colonial government that they would control politically and economically. Think back to the chapter on eugenics, where Francis Galton wrote an article in the newspaper suggesting that Chinese people be imported to Africa, so that they could essentially be used as pawns to establish a colony, this is very much the same concept.

Sure, a great number of Jewish people do live in Israel but they do not have control of their government, economy or their military, but are in fact oppressed and manipulated by all of those institutions. The aristocracy in Great Brittan has more control over Israel's domestic and foreign policy then the people actually living everyday lives inside the country, the same goes for people living in America as well. The British elite have much more say in major American policies than the taxpayers and voters inside the country do.

The creation of the state of Israel is extremely similar to the creation of both Australia and the United States. In each case, the aristocracy within Great Britain wanted to set up a colony in a faraway land where there was already an established native civilization. In every single case they did not launch a military invasion but simply sent exiles, refuges and prisoners of war to live in the area and establish a stronghold. Of course the prisoners were always told they were being sent to a promised land or paradise, but in reality they were being used much like pawns are used in a game of chess. They are sent to the frontlines of the area that the elite wish to conquer, and they fend for themselves until a workable civilization is established. At that point, the civilization is exploited and overtaken by the colonial powers that sent the refugees there to begin with. Although things are somewhat different in America because of the revolutionary war, Great Britain still has a lot of control over our economy and our political system as well. This same situation is taking place, but to an even greater degree in both Australia and Israel.

When the state of Israel was created in 1948, anyone that happened to be living within the borders drawn by the United Nations, who was of Arab or Palestinian descent was forcibly expelled from their homes. This is not slander or speculation, this actually happened, and it created the world's largest refugee population. 6 Million People were forced into exile, in different parts of the world because of their heritage. Since then these refugees have lived in camps or in the ghettos of Palestine because they are not permitted to buy or sell property and are banned from employment. This goes for refugees inside Palestinian territory, the West Bank, the Gaza strip, Lebanon and other parts of the Middle East. They are given no chance of obtaining citizenship and are denied many of their basic human rights. A young Palestinian by the name of Ali Abdul Bari runs a peaceful activist organization called Esha. In an interview with the independent press he said "*The media talk about Gaza as a centre of starvation, but that's not true. What we are lacking is our freedom: We have a sea, but we can't use it. We have air, but we aren't allowed to build an airport. We want to be able to depend on ourselves.*" [1] This is the true sentiment of the Palestinian people, not the crazed rhetoric of the areas so called "leaders".

The people of Israel have a nationalistic militant government that doesn't represent their will, while on the other end, the people of Palestine also have a nationalistic militant government that doesn't represent their will. The so called "leaders" of the

Palestinian territories are Hamas and Fatah, they are two militant Islamic factions that in no way represent the people of Palestine. They are at war with each other, at war with Israel and at war with the people of Palestine as well, their regimes are a massive barrier in the peace process. They refuse to negotiate with each other and refuse to take place in any peace processes, as ceremonial as they may be. They openly spit hateful rhetoric that gets people on both sides fired up, and escalates the tension in the region. Israeli people begin to hate Palestinian people for things that their government did or said and vice versa. Hamas often calls for the complete destruction of the state of Israel and exile of the current Jewish population. This is obviously a bad idea and would simply compound the region's problems by creating yet another human rights crisis and refugee population. This political stance also ensures an ongoing conflict, because if both sides will not quit or negotiate until the other is destroyed, then conflict could go on forever.

To understand how Hamas and Fatah really work and who they serve, one must ask themselves a few questions. How did they get so powerful if they don't have popular support? Where did they get their weapons and resources from in a poverty stricken area like Palestine? Most of all, who benefits from them being in power? The answer to all of these questions is short and simple, The UK, the United States and Israel, or more appropriately the MI6, CIA and the Mossad. Remember, secret service organizations operate together across borders, many times without the knowledge of the governments that they apparently work for. In June of 2008 the Prime Minister of Israel Ehud Olmert admitted that Israel's secret service Mossad transferred millions of dollars to the Hamas government every single month for years. The same people that are being condemned in public by the west and Israel as being terrorists are receiving millions of dollars for weapons from these very governments. This allows the conflict to escalate and serves the elite at the expense of the average people in every country.

In spite of Hamas' refusal to negotiate, there has still been a very one sided and controlled "peace process" of negotiations that have taken place between the Zionist government in Israel and another Political group called the "Palestinian Liberation Organization". The Palestinian Liberation Organization claims to represent the Palestinian people, but of course just like Hamas and Fatah, they do not. The details of the peace conferences were hazy in the media for years, until 2011 when 1,700 declassified diplomatic cables were released through two different international media outlets, The UK's "Guardian" and the Arabic "Aljazeera". These cables showed detailed exchanges between the Zionist regime and Palestinian Liberation Organization that were hidden from the whole world.

The files showed that a whole decades worth of behind the scenes negotiations took place between representatives on behalf of both nations (With the US as a strong 3rd party of course). The problem with the content of these negotiations is that both the PLO and the Zionist government were both making decisions that were in direct opposition of their nation's public interest. The Zionist "leaders" of Israel refused to accept various peace offers suggested by the PLO that the people of Israel would have had no problems coming to terms with. The reason why these terms weren't accepted is because the war with the Palestinians provides the Zionist Government a pretense for constant militarization and homeland police state. This is the same tactic used by the American Government in their ongoing "war on terror", a constant war state is perpetuated and drawn out by the establishment to ensure the central government more power. On the other end, tyrants of the Arab world take advantage of this crisis to impose the same kind of wartime mentality on their people. The global elite also stand to make a lot of money in both the war on terror and the Zionist war in Palestine, through their arms dealers, oil companies and other multinational corporations.

So the western governments and corporations, the Zionist elite in Israel, and the elites of the Arab world are all benefiting politically and financially from the continuation of this horrible conflict in the

Middle East. This is exactly why the aforementioned parties just can't seem to come to terms and bring an end to this bloodbath. In every major war it is the common people of each nation who are the biggest victims and the elite of those same nations who reap all the benefits and use the lives of their citizens as bargaining chips behind closed doors. The Palestine papers resulted in the resignation of Saeb Erekat, chief negotiator for the PLO. The leaked documents proved that he was willing to abandon millions of refugees and showed no consideration for the needs of the people he was apparently representing. This is the typical nature of the relationship between politician and citizen throughout most of history.

It is also important to mention that the creation of Israel was not an issue that was brought forth by the Jewish refugees, but was championed by the ruling class of the United Kingdom through the United Nations. Although the state of Israel was created after World War 2, the push for Zionism and a Jewish homeland in Palestine began on the record in 1917, when the "*Balfour Declaration*" was printed. This declaration was not something that developed in parliament or among the Jewish people, but it was actually a letter between British aristocrat Lord Arthur Balfour and Lord Lionel Walter Rothschild. Some researchers even believe that it was the work of Rothschild himself, but either way, Lord Balfour is quite easily linked as a close associate of the Rothschild dynasty, which strongly implicates their involvement. Rothschild was the representative of the "English Federation of Zionists". This was the same group of people that would fund Hitler's rise to power and ignore the genocide of the Jewish people who they claimed to be so concerned about.

In the western media and Israeli schools, people are taught that the state of Israel was created specifically so there could be a Jewish homeland in the Middle East. The United Nations apparently did that out of the kindness of their heart for the Jewish people. I highly doubt that there were not any ulterior motives on the part of the western aristocrats that initiated the creation of Israel. The United Nations was simply carrying out policies that they already wished to establish by exploiting the crisis that the Jewish refugees were facing. In other words, the creation of a Jewish homeland was only one side effect of the western powers establishing their base in the Middle East, a side effect that they used to their advantage as a public relations tool.

The people who are truly behind Zionism are not Jewish nationalists, they are elitist globalists who use nationalism and religion as a political tool to cultivate support for their non-ethnic imperial agenda. The Rothschilds may claim to be of Jewish descent but they are only "Jewish" in the same way that George Bush is "Christian", it is just a part of their public image that is in place so the common people can relate to them. Along with apparently being Jewish, the Rothschilds are also prominent Catholics and they basically run the treasury department at the Vatican. They play every possible side they can to gain as much control as possible and to more or less buy anyone who might stand in their way.

In reality, the global elite and their puppets are the ones calling the shots in the US, Israel and the UK. These people are not Catholics, Christians or Jews but they are in fact practicing Satanists. I know it might sound a little bit farfetched at first to think that the most powerful people in the world are Satanists, but if you do some research into what Satanism is all about it makes a whole lot of sense. The modern satanic religion actually has nothing to do with "devil worship", as described by Anton Lavey, author of the satanic bible. Modern Satanism is rooted in hedonism, self-indulgence and attention to very primal human triggers, which perfectly describes the kind of lifestyles that are led by members of the ruling class, and the societies they create share these same values as well. Think about it! War, domination, destruction, exploitation, taxation, mind control, manipulation and deception. Do those sound like the ideals of a Christian, a Catholic, a Jew or a Satanist? I think the answer should be obvious. Actions speak louder than words, especially when those words are coming from a group of people that have a consistent record of violence and pathological lying.

As I explained earlier, The Rothschilds were one of the primary sponsors of the Third Reich in Germany. Without their loans and oil companies, Hitler would have never been able to turn the Weimar republic into a threatening military superpower in such a short amount of time. The Rothschilds were not the only prominent family to claim Jewish heritage yet betray the Jewish population of Europe during Hitler's genocide. George Soros, the billionaire globalist who has been responsible for crashing markets all over the world admits himself that "his character was made" when he was working for the Nazis as a teenager, snitching on other Jewish families so they could be robbed by the thuggish regime and sent off to concentration camps.

On December 20, 1998 during an interview with Steve Kroft on "60 Minutes" Soros admitted that he worked for the Nazis in this fashion. When asked in the interview if he had any sense of guilt he replied "*Well, of course I c–I could be on the other side or I could be the one from whom the thing is being taken away. But there was no sense that I shouldn't be there, because that was– well, actually, in a funny way, it's just like in markets–that if I weren't there–of course, I wasn't doing it, but somebody else would–would–would be taking it away anyhow. And it was the– whether I was there or not, I was only a spectator, the property was being taken away. So the–I had no role in taking away that property. So I had no sense of guilt.*"[2]

So when the aristocracy and so called "leaders" claim to be a part of some ethnic, religious or social group remember to pay attention to their actions instead of their words. Many times actions that are taken by the aristocracy result in the death and impoverishment of the very people they are claiming to represent. Their loyalties are centered on wealth and power and are not influenced by any other social, ethnic or religious factors, those are merely the false divisions that they use to splinter the slave class into feuding sects.

The UK is the base of operations for the ruling class, and most of their policies are carried out through the politicians in that country as well as their colonies. Coincidentally, just after World War 1, the League of Nations mandated Palestine and Mesopotamia to the UK in 1921, just 4 years after the British oligarchy produced the Balfour Declaration. After World War 2 since the UK was already in control of various Middle Eastern states, the establishment began drawing more lines in the sand that would disrupt local diplomacy and open up the region to civil war and western influence. Another quick example is that of Afghanistan and Pakistan, it was once one nation with one people and was split up by British imperialists as a part of their divide and rule strategy. This happened all over the Middle East but is far more pronounced in the areas around Israel because of the refugee populations.

The main issues that are still controversial today are the displacement of the Native Arab's that once occupied the region, and the constant expansion of new Israeli settlements. There is a bitter war raging between the Zionist government and the Arab people that inhabit the Middle East due to these issues. This feud is extremely tragic when considering that the people on both sides of the conflict who are caught up in the fighting are both refugees and victims of imperialism. Many of the Jewish people that are now inhabiting the Middle East are descendants of people who were displaced themselves at the hands of Hitler's evil regime. Even living within the state of Israel, much of the Jewish population are themselves subject to oppression at the hands of the Zionist government.

When the state of Israel was created instead of integrating the Arab and Jewish cultures together, the ruling class put policies in place that would force the Palestinian people onto unfertile ghettos, separated from water sources and food growing lands by giant walls. The Palestinians were also not given the right to organize, own property, or work, and without these basic freedoms they remain refugees. These policies would result in a growing hostility between the two groups which eventually flared up in physical violence. This violence has spread all throughout the oil rich Middle East and has allowed the western establishment to have a permanent involvement in the region's affairs, just as they planned.

Israel is facing a situation much the same as the United States, where their major political parties are heavily influenced by global banking interests. The international bankers use these nations and their militaries as pawns to carry out their globalist agenda. In America we have the Democrat and Republican parties that appear to be different but are really controlled by the same global interests, while in Israel the elite pushes their policies through the dominant "Zionist" political party. It is many times misunderstood in the media, but Zionism has no link whatsoever to Judaism or to Jewish heritage, it is simply a political party just like the American Republican party or the British labor party. The Zionist party is the long arm of the western establishment in the Middle East, who have hijacked the Israeli government since its inception and are forcing its military to take actions that the Israeli people would not agree with if they had all the information. This is exactly the kind of situation that the United States is caught up in.

The United States and Israel are essentially colonies that are controlled financially and militarily by the elite from within the United Kingdom, which is why there is such an unbreakable alliance between the governments of these 3 countries. This is also why all 3 countries have the same economic and military policy, because they are not independent nations who act in the best interests of their people, but are actually ruled by an alliance of bankers and aristocrats. The American government and military conducts its business overseas against the will of the public and on behalf of the corporations that run the country via the economy. These corporations are primarily the banking and energy cartels that are owned by the Rockefellers, Rothschilds and other ruling class families. Israel works in very much the same way, the government has an agenda which is against the wishes and the best interests of the people, but they use propaganda and fear to push public opinion in a direction that

263

suits their agenda. The issues unfolding in the Middle East have absolutely nothing to do with religion or ethnic conflict, but are politically and economically charged issues that have been propagated by western imperialism. Antagonizers and so called "leaders" on both sides of the conflict use nationalism and racism as a tool to manipulate their people into the battlefield, but that is not the reality of the situation.

Though the issues in the Middle East may seem complicated with how drawn out the peace talks are and how much the media confuses the issue, things really are not that difficult. It is important to address the corruption that exists within the Zionist government or else the international banking cartels will continue to use Israel and its people for their own imperialistic needs. They are the ones who are creating and profiting from these conflicts, not the Israeli or Palestinian people. The Israeli people are forced into military lives and convinced to fight a war that isn't theirs, while the Palestinians are sold out and manipulated by their "leaders" as well. Both the Palestinian and Israeli people are honest, decent human beings that just want peace. The average citizens of both groups are tired of the fighting and really wish to live in harmony with their fellow human beings. A Gazan writer named Talal has written for Palestine's "Al Yam" newspaper for 15 years and has a pretty good grip on the situation. In a 2011 article he said *"Even before the events that split our government and pit Hamas and Fatah against each other, youths weren't well organized. They didn't get much support from outside, or inside. The political factions were only interested in using them as employees or fighters"*. [3] This is the same way that the Zionist government looks at their people, and this attitude is common among the ruling class in the US and the UK as well.

The Palestinians have been tossed out into the wilderness, displaced from their homes and most of them are only asking for the ability to work, trade and own property. To be given this freedom would prevent them from being displaced again and would establish a proper economy so the Palestinian people can have a fighting chance to become a thriving society. The American government, which is also a banker backed colony, used these same policies to wipe out the native people that inhabited North America. The Native Americans were also treated as exiles on their own land and were pushed further and further away from their homes until the only places left for them were small reservations that were mostly in the desert. This is the kind of policy that the ruling class wishes to carry out in Palestine using the Zionist party as a political front.

This is not an ethnic issue. The "leaders" of these countries want people to think that it's an ethnic issue, because it distracts people from the real issues that are at the root of these problems.

The refugee crisis is not something that the Palestinians should hold against the Israeli people, as they were just refugees themselves at the time when the state of Israel was created. Besides, the citizens within the country have no say in their government's actions anyway. The root of the crisis lies with the United Nations who actually made the decision to expel the native population and the interests that forced the UN to take these actions. The militant rulers like Hamas and Fatah are also responsible for escalating the conflict as is their counterparts in the Mossad and the current Zionist regime. Even the PLO who was apparently making an attempt at peace was ready to sell their people down the river for some political advancement.

It is extremely important to emphasize that the people of Israel should not be vilified and punished for the actions of their "leaders". They are very much in the same predicament that the citizens of the US and Europe are faced with. In all of these areas including Israel there is a strong counter culture movement among the youth. The young people in Israel are not happy with the actions of their government and their military. Military service is required for all male citizens which gives the young people a constant reminder of the realities of war. This is actually having the same kind of effect on the youth that the draft did for the youth in America during the 60's and 70's, its waking them up.

A large number of potential Israeli military enlistees are growing disenfranchised with their government and they are rebelling, partying and seeking a less aggressive lifestyle than the one that has been chosen by their "leaders". Not every Palestinian is a terrorist, nor is every Israeli a trigger happy jarhead. This may be the image that Hamas, Fatah and the Zionist regime want for their people, but this is not the kind of future that the young people of both territories wish to create. In 2011 there was social unrest and mass protests all over Israel, because Israeli citizens were unhappy with the actions of their government. There is also a very strong antiwar movement growing among orthodox Jewish Rabbis who are coming out and saying that the actions of the Zionist government are a complete contradiction to the teachings of Judaism and that the current regime is actually doing more harm than good for the Jewish community.

There has been a very strong but unreported resistance to Zionism within the Jewish community long before the creation of the state of Israel. On April 20, 1922, Rabbi David Philipson, testified before the House Foreign Affairs Committee, disagreeing with the proposition to make Palestine "the national home of the Jewish people." He insisted that, "*No land can be spoken of as the national home of the Jewish people, as Jews are nationals of many lands.*" Rabbi Phillipson was a part of a powerful but largely ignored movement that is still a force today. Yakov M. Rabkin is a professor of history at the University of Montreal and he has recently written a book about this resistance called "*A Threat from Within: A Century of Jewish Opposition to Zionism*". In his book Rabkin says "*Zionism constitutes the most radical revolution in Jewish history. Opposition to this nationalist conceptualization of the Jew and of Jewish history was as intense as it was immediate. Even those rabbis who at first encouraged settlement in Palestine in the closing decades of the 19th century felt obliged to turn against Zionism. What made the Jews unique, they declared, was neither the territory of Eretz Israel nor the Hebrew language, but the Torah and the practice of mitzvahs.*"[4] These Rabbis and many other people of Jewish faith feel that the emphasis on Zionism takes away from the true teachings of their culture and that the Zionist regime doesn't embody Jewish values or properly represent Jewish people of the world or those in Israel.

These problems that face this region can actually be resolved quite easily, but it would only happen under conditions that the ruling class would absolutely detest and refuse to accept. The people who have been displaced and are refugees as a result of this crisis must have any kind of employment blocks removed and should be offered citizenship wherever they happened to be displaced. This will at least improve their quality of living while they decide where they are going to start anew. When it is time for them to start anew they should be given amnesty and citizenship in any country which has a population that can sustain them. Any funds that would be needed to make this better life possible should be provided by the United Nations and their subsidiary groups, the World Bank and the International Monetary Fund as these are the powers responsible for creating the refugee crisis and pillaging the entire planet. I definitely don't agree with how these groups acquired their resources to begin with, but now that they have managed to steal a great majority of the world's wealth, we should make sure that money is actually returned in a way that will benefit society.

Both sides in the conflict have been misled, abused and exploited by their self-appointed masters. As with almost every large scale conflict in the world, the key to a peaceful resolution lies with the ability of the people to realize that there is no reason for them to be fighting.

QUOTE SOURCES AND SUGGESTED READING
[0] The portable Mark Twain - Mark Twain, Tom Quirk (2004)
[1] http://www.globalissues.org/news/2011/02/27/8681
[2] Dec 20, 1998, 60 Minutes, Steve Kroft with George Soros
[3] http://www.globalissues.org/news/2011/02/27/8681
[4] A century of Jewish opposition to Zionism - Yakov M. Rabkin

"Fascism should rightly be called corporatism as it is a merger of state and corporate power" -Benito Mussolini (Politician) [0]

47. The Birth of the Corporate Beast in America

In 1868, just a few years after Lincoln's assassination, congress passed the 14th amendment which was apparently designed to give rights to freed slaves. While freed slaves did receive some kind of legal recognition through this act, it still changed nothing about the reality of their situation.

However, the 14th amendment carried with it the insidious government granted legal privilege of corporate personhood. This was a point that corporate lawyers concealed within the language of the amendment to give corporations more legal power in the courts, as well as give the courts more power in the realm of business. The corporate personhood clause states that corporations deserve the same rights that are apparently guaranteed to a "person" or "citizen" in the Constitution. Since this act was in place, corporations have been legally considered a "person" in the court of law. This was such a serious implication because now the people that are actually behind the actions of the "corporation" can no longer be held accountable for the crimes that they commit in the name of said corporation. This kind of idea is not new, this has always been the policy preferred by the ruling class, as it allows them to commit atrocities and get away with it.

In the 18th century in the parliament of England, Edward Thurlow said *"Corporations have neither bodies to be punished, nor souls to be condemned; they therefore do as they like."* Thurlow was as right then as he is today, if people that run corporations are not personally held accountable for the actions they commit at the head of that corporation, then they will take advantage of that and do whatever they want. The same goes for government as well; governments and corporations are both proxies that the ruling class hides behind to avoid punishment for their crimes.

268

There's nothing wrong with owning and running a "business" or a "company", entities which are completely different from a corporation. A corporation is an entity which is legally protected and subsidized by the government, while a company is a privately owned business that depends on its reputation to survive, instead of special privileges and handouts.
Unfortunately, in today's markets even the most well intentioned small business owners are forced to become corporate themselves just to contend with all of the licensing and regulation that is required by the government. When the government talks about "regulation" they are typically ignoring the major corporations, but regulating the small fry competition that threatens to disrupt the monopolistic nature of the current industry. This situation is often called "regulatory capture" and is a type of "corporate welfare"

It became apparent early in the 20th century that the 14th amendment had nothing to do with equal rights for freed slaves. By 1910 there were 307 cases brought before the judicial court in which the 14th amendment was cited, 19 of them cases were freed slaves fighting for equal rights, while 288 of them cases were corporations delegating for legal position. This legal loophole allows corporations to claim the same rights as a human being, which in turn makes it impossible to hold anyone accountable in the industry. This is one of the major reasons why we have huge monopolies in the energy, food and medical markets. Through the course of American history the aristocracy has consistently pushed for protections for their corporations and extension of their powers. Meanwhile the individual rights of citizens have been relentlessly attacked and continue to dwindle as time passes.

In the beginning of the 20th century, corporate corruption was one of the most debated topics of the time. In 1906 in an attempt to gather support and distance himself publicly from the aristocracy, the president at the time Theodore Roosevelt said *"Behind the ostensible government sits enthroned an invisible government owing no allegiance and acknowledging no responsibility to the people. To destroy this invisible government, to befoul the unholy alliance between corrupt business and corrupt politics is the first task of the statesmanship of the day."* Unfortunately, just like many other presidents, Theodore Roosevelt's time in the white house was spent protecting the aristocracy instead of policing it. What he was really looking to do was expand the size and reach of government and in order to gain public support for the cause he latched on to a key issue of the time and sought to exploit that issue for political gain. Theodore Roosevelt came to be known as a "trust breaker" and a hero for the common man exactly as he had intended to, but this of course was only campaign politics, as it always is.

This kind of hypocritical pandering is a typical part of the American political process and is seen to this day. The same way that Obama got "elected" on promises of closing Guantanamo bay, ending the war in Iraq and getting tough on big business, yet did nothing of the sort once he got into office. He actually ended up expanding the war into a half dozen different countries and signing a bill that authorized the indefinite detainment of American citizens without trial. The same way George Bush condemned the corrupt behavior of "a few bad apples" on Wall Street like Enron, but before Enron was exposed as a fraudulent organization, the CEO Ken Lay was a top consideration for Bush's "secretary of energy".

In short, the government and corporations are on the same team, and in many cases the reason why certain corporations enjoy monopolies, is because of legal protections and financial subsidies provided by government.

"Foreign aid is when the poor people of a rich country give money to the rich people of a poor country." - Johnny Hart (BC Comic Strip) [0]

48. The Sweatshop Economy

As the most recent great depression in America deepens, there is a lot of confusion and misinformation about how the job market works, and why the unemployment rate is so high. Between World War 2 and the invasion of Iraq, the United States was at the forefront of industry, offering well-paying jobs and opportunity. Now it seems like the well has dried up, leaving a large number of Americans unemployed and in poverty. What is most interesting about this situation is the fact that all of the manufacturing and factory jobs seem to have vanished, yet corporations are still able to produce their products in record numbers. If these industries are no longer creating jobs, then where are the products being manufactured?

Most corporations have outsourced their factories to foreign countries where the authorities are extremely corrupt and there is already a culture of oppression and widespread slavery. Hundreds of thousands of jobs every year are taken from this country and moved overseas where corporations take advantage of the desperate workers and basically run slave camps. In 2010 while the unemployment was at record highs, US companies created 1.4 Million jobs abroad. Meanwhile, in the US, those same companies struggled to create half that number.

It is far cheaper to run a factory in a 3rd world country where property rights are nonexistent, and people have no choice but to work for slave wages. In outsourced factories conditions are horrible, workers are subject to grueling 18 hour shifts for just pennies a day. Some of the biggest companies in the world such as Nike, Gap and Monsanto have been fined millions of dollars after sweatshop operations have slowly been exposed over the past two decades. Unfortunately, even after paying steep fines like this, it is still cheaper for these companies to outsource their labor than to run a business in the Unites States where they are heavily taxed and where workers expect better conditions and pay. Things are far from perfect here in the west, we still experience our fair share of oppression and poverty, but to watch the existence that our brothers and sisters in the developing world are needlessly forced to endure shows us a whole other level of struggle. It is often suggested in mainstream circles that these horrid conditions exist because there is not enough government intervention in the marketplace, when in reality it is not difficult to see that the complete opposite is true.

To truly understand why this situation exists, and how things have gotten to where they are today, it is necessary to examine the causal factors to see why these unfavorable conditions continue to thrive. It is often said that the people who are caught up in this mess have entered into their agreements to work in sweatshops voluntarily, and are better off than they were before they started working there. It sounds appalling to even mention, but it is sadly true. Which begs the question, why were they living in such dire straits to begin with? Why aren't these people running their own companies and employing one another? Why don't they have the ability to opt out, and just live on their own property where they could farm as their ancestors probably did? Surely this would be a better existence than long hours and low pay, but unfortunately the indigenous do not have this opportunity because their property rights have been violated generation after generation, by local and foreign governments alike.

The developing countries that are currently riddled with poverty were once abundant in natural resources, as they still are today. The people whose ancestors homesteaded this land, tilled the soil, planted the crops and hunted the grounds, they are the ones who have the rightful claim to the property, and all of the resources that it possesses. Unfortunately, there is not really a place on this earth that is truly civilized in their respect for property rights, and the developing world is even farther behind. This means that in the past and present, instead of trading and

272

negotiating over land and natural resources, people, primarily those in power have had the ability to use force, fraud and coercion as the primary means of achieving said land and resources.

This ability to use falsely legitimized force to root people from their ancestral homelands, and then to use further force to control their actions, are without a doubt the primary causal factors behind the dreadful labor conditions in the third world. This is not just an abstract theory, the proof of this can be seen in every government action taken in developing countries. It can be seen in the military aid that is given to third world dictators to suppress their people, in the tough trade laws that make it impossible for anyone to become self-sufficient and in the massive involuntary evacuations and displacements that have created massive refugee populations.

To sum up the labor situation in the developing world, local governments sell or give away land that they do not rightly own to larger governments. Those larger governments then become the sole holders of property in the area, and begin to set up their own factories using corporations. Since most of the usable land has been stolen by these groups, the factories that spring up in the area will have an unnatural advantage that will result in the establishment of a monopoly. This leaves the people who had their land stolen with only 2 options, work for the monopoly and have a terrible life, or live on a reservation style wasteland and live a horrible life. This is an absolutely sickening predicament that has no place in a civilized world, but it is so important to reiterate, that this is not a natural situation, this is not the result of freedom, or of a free market. Quite the opposite, this situation has come about as a result of state violence and a primitive disrespect for property rights.

To clarify this point, lets imagine a world that actually was free, where homesteaded property rights were accepted and where people were free to do whatever they wished so long as they did not hurt anyone else. Say that a group of indigenous people had a right to land that was rich in oil or mineral resources, they would have limitless options, compared to what they experience today. They would have the ability to sell parts of the land, or just sell the resources, they would even have the ability to rip up every offer that was tossed their way and keep the land to themselves for sentimental and preservational reasons.

Now, say for example that this group wanted to turn their small village into a thriving technological community. Well, without heavy trade restrictions and intellectual property laws, they would be able to observe what was going on elsewhere in the world, research how to build what they wanted to build, then copy and create whatever they wanted. Any extra supplies that were needed would be easy to come by. Since this community would have inherited such a wealth of property and resources from their ancestors that it would not be difficult to trade and barter for whatever was required.

With options and possibilities like these, no one would want to work in a factory for three cents a day, so these factories would not even exist in the form that they do now. In fact, without the falsely justified violence that statism allows, this situation would have never been able to take form to begin with.

Cutthroat practices are openly accepted if you have enough money or the right political connections. Manipulation, lying, intimidation and even murder are all commonplace in the political and corporate world. Multinational corporations take this behavior to a whole new level because they are completely above the law and very influential in politics. In developing countries, corporations are oftentimes more powerful than the local governments and even have their own private armies to keep workers in line and reporters out of their factories.

Most of the people in this country believe that slavery is just an ugly part of our past, something that ended years ago and no longer affects them. However, Slavery did not end with the civil war like many of us would like to believe, it was just transferred to distant lands away from the concerned eyes of the American public. Sweatshops are the new corporate plantations, which have for the most part stayed out of sight and out of mind because of the distant location of their factories.

QUOTE SOURCES AND SUGGESTED READING
[0] Johnny Hart (BC Comic Strip)
[SR1] Slaves to Fashion Robert J. S. Ross
[SR2] Advocacy Across Borders by Shae Garwood

"In every scheme that worsens the position of the poor, it is the poor who are invoked as beneficiaries." - Vandana Shiva (Activist) [0]

49. Third World by Design

"Third World" is a term that originated during the cold war, to describe countries that weren't allied with the Soviets or the west. Although they had no alliance or affiliation, these countries were still colonized by both sides of the cold war. During this time, the governments of these countries were influenced by both the Soviet Union and the United States. Businesses from both nations had also moved in to exploit the people and resources of the colonized areas, a practice that had already been taking place for centuries. When the cold war was over, the military and spy operations within the colonized countries ended, but sadly the exploitation did not.

Two of the largest corporations in the world, the International Monetary Fund (IMF) and the World Bank are the self-appointed "developers" of poor third world countries. However, under their carefully crafted public image, these corporations are doing incredible damage to developing countries for their own political and financial gain. The IMF and the World Bank are actually holding back progress in these countries through their complicated international trade laws and bureaucracies. The decisions that are made by these organizations disrupt the lives of millions in the third world, displacing them from their homes, staking claim to their natural resources and monopolizing their economy.

Prior to the establishment of these organizations in the third world, the people were able to grow food and hunt in the wilderness of their country, but those times are gone. These government appointed corporate interests have basically seized all of the land in these developing countries and claimed that they own it. This process can be described as neocolonialism or diplomatic imperialism.

276

There is no reason why global poverty should be a problem, it is obvious here that there is something more to the situation. A population should only be in a time of struggle during some unpreventable natural disaster, like a drought, famine or flood. Any other catastrophe is usually going to be manmade, and if it was manmade it's safe to say it should have never happened in the first place. In most cases it is not natural disasters that are responsible for the condition of the third world. Many of these areas were once abundant in natural resources, before western countries came in and industrialized their lands. Now the people are cut off from their homes and pushed off into infertile wastelands because their corrupt government sold out to western governments and corporations. After having their only means of survival taken away they are expected to pay money for food, water and clothing, which they once had the ability to provide themselves by using the property that was taken from them. There was once a time when these people were able to live naturally off the land, and that was the life that they were accustomed to for many generations. Today, most of them have been forced off their land by the military or corporations and forced to contend in the weak job market and poor living standards within the overcrowded cities.

Any third world country that you take a look at always has the same story, corrupt politicians have sold out the country's resources and finances to the elite western business and political interests. When multinational corporations enter into a third world country they set up sweat shops, pillage whatever resource it is that they are seeking and are then protected because they are working with the local puppet regime. This is why it is so important to our government that countries be "cooperative" with the interests of the United States. By "cooperative" what they mean is basically a puppet government that won't stand up to western corporations and governments.

Whenever a "leader" actually does stand up for their people they are vilified by western governments, even if they are the most humane person that the nation has ever seen. There is a great deal of wealth in 3rd world countries, but it is hoarded by the aristocracy and is not accessible to the overwhelming majority of the population.

This imperialistic global trade system is made possible by complex trade agreements such as the "North American Free Trade Agreement" or NAFTA. This agreement and many others like it come from a multinational group of elitists called the World Trade Organization or WTO. The policies put into place by this organization benefit only the owners and shareholders of a few specific corporations. "Free trade agreements" are very poorly named, and represent ideas and policies that totally oppose free trade. These are nothing more than charters for government granted corporate and legal monopolies, giving specific corporations powers that other individuals and companies do not have.

One of the most articulate and on point descriptions of "free trade agreements" that I have come across was from a researcher by the name of David Icke. In his incredible book "...And the Truth Shall Set You Free" he writes *"free trade is the freedom of the strong to exploit the weak. It is the means through which multinationals, subsidized by their governments via the overseas aid budgets and other hidden channels, operate "cartelism" against the interests of the general population. It is the freedom to create dependency on a system which only the few control, and use that dependency to manipulate at will. The freedom to move production from high wage industrialized countries to the sweatshops of the third world, savagely exploiting the native population. The freedom to steal their food growing land and to destroy the industries and incomes of those in the developed world also. In doing this, the elite create anger, despair, and division, the perfect combination for manipulation. That, my friends, is the "free trade" the economists, politicians, and news correspondents tell us we desperately need more of."*[1]

The British and United States governments are intent on

278

maintaining dominance in the third world, through conquest and diplomacy both, because they depend on the regions resources and cheap labor for their global power. Many times throughout history, the western imperial powers have proven that they will do anything to keep their colonies abroad. This is responsible for the vast majority of wars that take place, wars that are carried out against the will of the public in most cases. The US does business with tyrants who will be portrayed as saints in the press as long as they welcome multinational corporations into their countries. However, if a "leader" refuses to open up his borders to western influence, he is vilified and marked as an enemy.

In the 1980s, the CIA led covert operations to overthrow a popular "democratically elected" government in Nicaragua because they were less compliant with western businesses then the former totalitarian regime. The new regime was less corrupt and did not want their people to be exploited by foreign corporations. Hundreds of thousands of innocent peasant farmers were killed simply so the US could establish a regime that was friendlier with their businesses. Some of the most brutal death squads in Central America during that time were trained by the US government so they could prevent the peasants from establishing a free society. This war for trade and political dominance continues in Central America to this day, and the government continues to support fascist regimes with financial military aid, weapons and training. This is what they call "humanitarian aid", more of the deceptive language that is used to mask the harsh reality of what we're dealing with.

The same goes for the Middle East, Saudi Arabia has one of the most oppressive feudal regimes in the Middle East, but they are praised by American politicians and businesses because they play along with the global trade game. Africa is no different, in 2010, ten years' worth of classified diplomatic files were released through the whistleblower website Wikileaks, showing discussions between American and European diplomats regarding Zimbabwe's natural resources. Throughout the whole decade of discourse between various diplomats it was apparent that the western governments had no interest at all in the human rights violations or poverty that was taking place in the country. All of the discussions were concerning how the current regimes policies would affect business and trade for multinational corporations. This is just one of the recent stories that have surfaced in the United States, but the pillaging of the third world is taking place every single day all across the globe.

The IMF, The World Bank and other multinational corporations make promises in the countries that they do business in, but have never followed through on any of them. As soon as they have conned their way into a country they immediately build infrastructure that western companies use when pillaging the areas natural resources, displacing millions of people in the process.

Every year multinational corporations pay public relations firms millions to clean up their image and cover up the cruel reality of globalization. PR consultants are masters of deception and are thoroughly educated in advanced persuasion techniques. If the multinational corporations that are impoverishing these countries were actually providing a public service and had nothing to hide there would be no need for a tremendous public relations budget.

The revitalization of the third world is only possible through allowing the people to have control over their own land, resources and economy. There should be an incredible public outcry across the whole world about this, but there isn't because the issue is so misunderstood. The establishment shrouds the roots of poverty in mystery when the whole situation can be explained quite easily. Most third world countries are abundant in natural resources and are actually quite wealthy, but all the wealth is held in the ruling regime, who leave their people to starve. This local regime gets huge payouts from western corporations and governments to let them come into their countries and pillage their natural resources. The common people get nothing from these payouts and in the process lose their natural resources and their land.

QUOTE SOURCES AND SUGGESTED READING
[0]Staying alive: women, ecology, and development - Vandana Shiva (1989)
[1]And the Truth Shall Set You Free - David Icke (1997)

"Three hundred men, each of whom knows all the others, govern the fate of the European continent, and they elect their successors from their entourage" - Walter Rathenau [0]

50. Royal Landlords

The fact that a very tiny percentage of the world's population maintains control of all the land and resources on the planet is another one of the serious issues of the 21st century that no one wants to face. The facts are all on public record, and all of the statistics that I used in this essay have been taken from the "world wealth report of 2007" released by Merrill Lynch/ Cap Gemini.

The people who are responsible for poverty and hunger are in fact those who are keeping food and resources away from the rest of the human population. This group I am referring to consists of less than 1% of the population, they are the royal bloodlines and multinational corporations that covertly rule over the entire planet. Whether we want to admit it or not these people have total control over the world's population by maintaining a monopoly over everything they possibly can from energy resources to food and water. These monopolies are always achieved and maintained through governments, because governments act as the mechanism of force for the aristocracy.

Hundreds of years ago, the royalty of Great Britain were hell bent on world domination, like many other European nations at the time. After centuries of violence and conquest the British royalty were able to dominate most of the world through political and military force. It was said that "the sun never set on the British Empire" because there were so many areas throughout the world which the British had colonized, that it was always daytime somewhere in an occupied territory of Britain. Even today the Queen of England's real estate takes up 1/3 of the earth's surface! That's one family owning more than a quarter of all the land in the world, while 85% of the human race owns no land at all! This is not what humanity is about, something is horribly wrong with this situation. The royal family may have the lion's share of land to their name, but other elite families also have a large wealth of stolen property as well, which they have acquired through generations of conquest

Land is not scarce, if it were to be divided up equally there would actually be 5.2 acres available to every man woman and child in the world, and that isn't even including Antarctica. Now I'm not suggesting that we divide up the earth into 7 billion 5 acre sections, but these figures should help you better understand the gross disparity of land ownership that exists between the ruling class and the rest of us. Most average people don't have the luxury of owning much of anything, instead they are piled into slums and ghettos where they have little privacy or personal property. For the rest of us the idea of *owning* an entire content is not within the realm of our understanding, we are too busy struggling to stay alive and feed our families.

There is no reason why the real wealth of this world should be in so few hands. Literally 99% of the world's population struggles to keep their families fed and in safe housing, while the privileged spend their days figuring out how to hide or whitewash this exploitation. They know that if the majority of people were to figure out that they were being taken advantage of so others could live lives of luxury, things would change very quickly. It is our hard work and creativity which they feed upon. Without having people under them to keep things running, their game would fall apart. The ruling class consists of the people that have given us our corrupt education systems, media and politicians. All of these institutions have been manipulated in order to imprison the minds of the struggling, hardworking people of this planet.

The ruling class has stolen nearly every last piece of land on earth and they use their control of this land to keep the world's population under their thumb. Through the strict enforcement of international law and strong arm collection of property taxes "the powers that shouldn't be" are able to use their stolen land to enslave their helpless subjects and keep them dependent. This is exactly how the feudal lords maintained control over their peasant underlings during the Middle Ages. For all intents and purposes it has been the same royal families that have had control of this land down through the centuries. So even though the names and financial systems have slightly changed, the general structure of our social system and the bloodlines that benefit from it have stayed the same.

Land ownership should be decided according to direct homesteading, if you are living in, or making use of a particular piece of land or property, then that belongs to you. Claiming large areas of land by planting flags or drawing lines on a map is not a legitimate way to homestead property.

QUOTE SOURCES AND SUGGESTED READING
[0] The global game for a new world order by Tariq Majeed
[SR1] The Leviathan by Thomas Hobbes
[SR2] The tax exempt foundations by William H McIlhany
[SR3] Undue Influence: Wealthy Foundations, Grant Driven Environmental Groups and Zealous Bureaucrats That Control Your Future by Ron Arnold
[SR4] Who Owns the World: The Surprising Truth About Every Piece of Land on the Planet by Kevin Cahill

"I have no doubt that we will be successful in harnessing the sun's energy.... If sunbeams were weapons of war, we would have had solar energy centuries ago." - Sir George Porter (Chemist) [0]

51. Cursed Dinosaur Blood

Anyone with open eyes can look around and see that our world is dying. Looking deeper we see that a small group of very powerful people have taken control of how we live and the mark we leave on our planet. Dangerous and destructive resources such as oil are not needed for energy or product development. There are countless other natural, renewable resources that could completely replace oil. The natural alternatives to oil would make energy and household products cheaper for the average consumer in the long run, but would cost entrenched monopolies a considerable amount of money and radically change the balance of power on this planet. As usual, it all comes down money and power, just as we have seen countless times throughout history in the horrors of slavery and war.

The ruling elite push for oil dependency because it is a resource that they have a monopoly over. Having total control of our primary source of energy is one of the fundamental scams that they have used to maintain power over humanity. If we were to progress as a species and discover cheaper, cleaner solutions and no longer need their oil, they would not only lose one of their main industries, but they would also lose their ability to restrict travel among the general public. Most eco friendly energy would be free and can be grown or harvested by anyone, which completely takes away the ability to control the market and the population by manipulating the energy supply. So it makes perfect sense that they would buy the media, bribe government officials and use their money to stifle any kind of progress in developing cleaner fuels.

Today, one of the biggest businesses in the world is the tightly

285

controlled oil industry. At the very height of this goliath sits the same people who control the media, the banking industries and most multinational corporations. The very first oil company in the world was none other than John D. Rockefeller's Standard Oil, established in 1853. He inherited an abundance of petroleum resources from his father William who peddled oil for 25$ a pint as a cure for warts, snake bites, cancer and impotence. To this day control of the entire oil industry has remained in the hands of the Rockefellers and a few other aristocrats spread across the world.

John D. Rockefeller formed Standard Oil in 1853 and shared a monopoly on the world's resources with a handful of elite families for a number of years. Eventually, the public became extremely suspicious and the company was forced to splinter off into a handful of different subsidiaries, that are all still a part of the Rockefeller's oil empire. It has been almost impossible for any other companies to compete with these giants, so of course after time any contenders end up fading away. The oil cartel that started with standard oil and still controls the oil trade to this day has been called the "seven sister's oil cartel" or more commonly known today as "OPEC'. Many people have the misconception that OPEC is influenced by Arab "leaders", just because the oil is being exported from Arab states, but in reality this cartel was formed by leading American and European companies, then was later handed off to puppet regimes in the area.

The first trace of this cartel was an agreement signed on September 17, 1920, between Royal Dutch Shell, Anglo-Iranian (aka Amoco aka BP), and Standard Oil. This agreement was set up to fix prices and dominate the market, but came under the guise of an innocent trade deal. Over the years these large companies have splintered off into many smaller subsidiaries to create the illusion of competition and to divert attention away from their monopoly over this prime resource. For example, the company that we know today as BP was once Amoco, before that it was Anglo-Iranian, before that it was Anglo-Persian, and before that it was just plain old standard oil. That's at least 5 name changes in a hundred years and no doubt they're going to be forced to change their name again after the BP deep horizon oil spill in the Gulf of Mexico. Rockefeller's Standard Oil has today splintered off into many different companies, but remains in the same hands. Who is standard oil today? Almost everyone! Exxon, Mobil, Chevron, BP, Texaco, Gulf, Sunoco are all products of standard oil! Crazy isn't it!?

By owning all of the major oil companies and guarding the pipelines with military forces, the cartel is able to control the flow of oil to refineries which gives them the power to raise or lower the price of the commodity. With this kind of monopoly on the world's primary source of energy and trade, this cartel has an extreme interest in suppressing the development of any other possible energy source. It is a tried and true business model of the ruling class to eliminate any possible competition in order to maintain dominance of the many industries that they have their hand in. A monopolized industry is the only option for these people, John D. Rockefeller once said "competition is a sin".

It is an insult to the intelligence to suggest that this one finite limited resource is the only way that we can power our societies. It doesn't even make logical sense for our species to build our lives around a resource that won't be around for much longer, to do so is to ensure widespread panic when the resource inevitably runs out. Although, it is important to mention that the scarcity of oil is heavily debated.

Real technological progress is not accepted in our society if it threatens to upset the established order, this point was made abundantly clear almost a hundred years ago when revolutionary genius Nikola Tesla announced to the world that he discovered a way to wirelessly harness free energy from thin air! This project was met with total objection from the establishment and they destroyed his whole campaign because it would put an end to their stranglehold on energy. Throughout his life, Tesla made countless contributions to science and the development of human understanding. Unfortunately, due to the fact that most of his ideas would have worked to free humanity from economic slavery, his work was silenced and the powerful implications of his discoveries were covered up for generations.

Tesla could never get any investors to implement his free energy plans because the investor would never get a return on their investment, since the product's goal was to not make any money. From an investors perspective it would be a very foolish thing to invest in, so Tesla died a broke man with many of his ideas stolen by people who then implemented those ideas in such a way that they were profitable or violent, thus undermining the original intent of the invention. When Tesla died in 1943 his house was raided by the FBI and all of his plans, notes, experiments and inventions were stolen to be used for military purposes. He refused to work with the establishment during his lifetime because he knew that they would use his knowledge for war, a concept that he was morally opposed to.

We have the intellectual capacity to pretty much decide the fate of the planet, this is no mistake, this is our responsibility and as a whole we are failing desperately. This responsibility will not be met sitting on the couch waiting for the fools in power to fix the problem. We must educate ourselves about how things work so we ourselves can offer better solutions that will render their oppressive ideas obsolete. Instead of working to lower emissions or improve gas mileage, we need to push our technology in a more innovative direction.

The solutions that are being offered by the establishment are only temporary "Band-Aids", which still use their controlled commodities as resources. This approach is an effort to direct attention away from the problem, while still maintaining control over the world's energy supply.

If it was up to me, there wouldn't be no such thing as the establishment. - Jimi Hendrix (Musician)

52. The Broken Window Fallacy in War and Bailout Propaganda

What is a fallacy? A fallacy is basically a false idea that acts as an obstacle, which prevents someone from understanding a particular topic. Fallacies are quite often used in arguments as deceptive maneuvers to mislead a person who is attempting to determine truth and make sense of a situation. Within the studies of logic, many of these fallacies are identified and given specific names. This way, someone can more easily spot a misleading idea before it enters their consciousness and becomes a part of their worldview.

I'm sure that it will come as no surprise to you, but the political world is consumed with fallacies. Most of the information that you will find in the mainstream media, in public schools and in government speeches are riddled with deception, lies and fallacies.

As an organization comprised of human beings that claims ownership over other human beings, the government itself is one giant fallacy.

To sustain an organization that is rooted in lies and uses violence in its every interaction, it is necessary for them to employ fallacies on a constant basis to justify the destructive and irrational nature of their actions. One of the most frequently used fallacies in regards to economics, especially in times of war is "the broken window fallacy".

"The broken window fallacy" is a term used to debunk the popular but false argument that the destruction of property stimulates economic growth by creating messes that people will eventually be paid to clean up. This is one of the arguments that we typically hear to defend war. People say that war is good for the economy because it creates jobs. However, the fatal flaw in this logic is that it fails to consider that a better outcome could have been possible, had war resources been used for creation instead of destruction. The broken window fallacy was coined by French economist Frederic Bastiat in the 19th century in his essay *"That which is seen, and that which is not seen"*. He used a parable about a broken window to describe the situation that we are talking about here. In his story, the witnesses of the destruction assume that the broken window is good for the economy, because they are only thinking about the profit of the window maker, but overlooking the potential loss incurred by unseen third parties, primarily the owner of the window and the businesses that he would have invested in otherwise. War is the most obvious example of this fallacy, but it can also be seen in the recent financial bailouts or even the very process of taxation to begin with.

In the case of the bailouts, our broken window is the untold trillions that were transferred from the general public to various quasi-state corporations just after the massive financial crash of 2008. At this point, no one can be sure of exactly how much money was transferred through these bailouts, but the official figure continues to climb as more independent research and investigation is carried out. The mainstream media will have us believe that these bailouts were necessary to save jobs and prop up the US economy, but when we take a closer look we can identify this as an obvious use of "the broken window fallacy".

Digging deeper into the broken window kind of mentality, we can see some very serious philosophical consequences that come as a result of finding joy in destruction. This kind of thinking makes ethics completely irrelevant, because it allows people to rationalize actions that truly should have never been tolerated to begin with.

"Politics is the entertainment branch of industry"
- Frank Zappa

Section 8

Politics

53. -Newspeak: A Language of Deception
54. -Right? Left? WRONG!
55. -Beyond the Good Guy and the Bad Guy
56. -This is What Bureaucracy Looks Like!!
57. -Fascism...For your safety
58. -The Prison Industrial Complex
59. -Dare to Resist the War on Drugs
60. -8 Reasons to End Prohibition
61. -Tricks of the Trade

"I just want you to know that, when we talk about war, we're really talking about peace" - George W. Bush (Politician/War Criminal) [0]

53. Newspeak: A Language of Deception

Anytime a politician speaks to the citizens of their country a con job is taking place, there is always some kind of angle or tactic being used to persuade the people. The most popular tactic used in America's current political landscape is "newspeak", which is basically when someone sugarcoats what they are saying with fancy language so it comes across less offensive, and hides the true nature of what they are saying. This term originated from George Orwell's famous dystopian novel "1984", where politicians manipulated language to deceive the public.

The best description of this phenomena is revealed in Orwell's essay "politics and the English language". In this piece Orwell says *"The words democracy, socialism, freedom, patriotic, realistic, justice, have each of them several different meanings which cannot be reconciled with one another. The word "fascism," he said, had no meaning "except insofar as it signifies 'something not desirable.' Statements like 'Marshal Petain was a true patriot,' 'The Soviet press is the freest in the world,' 'The Catholic Church is opposed to persecution,' are almost always made with intent to deceive."* If politicians were clever in Orwell's time, they really have perfected their game over the years to be even more conniving.

Newspeak has infected American politics on such a level that politicians almost never say what they actually mean. The most oppressive pieces of legislation to come through our government always have names with positive connotations, using words like "freedom" "safety" or "peace" when in reality, the language within the legislation sets up a completely different policy than is implied in the title. The most popular example of newspeak in recent legislation is the infamous "patriot act" which I have discussed many times throughout this book. If they were really being honest they would have called it the "police state act", or something to that effect. Unfortunately, the oppressive patriot act is not alone, every single day our government passes new laws with happy, joyful names that contain the most abusive and autocratic policies that you could possibly think of. This is reminiscent of when the department of war changed their name to the department of defense in 1949 and then proceeded to carry out more wars of aggression than any dictator in recent memory.

In 2010 alone there have been countless attacks on our civil liberties and freedoms through oppressive legislation riddled with newspeak. The "Food Safety Bill" didn't make food any safer, it just gave the FDA more control over the food supply and allowed bio-tech food corporations to become even more powerful in the food market. This bill actually made food more dangerous, controlled and expensive, yet it was called the food "safety" bill. A similar situation was that of "net neutrality", which is the belief held by most Americans that the internet should be free, open and unregulated. The government obviously does not adhere to this belief, because they are threatened by the ability of normal people to have a voice through the internet. So in order to slip through legislation that allowed them to regulate the internet, they had to give the bill a name that wouldn't tip the public off about what they were actually doing. They called their bill, the "net neutrality act" which once again was anything but. The government claimed that this bill would regulate the current internet service provider's, not American citizens, but this really just opened the door for the government to get their hands on the internet. As usual, had the politicians actually told the American people the truth about what was going on, and told them what they actually wanted to do, there would be outrage among the public. This is the same way that President Obama promised the American people that he would end the Iraq war by 2011, only to leave 15,000 troops in the country who were then renamed as "diplomats".

"Constantly choosing the lesser of two evils is still choosing evil."
- Jerry Garcia (Rock Musician) [0]

54. Right? Left? WRONG!

Most Americans in the 21st century are totally convinced that they live in a free society, where they have a say in how their country is run by electing officials to represent them in government. Unfortunately, these assumptions are unfounded, because the voting system in America as well as many other countries is rigged to meet the needs of the ruling class. An illusion of choice is presented, but there is no choice. Even those who are still duped by the voting scam will admit that they are forced to choose between "the lesser of two evils". We are told that this is our only option, to choose one of the rich aristocrats that will no doubt bring us war, poverty, corruption and corporate control. This is not freedom! To choose between evil and evil? What kind of choice is that? What kind of freedom is that?

In the realm of politics, economics and religion there exists many "false dichotomies" in which there seems to be a narrow field of two options to choose from, when there is actually a larger set of possibilities beyond those guidelines. In other words, you are asked to choose between black and white, leaving you to think that the only colors in existence are black, white and maybe gray, when in reality there is a whole palette of different shades and tints that were left completely out of the discussion. The statement, "*If you're not with us, then you're against us*" is a classic false dichotomy, because it presents two options, both of which amount to violence, while completely neglecting the option of remaining neutral. Likewise, the traditional two-party political system in the West is a striking example of a false dichotomy.

Regardless of party affiliation, the vast majority of politicians are completely out of touch with the people whose lives they are in control of. Most politicians come from wealthy families and know nothing of the struggle that most of us experience on a day to day basis. Whether the candidate is a democrat or a republican they will still be making decisions from the perspective of an aristocrat. Additionally, both parties are bought and sold in every election. Lobbyist and their bribes carry more weight than public outcry or moral obligation.

Our country is run by greedy, power hungry goons that see themselves as a higher class of people than the rest of us. They will never tell us this directly, because they know we would not stand for it. However, quite often politicians slip up and their lack of compassion shows through. For example, during hurricane Katrina, one of the worst disasters in recent history, a member of the Bush family showed just how much compassion the ruling class has for the rest of us. While visiting an overcrowded refugee shelter in Houston, Barbara Bush said on live television *"What I'm hearing, which is sort of scary, is that they all want to stay in Texas. Everyone is so overwhelmed by the hospitality. So many of the people in the arena here, you know, were underprivileged anyway, so this is working very well for them."*

This lack of compassion is just as prevalent in the Democratic Party as it is in the Republican Party, although the democrats try to portray themselves as the heroes of the working class. While running for president in 2008 Barack Obama showed his disdain for the working class of this country when speaking about the economic struggles in small towns. He Said *"You go into some of these small towns in Pennsylvania, and like a lot of small towns in the Midwest, the jobs have been gone now for 25 years and nothing's replaced them ... And it's not surprising then they get bitter, they cling to guns or religion or antipathy to people who aren't like them or anti-immigrant sentiment or anti-trade sentiment as a way to explain their frustrations."* Instead of addressing the serious concerns that these people had, Obama ridiculed them, showing a total lack of respect for their lifestyle, as well as some of their natural born rights.

The current two party system isn't just broken, it's inherently corrupt. The very concept of representative government itself is in no way free. Our elections are ceremonial at best. When power changes hands between political parties, only the banner changes, the agenda stays the same. Regardless of which party is in control, war, oppression and corruption is the dominant policy. Outside of the two "main" political parties there may be some decent hardworking politicians out there who are actually trying to do the right thing. These independent parties would win by a landslide in every election if only there was an even playing field. But the playing field is far from even, most people don't even realize that there are more than two parties to vote for!

In 2008 there was a great deal of hype surrounding the possibility of there being the first African American or woman president. All that hype was of course surrounding the pro war, pro globalization, corporate candidates Barack Obama and Hillary Clinton. Meanwhile, there was a black woman with much more radical ideas running for the same office. Cynthia McKinney represented the green party in that year's election and wanted to end the war, end the illegal income tax, legalize marijuana and clean up Wall Street. These are all issues that would appeal to your average American in such a way that if she were given a shred of media coverage or an equal chance to debate she would easily have been the most popular candidate. Unfortunately, new ideas that would benefit the people and take power away from the elite are smothered by politicians, Wall Street and the media alike.

Barack Obama won the presidential election in 2008 because the public was fed up with what they saw as "Bush era republican policies" and they wanted a change, which is what Obama was promising. The people were tired of wars, corporate corruption and police state legislation like the patriot act. Obama promised to put an end to all that, but as soon as he was "elected" he forgot about his promises and continued business as usual in Washington. Nothing changed about foreign or economic policy, more troops were sent to war, more lies were told and more bailouts were given to corporations who were responsible for the economic collapse. The democrats and republicans may have some small insignificant differences that play on people's emotions, but when it comes to all the important things that affect everyday life for average people, there is a "bipartisan consensus" to protect the ruling class.

This bipartisan alliance against the working class citizens results in a one party system that gives the illusion of being a two party system. This leaves no choice for the majority of the country who just want to live honest lives without wars and Wall Street scandals. Sadly, that isn't an option here in the "land of the free", we don't have a choice about those things. The only thing that Obama *apparently* did in the best interest of the American people was his highly publicized health care reform. Yet the changes in the health care system were primarily to benefit the large pharmaceutical and insurance industries which are extremely powerful in Washington.

The democrats and the republicans are like the Crips and the Bloods of the political realm. One is red, one is blue and it's a bad idea to get them in the room with one another, but when it comes down to it, they're both gangsters in a turf war. The democrats may provide a maternalistic form of authoritarianism, while the republicans offer a more paternalistic authoritarian approach, but both options are still authoritarian. This country cannot take four more years of madness, war and corruption. This volley back and forth between red evil and blue evil has brought our society to the brink of total collapse. Both evils only offer us more of the same corruption that got us into the mess we are in. It is not difficult to see that democrats and republicans represent two sides of the same oppressive coin. It's like being forced to choose between Coke and Pepsi, when what you really want is a glass of water. Both options given are the same well-disguised poisonous garbage while the healthy alternative is left completely out of the discussion.

"If you want government to intervene domestically, you're a liberal. If you want government to intervene overseas, you're a conservative. If you want government to intervene everywhere, you're a moderate. If you don't want government to intervene anywhere, you're an extremist." — *Joseph Sobran (Journalist)*
[0]

55. Beyond the Good Guy and the Bad Guy

The history books show a world drama in which the good guys and the bad guys battle it out for military and economic supremacy. Those who fit into the good guy role change depending on which nation's history book you are reading. Each story is very different yet all of them have their own respective "official account" of what has happened in the past. These official versions of events are always handed down to the people by the governments and rulers who play starring roles in these historical dramas. This situation shows an extreme conflict of interest and bias on the part of those who are writing history. The issues are crafted to shift blame, whitewash crimes against humanity and project a good guy/bad guy mentality. This results in a cartoonish view of history, where war, conquest and blind nationalism are painted as laws of nature.

It is this good guy/bad guy mentality which shields most of us from the truth and brutality of what has taken place at the hands of politicians and monarchies. These labels attach a characteristic image to historical "leaders' and allow us to skip right over the issues that made these people who they are. Regardless of nationality, political party or belief system, the underlying belief in authority is what is responsible for the most unspeakable crimes against humanity.

The prepackaged history that is fed to us insists that entire countries were to blame for the atrocities that were committed by various political organizations in the past. However, it is the specific policies, attitudes, systems and leaders of these movements that are to blame for these social injustices, not their

298

flag, nationality or country. It is the use of institutionalized control systems that are responsible for the darkest, most shameful events in history. In the name of socialism, communism, democracy or just plain old "progress" our governments have created social inequality and genocidal military machines to expand their dominance over the human family.

The most ironic example of this situation exists within the historical American portrayal of the Nazi party. Most people in America have a negative opinion of the Nazi party from the third Reich in Germany, and rightfully so. This was a political system responsible for genocide, racism, extreme social dominance and dehumanizing programs which terrorized the whole planet. What is interesting about this situation however is that American history doesn't necessarily condemn the Nazis social policies, but only sheds light on the political party and the bad guy.

Following the cold war, the western democratic governments presented the idea that the authoritarian rulers of Europe and Asia were so harsh because that's just how people in those countries were. In reality, the atrocities that were committed under authoritarian rule are typically carried out against the wishes of the public. If we look beyond the good guy/bad guy mentality that we have been taught to accept we can see that both sides of the fence are responsible for the same horrors. Each government has their own brand of torture, imperialism and greed, while the average citizens are scared, docile people who just want peace.

It is important for us to take a hard critical look at the policies that all governments are carrying out instead of just identifying with nationalistic labels. There are no "good guys" in war, anyone who is responsible for genocide, poverty or extreme social dominance should not be exempt from criticism because of the flag that they fly. This is the kind of attitude that Hitler expected of his people and this is the same attitude that the US government is expecting from us. If the United States

299

government participates in genocide, torture and terrorism, which official records show that they do, then they are in reality no better than the Nazis. This is obvious when seeing what our government did to the Native's during colonization, Africans during the slave trade and Japanese during World War 2.

In 1942 Executive order 9066 was passed by Franklin Roosevelt which called for the "relocation" of Japanese Americans living within the United States. It was this executive order which allowed the US government to keep hundreds of thousands of Japanese Americans in internment camps for the duration of the war. These Internment camps were eerily similar to those used in Germany by the Nazis, although the Nazi camps were obviously more grotesque. The camps in American were still inhumane, and these details are many times left out of our history books. The Americans were never on any kind of moral high ground in World War 2 and they aren't in modern times either.

The only thing that sets modern day America apart from Nazi Germany is the different flag, different corporate economic system and a different set of gimmicks and scapegoats. Both are examples of institutionalized control systems that lied to their citizens so they could expand their empires across the world. Both empires used racism, propaganda, genocide and economic warfare to control their enemies as well as their own citizens. We have seen the detrimental impact that these dominating control systems have had on societies in the past, so we must have the good sense to put an end to this cycle of tyranny. Any regime that wages wars, creates poverty and exploits people is inherently evil, regardless of what flag they are waving or what is written in their constitution.

"I never would have agreed to the formulation of the Central Intelligence Agency back in forty-seven, if I had known it would become the American Gestapo." - Harry S Truman (Politician) [0]

56. This is What Bureaucracy Looks Like!!

Any of us who grew up with government schooling were given a very inaccurate view of what bureaucracies are all about. This should not be so much of a surprise because the school system itself is a bureaucracy, so they have an obvious bias. The last place that we should expect to find information critical of the establishment is an organization that is a primary fixture of that establishment. Sadly, the true face of government programs is far different from what we are told in school, and in the mainstream media.

A bureaucracy is the absolute worst kind of monopoly because it is a monopoly with a limitless bankroll. Therefore, it doesn't matter how unproductive and unpopular it is, there will always be funding for it. In fact, there is actually far more incentive for bureaucrats to do a poor job with the task at hand, than to provide meaningful services to the community. Why is that you ask? Because bureaucrats actually get paid more money when they do a poor job, and they even run the risk of becoming unemployed if they complete the stated mission of their department. I know it sounds crazy, but this is actually the way things work.

Bureaucracies are established to fix some sort of perceived social problem; at least that's what we are told anyway. Now, if they were to actually achieve their stated goal, then there is no additional task for them, and their job becomes obsolete. On the other hand, if they are able to corner whatever market they are in, prevent anyone from doing a better job and just let the problem fester, they are able to milk their mission until the end of their lives. To make matters even worse, when they can prove that they are desperately failing at their mission, they are always rewarded with more money. Could you imagine screwing

301

everything up at work and then being rewarded with a bonus from your boss? What kind of behavior would that encourage you to adopt? Well this is what happens every single time that a bureaucracy demands "more funding" for problems that they haven't put a dent in throughout their whole existence.

What is also very interesting about these various government monopolies is the fact that they are always focused on pivotal control points, which render populations helpless and dependent upon the state for survival. I promise you this is no mistake. The intent of these organizations is without a doubt to control very specific aspects of our lives, which is why the government insists that they are the only ones able to provide these services. This is a strategic maneuver which is targeted at specific trade sectors that are absolutely vital to the lives of individuals. The idea here is to enslave people by keeping them so sheltered that they forget how to take care of themselves, or even forget that they have the ability to take care of themselves. This is all done under the guise of providing security, protection and "help for those in need".

Unfortunately, these programs do very little to help anyone in the long term, aside from those who are employed by them maybe; and, of course, those who are seeking to control the population. Food, education, land, communications, trade and other choke points for a society are all controlled by supposedly benevolent state monopolies, that allow for absolutely no competition in their respective realms. Regardless of the public relations spin that these organizations are given, their actions in relation to average people show us that it's all about control.

Even the most popular of bureaucracies such as the EPA are still more concerned with controlling people, land and resources than they are with achieving their stated goal of environmental protection. How do we know this? Well let's take a look at some of the most recent actions taken by this organization that is apparently so concerned with the environment. This past January the EPA was involved in a nasty legal dispute with a family who wished to build a private residence on land they owned for years in the state of Idaho. Meanwhile this same organization has spent the past 10 years hiding and downplaying the environmental consequences of natural gas fracking.

When we look into the actions taken by these organizations it becomes obvious that they were not established to help us, but to control us. When we see bureaucracies like the TSA and the Department of Defense (formerly the Department of "War"), the oppressive nature of these programs are even more obvious. It seems like everyday there is a new complaint against the TSA for their invasive groping procedures, their radioactive body scanners, or their authoritarian enforcement agents.

Restricting travel and land development are definitely serious transgressions, but the government doesn't stop there. They even want control of our bodies and everything that we put into our bodies. This most sinister aspect of modern bureaucracy is often overlooked, because by now most people are accustomed to the government putting their nose into every aspect of our lives. The Food and Drug Administration exists under the pretense that they are keeping the food supply safe for average Americans. However, when you see that companies like Monsanto are basically running the FDA, any claims to defend the food supply become laughable.

The toxic trash that passes for food these days is placed on every store shelf without question, while organic farmers are being raided for supplying their community with nutritious raw milk. Recently the FDA even went so far as to decree that our bodies are drugs, so they could have the right to regulate our bodies. This was around the same time they starting pushing through legislation that would actually make a lot of vitamins and supplements completely illegal, forcing everyone to depend on the chemical medication offered by big pharmaceutical companies. This is certainly not speculation; these types of organizations have been found with deep ties to big pharma monopolies time and time again. Just this year the Wall Street

Journal reported that the FDA had secret connections with Bayer, which greatly influenced their actions in Washington. Connections like these have also provided the motivation for forced vaccination programs, and other potential rights violations.

It is a commonly known economic fact that monopolies make for high prices and low quality, since a monopoly is guaranteed payment regardless of service quality, as they are the only show in town. Yet we allow massive coercive monopolies to manage the most vital aspects of our society and our personal lives. The organizations mentioned in this article are out of control because they can do whatever they want with absolutely no accountability to the community. Opening up these vital areas to competition by allowing members of the community to provide these services voluntarily would naturally encourage the kind of behavior that the community demanded. The TSA is becoming such a problem for travelers that this kind of approach is actually being considered. In 2013, the Senate passed a bill allowing airports to evict TSA screeners, and replace them with private security companies that might actually be held to integrity of their work. This is certainly not a solution that fixes the problem but it is a step in the right direction.

Monopolies encourage nefarious behavior, especially when that monopoly is given a license to use violence on others without consequence. This is the problem with the TSA and this is also why we see such authoritarian attitudes from police across the country as well. If the police in your district are corrupt, it's not like you can stop patronizing them and search for another security provider. However, in areas that the police completely neglect, there are actually private citizens taking matters into their own hands to provide security for their community. This has happened to a great degree in one of the nation's most dangerous cities, Detroit. In Detroit, the cops are absolutely worthless and corrupt, so the community fully understands that they cannot be counted on for protection.

To counter this problem, citizens have taken matters into their own hands to create security companies who are actually concerned with making the community safer, instead of just generating revenue. Sure they are still making a profit, but they are making a profit by providing a need in the community and receiving voluntary payments, not through extortion and exploiting nonviolent "law breakers". The bottom line is, everything that a bureaucracy does can be done far better and cheaper by people who are dependent upon community support for their economic survival.

"Those who would give up essential liberty to purchase a little temporary safety deserve neither liberty nor safety."- Benjamin Franklin (Colonial Politician) [0]

57. Fascism...For your safety

Recently there has been a lot of discussion about capitalism in the news and among activists. Many people are taking stances on either one side of the issue or the other, but very few are stopping to consider the fact that capitalism may have never even existed. If you examine most of the words used to describe our society, such as democracy, freedom, representative or capitalism, you will find that these words are simply abstract euphemisms which are used to disguise the true nature of our authoritarian civilization.

We are supposed to believe that we are represented by people who don't represent us, that we are somehow "free" in a situation where we are constantly being exploited and ordered around. Much in the same way that we are told we are "free" in our personal lives, we are also told that we are "free" in our financial lives. The word "democracy" is used to make our oppressive political system seem more benevolent and legitimate, while the term "capitalism" is used to give the impression that we operate under a "free market" economy. Obviously, neither is true.

Capitalism itself has been defined many different ways, but the rights to private property, as well as private production of goods and a free market economy, crossover between all of these definitions. Currently, none of the above rights are being fully respected in the United States and most Western countries that claim to be capitalist. Sure, at face value it may seem like these ideas are prevalent in Western culture, but when you take a look at property taxes, government subsidies for big corporations and the mountain of red tape faced by entrepreneurs, it should become painfully obvious that capitalism doesn't exist!

The system that we have in place today could more accurately be called fascism, mercantilism or cartelism. These words describe a system where the elite use their power in government to control the rest of society, as well as prop up their businesses by eliminating competition through the political system. The monolithic corporations that now exist would have never been able to grow into what they are today without the help of government intervention and protection. Without government intervention, the infamous lobbyists in Washington would become obsolete, because there would no longer be any ability to manipulate the marketplace through bribes or coercion. Government intervention and protection is the primary means by which the world's biggest corporations have devastated their competition and developed massive monopolies.

For any authoritarian government to stay in power they must convince their subjects that they are providing them with safety and security. This is the typical public relations scheme of every oppressive government, the idea that they are providing worthwhile services. This is sadly a myth. The government doesn't provide services, they monopolize services. In other words, they make sure that they are the only organization that can provide schools, hospitals, roads and other utilities to the public, because this creates a situation where the people are completely dependent upon the state for survival. This doesn't mean that a government is the only type of organization that is capable of providing these services. In fact, community groups and entrepreneurs would most likely do a far better job at providing these services because they would actually be judged by the integrity of their work, unlike politicians and monopoly corporations who get paid regardless.

In fascist countries there is really no line between government and big corporations; both types of organizations use legislative power to establish and maintain monopolies. When it comes down to it, both of these organizations rely on violence and threats of violence as a means of getting their way in the marketplace. Essentially, the government is an organization that is used to justify violence, from the military to the tax collectors, to the police. This constant use of force is said to be keeping us safe, but in reality it just instigates further conflict and makes our lives more chaotic and violent.

Oftentimes, when the government is providing a service they are actually doing a very poor job, but no one can really tell the difference, because there is no competition to judge it by. If you look at the goals that government organizations apparently set out to achieve, you will see that they always fail miserably. Therefore, if the government is claiming to provide maximum safety and security, it would be safe to assume that this goal will not be achieved. In the most authoritarian countries where the "leaders" claim to have established an extreme level of security, things are actually very unsafe and citizens in these kinds of countries live in constant fear. Just because there is a very high level of control does not mean that there will be adequate safety or order within a society.

The most controlling type of government in today's world is without a doubt a fascist one. Fascism is defined as an authoritarian system of government that has strong nationalist and corporatist values. A Fascist government never refers to themselves as such; to do so would be to admit that they run unjust and oppressive regimes. Fascism exists in many economic systems that claim to be capitalist or communist and can develop even in countries that call themselves democratic. In fact, most fascist "leaders" tell their people that they live in a free and democratic society so the public takes their grievances to the polls, instead of taking them into the streets where they could actually make an impact. Currently one of the most fascist nations on Earth is called the "Democratic Republic of North Korea". Likewise, the governments in America and the European Union are some of the most fascist regimes in history, yet they still claim to operate under systems of "capitalism" or "democratic socialism".

When the conditions for Fascism begin to develop in a country, the public is told that the increased security, taxation,

308

militarization and corporatism is for their own good. This is of course always an insidious and blatant lie, if history shows us anything it's that increased government power and control is never in the best interests of the people.

The public is needed to run the factories, fire the rifles, build the bombs and develop the empire, so for them to do all of this they have to be thoroughly convinced that it is in their best interest somehow. This is the only way a fascist regime can stay in power, by convincing their subjects that the institutions which are in place to enslave them are actually there to protect them. The easiest way to do this is to create a culture of fear, where people are so afraid that they allow the government to take extreme measures in the name of safety. This has been admitted by various politicians, even the former Secretary of Homeland Security Tom Ridge admitted that he was pressured to raise terror alerts to help Bush win the 2004 presidential reelection.

In the decade since 9/11 the terror hype has led to the rollout of a massive surveillance grid, draconian security legislation, multiple wars and a police state that would have been considered martial law two decades ago. This fear that is generated is nothing but baseless hype, technically you are statistically more likely to be killed by your own government than by a foreign terrorist. According to the National Safety Council you are 8 times more likely to be killed by a police officer than by a terrorist, 17,600 times more likely to die from heart disease and 404 times more likely to die in a fall. Crossing the street, eating fast food, driving to work or having a surgical procedure are all more dangerous than any existing terrorist threat in the world.

Unfortunately, most Americans don't realize that the biggest threat to their happiness is not a foreign enemy but the tyrants in charge of their government. Early US president James Madison warned "*If Tyranny and Oppression come to this land, it will be in the guise of fighting a foreign enemy.*" [1] Then 2 centuries later George W. Bush told the Iraqi people "*Your enemy is not surrounding your country, your enemy is ruling your country.*"[2]

Most Americans didn't understand the sad irony in Bush's statement, because it was something that could be said for Americans as well. Although Bush was just a puppet, it was his presidency that brought the TSA, The Department of Homeland Security, The Patriot Act and other authoritarian measures.

It is very rare for a terrorist to be stopped or apprehended with the help of the new laws and surveillance equipment, but it is very common for these measures to help law enforcement fine or imprison citizens for nonviolent infractions. With this in mind it should be very easy to see what the true intention behind the growing police state is, and who it is really intended for. It's not intended for the terrorists, but for me and you.

Today the most cutting edge technology is being used to set up intricate databases to catalog and keep records on every person on the planet. This is typical of fascist societies, the very same kind of measures were seen in Nazi Germany and Soviet Russia. The citizens of both countries were in constant fear of terrorist attacks, and helplessly gave up all their civil liberties to control freak governments, who then in turn carried out mass genocides against their own citizens. Joseph Stalin himself revealed the plan quite clearly saying *"The easiest way to gain control of a population is to carry out acts of terror. The public will clamor for such laws if their personal security is threatened"*. [3] Adolph Hitler Echoed *"Terrorism is the best political weapon for nothing drives people harder than a fear of sudden death"* [4].

QUOTE SOURCES AND SUGGESTED READING
[0] Respectfully quoted: By Library of Congress
[1] Liberty Quotes By Christopher Kalabus page 56
[2] George Bush State Of The Union address 2003
[3] Vile Acts of Evil -Banking in America By Michael A. Kirchubel
[4] Telling It Like It Is By Paul Bowden

"Drug money is used to rig elections, and train brutal corporate sponsored dictators around the world. They're trying to build a prison, for you and me to live in" – System of a Down (Heavy Metal Band) [0]

58. The Prison Industrial Complex

The prison industry is one of the fastest growing and top earning businesses in the United States. In the past 3 decades this enterprise has grown into a monstrous system of oppression that now houses over 2 and a half million people in the US. That is by far the largest prison population in the world, no country on earth has as many inmates as the "land of the free". Ironic isn't it? Since 1991 the violent crime rate in America has dropped at least 20%, while the amount of people in prison has increased by 50% in that time. These numbers show that the rapid increase in prisoners is largely due to over prosecution of nonviolent crimes. This has nothing to do with "cleaning up the streets" or making our society safer, this all about money and control. The prison system as it stands now does not make our society any safer, but instead turns average nonviolent offenders into hardened criminals by exposing them to such a harsh environment.

The sad truth is that the way our prison system has been structured has actually outlawed more than half of the US population. Nonviolent offenders have no place behind bars, if anything the savage conditions of prison will turn most people into violent offenders once they get out. Which is exactly what the prison establishment wants, return customers. The establishment that I'm referring to is the collection of state and private industries that make up the "prison industrial complex". Billions of dollars are made every year in this industry, one company alone "Wackenhut Corrections" makes over a billion dollars a year and they aren't even the biggest prison service in the country.

That isn't even considering the many satellite businesses that surround this industry, there are over 1000 vendors that specifically sell correctional paraphernalia. Even local phone companies cash in on the operation and install payphones for free because those phones can generate 15,000 dollars per year just from each inmate making 1 phone call every day. Those companies are just the tip of the iceberg, that isn't even counting the police, lawyers, wardens, politicians and food distributors that line their pockets through the incarceration of peaceful Americans.

Most of the people caught up in the prison system are from the working class and are doing time for petty nonviolent crimes. Usually if someone has enough money or influence they can avoid incarceration by cutting deals with the prosecution or paying off officials, this obviously isn't an option for most Americans. It has always been rare for someone from the upper class to end up behind bars. In the middle ages, peasants who were not able to pay high taxes or debts were thrown in dungeons called "debtors prisons", sometimes for their entire lives. Since these times incarceration has traditionally been a struggle of the working poor and lower classes and a tool for the ruling class to maintain power. It is quite common for political dissenters and protestors to be locked away simply for refusing to comply with the government, and in our culture it even goes several steps further.

The growing police state and the constant influx of oppressive, complicated laws are responsible for the massive increase in the prison population that has taken place over the past decade. Every single day for hundreds of years, new laws have been spit out of our legislative system, most of which have been designed to benefit the ruling class who work in finance and politics. The average citizen has very little time to spend contributing to the legislative process and even if they did, their opinion would hold very little weight next to the powerful lobby groups that dominate Washington. The ruling class is guilty of the most horrifying crimes against humanity and is responsible for the exploitation, displacement and murder of millions of people. These are the biggest criminals on the face of the earth, but the prison system wasn't built for them, it was actually built BY them. So the legal system doesn't represent absolute moral authority like it claims to, but it is simply a tool that has been created by the ruling class to maintain dominance over the population.

Our legal system has been specifically designed to oppress and weaken the lower class so the aristocracy can better control them. This is because the majority of the laws have been written by the establishment and most of the bureaucracies that enforce these laws have been created by them also. So they are the owners of this "casino", which means they call the shots. The injustice of the American prison system is illustrated by the high amount of illiterate, mentally ill and unemployed people that are incarcerated.

70% of the prison inmates in America are illiterate, and about 80% have a history of substance abuse. Despite these numbers the amount of drug treatment programs have been cut in half and opportunities for education have been greatly reduced in the past decade. That is because their goal is not to rehabilitate these people and groom them into productive members of society, their goal is to keep as many people in the system as possible.

The people who have been mistreated by the system are the ones who would be most likely to speak out against the injustice and inequality in our society. So if the establishment has them in and out of prison for most of their lives, chances are they won't be much of a threat, instead they will spend their time struggling to keep their heads above water in the corrupt legal system.

The worst thing about this whole situation is that this system is doing nothing to keep anyone safe. The propaganda that the police are "the good guys" here to "serve and protect" is the big lie that cloaks the violence and corruption of the state in an air of legitimacy. The first step to removing this false legitimacy and revealing the truth is to simply stop sugarcoating this violence in newspeak and stop pretending that the state actually does anything to prevent violent crime.

There are a lot of ideas and concepts in that last sentence, so let's delve deeper for a better understanding. As I alluded to earlier, a cold hard violent criminal is hard to come by in most holding cells and most county jails. This is because most people are naturally good and typically are not drawn to lives of violence until they are broken down and corrupted by years of moving through the system being treated like an animal. Another reason why there aren't a whole lot of violent offenders in prison is because it's a lot of hard work to catch them!! Cops get paid the same for locking up a pothead as they do for locking up a serial rapist, as long as there is a warm body in the cell, then Dudley Do-Right makes his quota. So it really makes sense that most cops go into work hoping for a good "easy" day where they don't get shot at. They are not benevolent saints that wake up in the morning and think about nothing else but trying to make the world a better place, although many of them may have convinced themselves of this much. Just like the rest of us, most cops take the easy way out in their day to day, which basically means letting thieves, murderers and rapists roam free while chasing around nonviolent offenders all day because they are easier to deal with and they pay the same.

Now onto the newspeak, which is one of the most fundamental propaganda tactics used to defend this growing police state. Luckily, this is one aspect that we do have a great deal of personal control over because instead of using the same deceptive language that police use to describe their actions, we can simply call it like we see it. Soft sounding words like "detainment", "arrest" and "police officer" subtly change our perception of the actions taken out against us. Police are people who are paid money to go around with weapons and force people to submit to the arbitrary commands of a central government, so rightfully we should call these people mercenaries, instead of police, because that's what they are. Furthermore, when someone takes you from your home, or any other place that you want to be, they are kidnapping you and

314

holding you hostage. Is this not exactly what happens when one of these mercenaries puts a nonviolent offender in a cage? Again, all these "legal fees" and "fines" are forms of extortion that are dressed up in pretty language to disguise the corrupt nature of what's actually taking place.

There are millions of solutions to these social problems that don't involve violence, unfortunately there just isn't enough people out there trying to develop these solutions. Most of the population spends their time rationalizing the current system and learning how to cope with it instead of actually working to devise solutions that would improve our society. Luckily, more and more people are coming to the conclusion that it is time for our species to advance past this kind of brutal approach to dealing with crime.

Stefan Molyneux for example, is a philosopher and writer who has dedicated years of his life towards developing nonviolent solutions to the many social problems that are currently being butchered by the establishment. He has created dozens of future propositions for how life would work in a free society. This includes the "Dispute Resolution Organization", or DRO, which is a system designed to deal with social problems in the most humane and voluntary ways possible. These social problems range from violent crime to trade and property disputes. This is just one person, and he has come up with plans that would replace every brutal aspect of the state with realistic and peaceful solutions. Maybe some of his ideas would work, maybe some of them wouldn't. Personally, I think they are great ideas, but that's not the point. The point is, if one person is capable of coming up with a few simple ideas that have the potential to make human interactions more peaceful, then just imagine what we can come up with if we are openly talking about these issues and working them out together.

"The war on drugs is a war on people... And people's rights are being violated. And your incarcerating and caging human beings often times who are simply victims of the sickness of addiction, Who have become sucked up in this giant war on drugs, Which in fact is a crime against humanity. The war on drugs is a war on people." – Corporate Avenger (Hip Hop Group) [0]

59. Dare to Resist the War on Drugs

Addiction to mind numbing street drugs like opiates and amphetamines are definitely a serious problem that our generation must overcome in order to have control of our own minds. Although the establishment groups theses poisons in with psychedelics, they are actually nothing like psychedelics. While psychedelics elevate consciousness and have little physical effects on the body, synthetic street drugs diminish the consciousness and do considerable damage to the body. The addictive properties of these toxic substances cause extreme turmoil in the life of anyone who is caught in their grip. Heroin, prescription pills and methamphetamines have enslaved a large portion of the lower class, who were just looking to momentarily ease the pain of poverty with substances that were everywhere in their communities.

The government has taken a strong public stance on the issue and has declared a "war on drugs", whatever that means. Yet lower income communities continue to be flooded with drugs despite the harsh legal penalties that go along with their possession. In the two decades since the war on drugs began, evidence has surfaced that explains why the drug trade has continued to flourish. There have been many cases confirming that the CIA and DEA have been importing and exporting drugs all over the world for decades. Even with the testimony of ex agents and air traffic control operators, the mainstream media has continued to ignore the evidence because they fear losing their jobs and ability to broadcast.

The first person to expose this secret operation was an air traffic

316

control person by the name of Rodney Stich. While investigating CIA drug trafficking, this former pilot became acquainted with a long list of ex agents that gave him classified information proving the CIA's involvement in importing drugs. Once Stich's research surfaced it exposed the true nature of the drug trade and encouraged other witnesses to come forward. The information that surfaced showed that the international drug trade was a booming business that the US and British covert organizations had a total monopoly over. Although Stich's work was all documented fact, his story was covered up by the puppet media and most Americans never even heard about it. Since Stich, there have been countless others who have spoken up and have subsequently been slandered by the media and attacked by the government.

In many cases the government and its agencies have gone beyond intimidation and have actually murdered witnesses. The most tragic of these situations to actually surface is the case of Kevin Ives and Don Henry, two innocent teenage boys who were murdered by police in August of 1987. The murder took place in a rural community just south of Little Rock Arkansas. The area is a hotbed for government drug smuggling activity and the boys accidentally stumbled upon a high profile drug deal taking place. This high profile drug deal was actually involving several CIA assets and was being protected by local police. When police discovered that their operation was uncovered they quickly took out the witnesses. After shooting the two young boys in cold blood, the police put their bodies on a set of train tracks and began a massive cover up that lasted several years.

Through her own investigation, Kevin's mother Linda began to expose the conspiracy that was behind her son's death, but she has yet to bring the officers that committed these acts to justice. There were also 6 people who had information about these murders who were hunted down and killed by the CIA, one by one, so the plot could be kept under wraps. Keith Mckaskie, Jeff Rhodes, Keith Coney, Gregory Collins, Richard Winters and Jordan Ketelson were all closely involved in the case and had sensitive information regarding government involvement in drug trafficking. Every single one of these people died mysteriously in the years following the initial murders. This whole case and everything about it was ignored by the media and all of the politicians, including the governor of Arkansas, who was Bill Clinton at the time. Clinton is said to also have very close ties to the drugs and ammunition that was coming in and out of the Mena Airstrip while he was working in the area.

Clintons extracurricular activities were exposed when a man named Larry Nichols was hired as marketing director of the Arkansas Development Finance Authority. It turns out that this organization was just a front for Clinton to launder black market money, and this all surfaced when Nichols was interviewed by "The Citizens for Honest Government Organization". In the interview he said *"For about two months I watched accounts accumulate money. And at the end of the month they zero-balanced. They're laundering drug money. There was a hundred million a month in cocaine coming in and out of Mena, Arkansas. They had a problem. They were doing so much money in cocaine, a hundred million. You, you create a problem in a little state like Arkansas. How do you clean one hundred million dollars a month? ADFA until 1989 never banked in Arkansas. What they would do is they would ship the money down to Florida, a bank in Florida which later would be connected to BCCI. They would ship money to a bank in Atlanta, Georgia, which by the way was later connected to BCCI. They'd ship to Citicorp in New York, which would send the money overseas."*[1]

Even with the media blackout, the facts are on public record, and government drug trafficking is so widespread that more cases are surfacing every day. In September of 2007 a CIA jet crashed in Mexico with 3.2 tons of cocaine onboard. The jet was on its way from Bolivia when it was spotted by Mexican helicopters that followed in pursuit. The chase resulted in the crash of the jet and the seizure of the cocaine. Upon inspecting the wreckage site, the Mexican authorities found no body or survivors, but did find several thousand pounds of cocaine. The serial numbers on the plane were eventually traced back to a company that transported terrorists for the US government. This story is not uncommon, there have been many cases where government planes have crashed in south and Central America with tons of illegal drugs onboard. On April 10 2006, Mexican police seized a DC-9 aircraft that was carrying 5.5 tons of cocaine, flight records showed this aircraft to be another CIA "terrorist transport" plane that was used to transport drugs. The pilot of the DC-9 aircraft also managed to escape from Mexican authorities.

Many times in recent history the CIA has expanded its drug cartel to include the US military. During the Vietnam War, the US government used their occupation as a basis for covert drug operations, which in turn helped fund the war and other secret projects. Drugs were transported on military aircraft and brought back to America, where they were eventually sold to the mafia and distributed on the streets. The same techniques are being applied today during the occupation of Afghanistan. When the US invaded Afghanistan in 2001, there was an immediate hike in the amount of heroin that was flowing out of the country. According to the United Nations Office of Drugs and Crime, after the US invasion in 2001 opium production in Afghanistan rose from 7,606 hectares in 2001 to 193,000 hectares in 2007. That is a 96% increase of opium production since the US has occupied the country. Now that the CIA has control of Afghanistan, 93% of the world's heroin comes from inside its borders. It is certainly no coincidence that in recent history we have seen a surge of drug exportation from war torn countries that were being occupied by western nations. During the Vietnam War the area surrounding Vietnam was known as "The Golden Triangle", a hotbed for heroin production. Now the Golden Triangle has taken a back seat to the "Golden Crescent", which refers to the area in and around Afghanistan of course.

Historically it is extremely common for governments to import and export drugs to fund covert operations and control populations. While this corruption takes place it is always hidden from the public, because it would create an obvious backlash and show the hypocrisy of government policy. After the years pass, things come to the surface and it becomes more difficult for the establishment to keep their drug operations secret. It did not take many years for the details behind the opium wars in China to be exposed to the world. This was probably one of the most historically famous situations where drugs were used by a government to get extremely wealthy at the cost of impoverishing others.

During the opium wars, the British government told their people that China was a threat to their way of life, but in reality the whole war was over the government trafficking drugs into Chinese ports. For years the British were making a fortune importing opium into China. The Chinese government was not happy about the opium trade, so they outlawed the drug in 1839 and tried to prevent British ships from importing the cash crop into their harbors. This attempt to stop imports infuriated the British, and they launched a full scale naval attack on China. From 1839 all the way through to the 1850's there was intense fighting between these two countries until China was eventually defeated. Upon defeat, China was forced to sign treaties which gave up their trade rights, opened up their ports to foreigners and made the prohibition of opium completely impossible. These agreements would go down in Chinese history as "the unfair treaties". This situation is ironically familiar to the current "opium war" being waged in the deserts of Afghanistan. Just before the US invasion of Afghanistan the Taliban made the cultivation of opium illegal just as the Chinese government did at the start of the opium wars.

As I'm writing this book there is a massive drug war developing around the Mexican border and thousands of innocent civilians are being killed. If it wasn't for drug prohibition this wouldn't even be taking place, bordering areas in both countries would not have descended into lawlessness and an untold number of lives could have been saved. By now it should also come as no surprise that the US government is heavily involved in the trafficking of these narcotics. In 2011 Mexican drug kingpin Zambada Niebla testified that his gang the "Sinaloa Cartel" was protected by US law enforcement for years before he was apprehended, the case is still pending today.

The war on drugs is an insult to the intelligence of the American people. There are mountains of evidence proving that the biggest importers of harmful, addictive, mind diminishing street drugs is the government. The drug laws that exist do not apply to the government agencies that bring these substances to our country. They are only designed to keep everyone else from this extremely lucrative business and give the establishment another reason to oppress people. We have seen this all before during alcohol prohibition, where the government, law enforcement and organized crime were all working together and making an unbelievable amount of money in the black market. When black markets are created, the crime rate goes up, taxes go up, prices go up and the police become more corrupt, all of this is inevitable. These are in fact the very consequences that any type of prohibition intends to create. To solve these problems all that we have to do is end all prohibitions, this would cripple the black market and drastically reduce violence. This would also drastically reduce the reach of the state, which is why it is looked at as such an impossibility. Drug laws don't do anything to prevent drug problems in our society, they only encourage violence, raise prices and criminalize half of the population.

QUOTE SOURCES AND SUGGESTED READING
[0] Corporate Avenger – FBI FILE – Freedom is a state of mind
[1] Larry Nichols Interview with the citizens for honest government organization

321

"Remember back in the day when they had probation? Now it's a plant that'll end you up in prison. What's your position on the status today? Alcohol is good to go, but smoke some weed no way, you get locked up, they simply throw away the keys" – Kottonmouth Kings [0]

60. 8 Reasons to End Prohibition of All Drugs Immediately

The drug war is one of the most misunderstood subjects in the mainstream political dialogue, even among people who are sympathetic to the plight of responsible drug users. It is rare for someone to come out and say that all drugs should be legal, but in all honesty this is the only logically consistent stance on the issue. To say that some drugs should be legal while others should not is still giving credence to the punishment paradigm and overlooking the external consequences of drug prohibition, or prohibition of any object for that matter.

There is no doubt that drug abuse is a serious issue in our culture, primarily because people are so depressed and beaten down that they self medicate just to be able to tolerate the average day. However, a prohibition policy is a policy of violence, because if you happen to be caught with any of these banned items you will be forcefully taken against your will and put in a cage, and if you dare to prevent this kidnap from taking place, you will inevitably be killed. This is the fundamental issue surrounding the drug war that we need to be focused on. Instead of bickering over how to slightly reform drug policy, or arguing about which drug is more harmful than the other, we need to be pointing out that prohibition itself is an inherently violent policy that rests upon the stone age concept of punishing people for possessing items.

As I alluded to earlier, there are many external factors that are affected by the drug war that many people don't take into account. That is because when you carry out acts of violence, even in the form of punishment, you then create a ripple effect which extends far beyond the bounds of the original circumstance to affect many innocent people down the line. The following list delves into those external factors to illustrate how drug users and non users alike, would be a lot better off if prohibition ended immediately.

(1) – Reduce Violent crime – The steady increase in violent crime over the past few decades is directly correlated with the escalation of the drug war. As we saw during the times of alcohol prohibition, when you ban any inanimate object, you create an incentive for people to get involved in the black market distribution of that object. Since there is no accountability, or means of peaceful dispute resolution within the black market, buyers and sellers are forced to resort to violence as their sole means of handling disagreements.

Eventually, this violence spills over into the everyday world and affects everyone's lives. No one could imagine Budweiser and Miller Lite in a back alley gunfight, but less than a century ago during alcohol prohibition, distributors of the drug were involved in shootouts on a regular basis, just as drug gangs are today. Of course, all of this violence came to an immediate end when alcohol was legalized, however, it was not long before the establishment found a new crusade in the drug war, which allowed them to continue the same policy, just with different substances.

(2) Improve seller accountability and drug safety - In the black market one of the major drawbacks is that there is no accountability among the people selling the drug. Since anyone can get kidnapped and thrown in a cage for even dealing with the stuff, it really doesn't make sense for people to be plastering their names and logos all over the drugs. In this age of corporate mercantilism, logos and branding may seem like a very tacky idea, but when looking at the black market we can see the value in such things. Someone who is selling a product with their name on it, is going to go through far greater lengths to ensure the quality of their product, as opposed to someone who would remain anonymous.

This anonymity creates an incentive for people to be dishonest with what they sell. This could lead to rip offs, or downright contamination of the drug with unwanted harmful substances. This is why there was bathtub gin that would make you go blind if you drank it during alcohol prohibition. This is also the reason why some of the harder street drugs today are cut with toxic chemicals that increase the chance of overdose ten fold. The fact that the drugs need to be smuggled also creates the incentive to make drugs more potent, and thus in some circumstances more dangerous. The increased potency and decreased availability inevitably leads to a massive increase in cost. The increased cost is a whole other issue with its own unique side effects in regards to drug safety. When the price of the real drugs go up, people just start huffing paint thinner, smoking bath salts and cooking up crystal meth in their basements, which is then even many times more dangerous than the unbranded drugs on the black market.

(3) – Reduce Drug Availability to Children – Many children have houses that are filled with alcohol, yet most of them find it way easier to get drugs than to get alcohol, even though alcohol is legal. Even if there were no legal age restrictions on alcohol, the societal and family norms would be just as effective at deterring children as a formal prohibition policy would. If we look overseas at countries that don't have age restrictions on alcohol, younger people are oftentimes much more mature and informed about its effects than children in the west, and are more likely to make responsible decisions about mind altering substances. In Portugal where drugs have been decriminalized for some time now there has actually been an incredibly obvious drop in drug use by school age children.

(4) – Reduce nonviolent Prisoner population – A vast majority of the prisoners in the United States are there for nonviolent, non crimes, many of which stem from the drug war. Currently, there are more people in US prisons than were in the gulags of Soviet

324

Russia at its worst. Putting nonviolent people in cages, bringing violence against nonviolent people is a horrible violation of natural law. According to the most cited Judge in the United States, Richard A. Posner, the government spends $41.3 billion per year of your tax money on law enforcement measures against mostly small time drug users.

(5) – Real crime can be dealt with – Even in areas with a declining homicide rate, the murder cases that are going unsolved are continuing to climb. Police departments and bureaucrats have a million excuses, but the drug war is one of the primary reasons for this occurrence.

If you look at the rate of incarcerations for drug offenses, and how incredibly often drug cases are "solved" and found in favor of the state, it becomes obvious that the police have more of an incentive in their day to day activities to hunt down drug users than murderers. These people aren't selfless public servants as the propaganda on primetime television would lead you to believe, they are average people just like you and me. They will even tell ya "im just doin my job", so like most of us, when they are on the job, they try to get the most amount of money for the least amount of work, and murder cases are really tough work.

A cop could even miss his quota by taking the time and effort to hunt down a murderer, instead of grabbing a kid with a bag of pot, which is a lot easier to find and a lot easier to catch. Quotas are another thing that many police departments deny, but time and time again evidence surfaces that proves otherwise. Recently a former NYPD officer has come forward saying that he would ticket dead people just to meet his quota.

(6) – Encourage genuine treatment for addicts – As a result of international drug treaties, most of the world has remained trapped in a punishment mindset when it comes to dealing with the social problem of drug addiction. While an addiction may be problematic for the person involved and everyone that they come in contact with, they are not a criminal until they actually hurt

325

someone or damage their property, and even then they are a criminal because of their aforementioned transgression, not because of their drug addiction. Even the treatment that we see today is not genuine because it is forced on people and does not address the reasons why they are doing drugs in the first place. In other words, today's treatment programs just try to bash the idea that "drugs are bad" into people's heads, instead of really communicating with these them, treating them like human beings and overcoming the underlying issues in their lives that are pushing them towards lives of drug addiction.

(7) – Prevent drug overdoses – As I mentioned earlier, most drug overdoses that happen today wouldn't occur if it wasn't for the artificially high potency of drugs that we see today. However, what is even more sad is that of those overdoses that do happen, many more of them could have been prevented, but were not because witnesses were too afraid of the police getting involved to call for help. 9 states out of 50 in the US currently have good samaritan laws to give legal amnesty to anyone who brings an overdosing person to the hospital, but that measure wouldn't even be necessary if prohibition wasn't a factor in the first place. The fact that people are actually afraid to call an ambulance in this country should really tell you something about the level that the police state has risen to.

(8) – Protect individual rights – Thanks to the drug war, merely on the whim of saying that they smell something, cops are now able to enter homes, search cars and totally violate the rights of nonviolent people. The drug war and terrorism are the two biggest excuses used to violate people's rights, yet according to the national safety council you are 8 times more likely to be killed by a police officer than a terrorist. The very existence of the drug war to begin with, or a prohibition on any object is a fundamental violation of natural rights that should not exist in any civilized society.

"Government: is derived from the Latin word gubernare, a verb, meaning —to controll combined with mente, a Latin noun, meaning mind. Government means: To control the mind." - Anonymous [0]

61. Tricks of the Trade

There is a war that has been raging for longer than any other political or religious conflict on the planet, and that is the struggle between the aristocracy and the serfs, the "exploiters" and the "exploited". This class of politicians, bankers and aristocrats has always been comprised of about 1% of the world's total population and for centuries each generation has spent their lives bitterly clutching onto their family's fraudulently acquired wealth. In order to continue a legacy of exploitation, they concoct a wide variety of deceptive plots that mislead the public and push them to accept their financial servitude. The same kind of trickery is used to silence dissenting viewpoints and extinguish antiestablishment movements when they manage to gather enough public support. These people have lived in luxury at the expense of the masses for centuries so it should come as no surprise that they carry out mischievous deeds in order to uphold their public image and continue their slave driving traditions.

The economic system as we know it is the fundamental scheme used by the ruling class to keep the masses in servitude. The economy is their game, which they have created and maintained with no concern for the public interest. By nature, a centralized economy favors monopolies and mega corporations which are owned by the richest people in the world. In today's economic climate it is nearly impossible for someone to start a small business and succeed because the big corporations have such an unfair advantage, largely due to government intervention.

Most of the largest corporations in the world are exempt from taxes and regulations because of their heavy influence in politics. Many of these corporations even push for higher taxes and regulations through political favors as a clever way of stamping out their competition. This means that small businesses will suffer and everyone will end up working for some different corporation, earning a menial income instead of having the freedom to work for themselves and earn a decent living, or even having the ability to work for a locally owned business.

American history is filled with cycles of long financial depressions due to the monopolization of industry. Many people believe that there was only one depression in the history of this country but there have actually been several each century. During these times of economic turmoil was where the ruling class greatly extended their fortunes by bleeding the lower classes and using them for slave labor.

These conditions within a society are enough to create rebellion among the underclass, even if the establishment does have the most elaborate public relations campaign in history, which seems to be the case today. During times of social unrest every facet of the establishment goes into self-defense mode and attacks any group that may threaten to disrupt the current order. This is especially true with law enforcement and the military. We are deceived into believing that they are in place to serve and protect the public but when push comes to shove, it becomes obvious they are only here to serve and protect the aristocracy and the status quo. Any time in history that oppressed people have peacefully resisted the establishment, they were met with police in riot gear and soldiers with guns drawn. Police have attacked civil rights leaders, union workers and other peaceful protestors in America for over a century.

In 1970, the National Guard murdered four students and badly wounded a dozen others at Kent State College in Ohio. The Students had assembled to protest the United States senseless invasion of Cambodia when they were shot by troops, all of the victims were unarmed. This incident sparked outrage across the country and prompted millions of students to hold national strikes. The Kent State Massacre was not an isolated incident, to this day our government uses tax funded physical force against activist groups that are speaking out for the good of the people and the environment.

In most cases, political protestors are nonviolent and do everything they possibly can to avoid clashes with the police. Demonstrators are well aware that they are out matched and are only assembling in groups and taking to the streets as a way of promoting their political ideas, this is the essence of free speech. This is an extremely powerful political freedom which is why it is met with such hostility from the establishment. Almost every single time there is a public protest, the authorities are unsympathetic and use heavy force to discourage protests from taking place in the future.

However, they don't attack the mob with guns blazing because they know it will further expose their oppressive nature and add credibility to the revolutionary movement. So agent provocateurs are used to instigate physical altercations between activists and authorities. Agent Provocateurs are people that work for the authorities, but pretend to be a part of an antiestablishment mob. While undercover, these agents commit acts of violence and vandalism to give the police a pretense to use force against the demonstrators. Once the agent smashes one window or throws one rock on behalf of the group they have infiltrated, the authorities are able to send in the Cavalry and turn the demonstration into a war zone.

Agent provocateurs have a long history of instigating violence at protests in the United States, this is why almost every time there is a public demonstration there are also police riots. The 19th century in America was filled with labor strikes and protests because of the horrible living conditions that new immigrants and the working poor had to endure while working in overcrowded factories. In 1886 there were 700,000 workers on strike throughout the US due to the inhumane conditions that the lower class faced working in sweatshop conditions. That year, in Chicago a large protest began on May 1st. Two days into the strike on May 3rd, 4 workers outside the McCormick Harvester company were indiscriminately killed by police during protests, and dozens of others were injured. The following day, the protests grew as a result of the murders, and prominent activists of the time began to call national attention to what was going on in Chicago.

The next day on May 4th, a bomb was set off in the midst of the protests and although there was no indication of who was responsible for the bombing, the blame was placed on the demonstrators and a witch hunt ensued. 8 of the most prominent antiestablishment speakers and writers of the time were rounded up for "inciting a murder" and executed. Their only crime was exercising their right to free speech and speaking out against the establishment. 3 of the 8 activists that were executed were speaking and were nowhere near the explosion, the other 5 weren't even in town at the time. The evidence that has surfaced since the Haymarket incident show that the blast was most likely set by an agent provocateur, in order to give the establishment an excuse to silence the growing political movement that surrounded workers' rights.

This strategy is still used to this day, every year at political conventions police double agents have been exposed while posing as protesters. By turning the protests into violence, the establishment is able to divert the attention of the protests away from the real issues and towards the chaos that's taking place in the streets. The media, which is merely a tool of the establishment, always paints protestors as violent and unreasonable people, to keep their revolutionary messages from gaining public support. An incident similar to the Haymarket bombing occurred in Greece in 2010 in the midst of antigovernment sentiments sweeping the nation. Agent Provocateurs set off two bombs in different government buildings, and later blamed the bombing on youth revolutionaries to discredit their movement.

When all else fails and the public finally begins to understand what the ruling class is up to, there is one final trick that they use to keep their power. When a revolutionary force rises amongst the people that cannot be stopped by the establishment, the establishment then pretends to accept the revolutionary force and they assimilate their own organizations into that movement. This tactic dates back to ancient times and is used so frequently it's unbelievable that people haven't caught on yet. When the revolutionary message of early Christianity threatened to overthrow the Roman church, the church simply made the Christian savior a part of their religion so they could then shape the future of "Christian" ideology.

This same kind of takeover happened in the beginning of the 20th century with the first organized worker unions. When trade unions first originated they were very outspoken and were constantly demanding that radical changes be made to their social and political structures. The people involved in these unions were also a political force in the country as well, and most of them were very critical of big business and government corruption.

Back then the unionists were called "communists" or "anarchists", now surely today they would be called "terrorists". After years of reacting aggressively with trade unions the establishment decided to take another approach and they gave the leaders of the unions a limited amount of political pull and convinced them to use the electoral system to air worker disputes instead of striking and protesting. The establishment then got what they wanted, the unions may have kept their organization and their titles but they no longer went on strike or protested but directed all their energy into worthless elections. Sure union protests still take place, but nowadays they are only aimed at slightly tweaking the oppressive policy that is in place, as opposed to radically changing the whole system.

A similar situation took place during the civil rights movement for African Americans, at the very march on Washington where

Martin Luther King JR. made his most famous speech, "I have a dream". When the government learned that the oppressed black people of the country were coming to Washington with revolution on their minds, they instantly switched up their approach and pretended to welcome the marching protestors with open arms. After the march, Malcolm X describes how the protest was hijacked and watered down by the establishment. When speaking of President Kennedy he said *"that old shrewd fox said "ill endorse it. Ill welcome it. Ill help it, ill join it! This is what they did with the march on Washington….They joined it, they became a part of it, took it over. And as they took it over, it lost its militancy. It ceased to be angry, it ceased to be hot, it ceased to be uncompromising. Why, it even ceased to be a march. It became a picnic, a circus. Nothing but a circus, with clowns and all… No, it was a sellout, it was a takeover. They controlled it so tight, they told those Negroes what time to hit town, where to stop, what signs to carry, what song to sing, what speech they could make, and what speech they couldn't make, and they told them to get out of town by sundown."*[1]

Malcolm X's description was spot on, even Martin Luther King JR. was insulted by how the civil rights march was taken over by the establishment. After the march on Washington was a letdown to the civil rights movement King began to call for a new wave of nonviolence that was "massive and militant", and it wasn't much after that when he was assassinated. Towards the end of his life due to his outspokenness on poverty and the Vietnam War, he became a target for the FBI in their COINTELPRO operation. King received many threats from the FBI and it is widely speculated that the establishment did have a hand in his assassination.

Again but more recently, after the economic meltdown of 2008 an antiestablishment movement was brewing called the "tea party". The people in this movement started out asking very serious questions about the criminal Federal Reserve Bank, the massive corporate bailouts and the income tax. Obviously this was a huge thorn in the side of the established order, so immediately they made steps to hijack the tea party. In just a few short months leading members of the Republican Party started identifying themselves with the tea party image but not the tea party message. Corrupt republican financiers such as the Koch brothers, began funneling millions of dollars into these "tea party" efforts. Just when it finally started to get any kind of media attention, the movement was co-opted and became represented by people who had nothing to do with the original messages or goals of the tea party.

In 2010 a financial blogger and ex-CEO credited with being one of the original "founders" of the tea party posted a very critical blog concerning the direction of the movement, saying it had been hijacked by the very people it was protesting against. His name is Karl Denninger and when denouncing the new tea party he said *"Tea Party my ass. This was nothing other than the Republican Party stealing the anger of a population that was fed up with the Republican Party's own theft of their tax money at gunpoint to bail out the robbers of Wall Street and fraudulently redirecting it back toward electing the very people who stole all the f*%#@ing money!"*[2]

Trade unions, the new tea party, the civil rights movement and one of the most popular religions in the world, these cases show just a few examples of the aristocracy's most sacred trick, be assured that they do this every single time they are faced with opposition. This trick can be described as the infection and subversion of counter culture movements.

The most deceptive and cunning villains of all time are not the work of fiction but are the wealthy families who control the world's economic systems and the bureaucrats that do their bidding. Whenever someone stands in the way of their growing financial empire, they immediately move into action and take out the threat in the stealthiest way they can imagine. If these interests were to publicly declare war and their agenda was exposed to the world then they would be looked upon with more disgust then the most brutal dictators in history. They only remain in power and in the good graces of the people because of their intricate web of deception and lies which they manage and perfect with every passing second.

QUOTE SOURCES AND SUGGESTED READING
[0] Peace Revolution Podcast Episode 23
[1] http://www.channel3000.com/news/26979885/detail.html
[2] We want freedom: a life in the Black Panther Party - Mumia Abu-Jamal (2004)
[3] http://market-ticker.org/akcs-www?post=16976

"We hold what is to come in the next generation, We hold the key to peace and prosperity
We have the tools to create a better existence, To end all things bad and to start a new beginning
This is the time we become something else, We are the future" – Toneshifterz (Rave DJs)

Section 9

The Future

62. -The Culture Battle Between Art and Propaganda
63. -Kindness and Cooperation
64. -We Are Winning
65. About the Author: John G. Vibes

"We have to stop CONSUMING our culture. We have to CREATE culture. DON'T watch TV, DON'T read magazines, don't even listen to NPR. Create your OWN roadshow. The nexus of space and time where you are -- NOW -- is the most immediate sector of your universe. And if you're worrying about Michael Jackson or Bill Clinton or somebody else, then you are disempowered. – Terrence Mckenna (Philosopher) [0]

62. The Culture Battle between Art and Propaganda

Every individual military conflict and case of economic slavery is made possible by some kind of cultural or philosophical mindset. All of the decisions we make throughout our lives are guided by our philosophical outlook and our cultural programming. Our ideas about the meaning of life, right and wrong, and human nature, will ultimately dictate our behavior. Tyrants would not be able to walk good hearted, self-respecting people into war and tax slavery if those people weren't first instilled with a personal philosophy that was receptive to those orders. This is why they so desperately control the education system and the media, to set the culture and ultimately control the overall mindset of the population. This is also why the counter culture is often viewed as a threat, because their role is to offset the established culture and push it in a direction that is not controlled by those running society.

Earlier in this book I discussed propaganda as a method of controlling culture and public opinion, to achieve destructive ends. Now I'm going to talk about how the common people of this earth can use the same methods, but with benevolent intent in order to push the culture in a more positive direction. If propaganda is what the establishment uses to create a culture of war, then art is what the average person can use to create a culture of peace. In times of oppression, it is very difficult for people to speak out against the constant tyranny, even when they do it's even more difficult to get others to listen. Art is a subtle way of getting the message out to the masses. This is useful because a lot of times people are so entrenched in the mainstream culture that they will become defensive when they come face to face with facts that call their worldview into question. However, if these same ideas are presented in the form of art, people are much less defensive and are more willing to approach the information with an open mind. Art is also used by activists who want to send a message but still remain under the radar.

This culture battle is all around us, almost every human creation is in one way or another either art or propaganda. Award winning movies, chart toping songs, children's cartoons, books and pretty much any form of media are filled with various philosophic and political overtones that are intended to speak to the audience. One of the top grossing films of all time "Avatar" may have seemed like a science fiction film at first glance, but with a closer look one will find that the whole plot was making a bold political statement. The creator and director of the film, James Cameron discussed the role that his political views played in the creation of Avatar.

In the December 2000 interview he said "*I think it's important for people to see the patterns in history... I think science fiction is a way of making history exciting by putting it in the future and taking you to a new planet and showing you exactly the same shit that's been happening for the last 2,000 years...Science fiction is excellent for that because if you want to make a comment about the Iraq war and American imperialism in the middle east, you're going to get a lot of people pissed off at you in this country, but you do it in a science fiction context where you do it at a metaphorical level, people get swept in by the story and they get to the end of the movie before they realize they have been rooting for the Iraqis*"[1] Cameron's other record breaking blockbuster "Titanic" was also very political, a film with class conscious social commentary hidden in a love story.

If you really examine some of the greatest works of art in history, you will find that the vast majority of the time, the artist was motivated by some kind of social cause. The art that really

337

moves people and leaves a lasting impression is rarely made with the thought of making a buck or climbing the social ladder. In today's culture, massive advertising schemes and flashy graphics are enough to catch most people's attention long enough to make a purchase, but you'll find that the works of art with real staying power are typically sending some kind of social message.

The original Wizard of Oz play was a subtle critique of the banking industry, most popular rock songs during the 60's were speaking out against the Vietnam war, early hip hop spoke out about civil rights and social justice, while at the same time almost everything that is approved by the FCC for television and radio is pure propaganda, designed to glorify materialism, authority and violence. Unfortunately, it is the information that is put out through the mainstream channels that is usually adopted as "truth" by the general public. This is why it is so important for us to not support the mainstream culture and actively work to create our own culture.

Now for the first time in history the internet gives average people access to unlimited, uncensored information and a place to share their opinions, free from fear of persecution. It's very easy nowadays for people to make a YouTube video, or put their music out to thousands of people, or start a podcast, the possibilities are limitless with today's technology. Our ancestors didn't really have the option to become the media, but we do. There is no need for us to feel helpless, or to resort to violence because we have the ability to reverse the direction of our culture peacefully.

QUOTE SOURCES AND SUGGESTED READING
[0] Terrence McKenna - lecture "Eros and the Eschaton"
[1] James Cameron discussing avatar in Vanity Fair" 12/11/00

338

"There is no path to peace, peace is the path" - Gandhi
(Activist/Philosopher) [0]

63. Kindness and Cooperation

As our reality descends deeper into chaos it is becoming impossible for the reigning cultural institutions to claim that there is nothing wrong with the way we are living. Our civilizations are built upon values of self-destruction which allow the most ruthless among us to set the general pace and attitude of our species. This means that our basic model of reality is shaped by the self-interest of those who have conned and murdered their way into power. The only ideas that are accepted into society are those which allow the ruling class to conduct business as usual and continue their corrupt existence. This is why insane ideas like "survival of the fittest" and "nice guys finish last" are held with such high esteem in authoritarian societies.

Our rulers are aggressive and emotionless people, so they tell the rest of us that we are supposed to be that way as well. We are given cultural norms based on the beliefs of the ruling class, and are told that this is the way that humans are supposed to think, act, feel and live. It is very arrogant for people to suggest that simply because we live a certain way now, and have lived this way for some time, that this is the pinnacle of human achievement and understanding. Every generation of our ancestors has had this same kind of arrogance regardless of how mundane their existence was. Things like slavery and human sacrifice were common in ancient life and seen as normal human activity just like our generation looks at war and poverty as some of life's "necessary evils". These practices were not devised by the average person and they do not benefit the average person. These were all created by one group of people that wished to dominate everyone else.

The idea of social superiority and inferiority was put forth by people who thought themselves superior to their brothers and sisters simply because they could manipulate and overpower

339

them. To carry on these barbaric policies in a sane world where people lived in love and cooperation would be impossible. For the manipulators to get away with their aggressions it is necessary for them to convince the rest of us that what they are doing is acceptable human behavior or "human nature" (whatever that is). This is when all hell breaks loose, because when the "leaders" of a society act nefariously then everyone else has the green light to behave the same way. This pattern is responsible for the depraved form that modern civilization has taken. People are not born violent and manipulative, but are made that way by sick cultures that encourage that type of behavior.

The cycle of domination and exploitation continues through the ages because we never make an attempt to do things in a different way. Religions, politicians and cultures may change but the basic way of doing things remains the same. To break this cycle we need a new approach entirely, as Einstein said "*The significant problems we face cannot be solved at the same level of thinking we were at when we created them.*" [1]

What he was saying was that if you are constantly trying to solve a problem using the same methods time after time then you're not going to get very far. This is kind of an extension on the idea of "trial and error", which says that when mistakes are made you should try a different approach. This idea has revolutionized science and technology but unfortunately hasn't been applied to politics, because we have governments throughout the world that are carbon copies of the ancient Roman Empire. That traditional model of Roman representative oligarchy fails completely somewhere in the world every decade and is then rebuilt with the same oppressive class structure, and same general policies, but a different label. Our planet cannot stand another rehash of this senseless power struggle, we need to find another way.

The solution is very easy, but for us to make this transition into a better way of living everyone is going to have to get involved and start being more kind and respectful in their everyday lives. Just because we are ruled by liars, thieves and hotheads doesn't mean that we have to display them characteristics within ourselves. For our ideas and our way of life to be taken seriously we will have to be more honest and ethical then those we are standing against. If the issues we are facing are due to a culture of violence and greed, then the only way to counteract that is to perpetuate a culture of love and understanding.

There are a lot of problems that do need our direct attention like dethroning the warmongers and banking cartels, and delegitimizing their authority. However, for us to truly sustain any kind of real civilization, we have to drastically change the way we think and the way we treat each other. All of the peaceful revolutionaries who have helped bring understanding to the world were aware of this solution and made it their life's work to share that message. Dr. Martin Luther King Jr. was one of these people, in one of his famous speeches he said "*Darkness cannot drive out darkness; only light can do that. Hate cannot drive out hate; only love can do that. Hate multiplies hate, violence multiplies violence, and toughness multiplies toughness in a descending spiral of destruction....The chain reaction of evil--hate begetting hate, wars producing more wars--must be broken, or we shall be plunged into the dark abyss of annihilation.*" [2] If we want to put an end to the violence and hate that we see in society then we are going to have to drop those ideals from our everyday lives. There is no way that we will ever be able to make a change in the world if we aren't able to make some changes within ourselves. We must represent a better way of life and lead by example with our own positive actions.

To get humanity and the planet earth back on the right track we need to take a more cooperative approach at how we run our societies and live our lives. One person could not possibly create an "ism" that will have the makings of a utopian society, which is not the kind of solution that will bring us peace and prosperity anyway. I've laid out some ideas that I feel are pretty good starting points However, if the world's population was

341

cooperatively working together, sharing knowledge and using their technology for the betterment of all humanity then we be living in a society more advanced then we could imagine. The common people need to get together and cooperatively construct a new paradigm for the future, instead of allowing our wicked "leaders" to decide the fate of humanity. We must work together and form a new society that works in the best interests of all people instead of a select few, while maintaining the principals of non-aggression, of course. This is the only path towards a truly civilized world, and for us to be walking that path we cannot participate in the same malicious activities as our corrupt "leaders".

QUOTE SOURCES AND SUGGESTED READING
[0]Pavement: reflections on mercy, activism, and doing "nothing" for peace By Lin Jensen
[1]Sustainability by design by John Ehrenfeld (2008)
[2]Strength to love - Martin Luther King (1977)

"They will not force us, and they will stop degrading us, and they will not control us! We will be victorious! so come on! Interchanging mind control, come let the Revolution take its toll......If you could flick a switch and open your third eye, you'd see that we should never be afraid to die, so come on!" – Muse (Psychedelic Rock Band) [0]

64. We Are #Winning

At the time I am writing this it has already began. The things that I have discussed in this book are now becoming widely understood around the world and the common people who represent the overwhelming majority of this earth are beginning to see how we have been exploited and manipulated for many generations. With the explosion of the internet, independent media websites have developed and are working to inform people about the reality of what's taking place in the world. Average people are taking advantage of social networking websites and using them as a political platform and a means to connect with likeminded people. In past generations, the ruling class was able to advance their agenda without the knowledge of the public because they had a stranglehold on which information was publicly available. Now with the internet, average people who are not controlled by the aristocracy are able to become the media themselves and bring uncorrupted information to the rest of the population.

As the truth begins to reach the masses, a new subculture of revolutionaries is being born and a whole generation is coming together in a way that has never been seen before. People who once saw one another as enemies are now realizing that they are facing the same struggles, that they are being exploited by their so called "leaders", just as a slave is exploited by their so called master. Christians, Mystics, Muslims and Jews are finally united in a universal fight against tyranny, poverty and oppression. The rich, the comfortable and the poor are all realizing that they are on the same side in a great "class war" that has been raging for centuries. This class war is really between the people who print the currency and the people who use the currency, not the "rich and the poor".

People of all financial and ethical backgrounds are realizing that they are all the same in the eyes of the ruling class. Soldiers are putting down their guns to join the protest lines, police are speaking out against the immoral war on drugs and scientists who have towed the party line for ages are finally starting to question the government approved, established version of reality. For generations, "the powers that shouldn't be" have taken advantage of our petty differences in order to divide and control us, but that time is over. People of different political affiliations are also beginning to learn that the people who they elect don't represent them. All of the wonderfully different people on this earth are realizing that they are on the same side, and that living together in peace isn't only possible, but it is absolutely necessary for our species' advancement on this planet.

Once the people become united and realize the immense power that they have over their freeloading "rulers" they become unstoppable. The practice of massive militant nonviolence is by far the safest and most effective method of removing corrupt regimes from power. When used correctly it works every time, without fail. This is among the biggest kept secrets in the world. What is most important though, is how the aftermath of the revolution is handled. It is incredibly easy for an informed, organized and morally conscious public to overthrow a corrupt regime, but the complicated part is preventing a power vacuum from developing for a new tyrant to fill.

We are watching a new era of revolution take place, where powerful tools like the internet are bringing people together, making their causes stronger and allowing them a place to record and express their struggle. The freedom of expression that exists on the internet makes it much more difficult for the ruling class circles and governments to control the flow of information that the public has access to. This is an advantage that our predecessors did not have. If a rebellion happened in one part of the world before modern methods of communication were developed, it was very easy for that movement to be disrupted without any other communities finding out about it. Now with the internet, activist movements spread out all over the world can join together and be just as informed and tight knit as the establishment that they are fighting against. The fact that the internet is shut off by the government in times of rebellion proves to us that this is indeed a very strong tool in the fight for freedom.

The internet is simply a tool, but the primary strength that ensures victory for the people's revolution is the incredible majority advantage that we have within the population. This is an unstoppable force because once the people understand that they are being exploited, it is only a matter of time before they refuse to partake in their own enslavement.

When revolution day arrives we must be clear in our intentions and not let our grievances be marginalized by vague terms like "equality" or "democracy". We need to have strong faith in our message and our cause, but not put too much trust into one specific "opposition leader". We must be very specific about the changes which are to be made and the future that we wish to build or else we run the risk of being led astray by a new tyrant and thrown back into another oppressive situation.

A revolution would threaten all of the wealth and power that the tyrants and aristocrats have been pillaging and hording over the generations, so they will without a doubt use every trick in the book to maintain their control over the population. These tricks include using controlled oppositions to make it look like someone new is taking over when in reality the new boss is taking orders from the same people and is often times just as bad as the old boss. As I discussed at length in "tricks of the trade" the elite has used many of the same techniques throughout history to maintain their power. To disable and counteract these kinds of sneaky tricks we must make fundamental changes to our political and economic systems. These changes will work to correct the injustice and violence that is threatening the existence of our species.

We can have a social system without having hierarchies, taxes, armies, politicians and prisons. We can also have an economy without poverty, exploitation, greed and insecurity. These things are possible, we just need to start making changes with how our societies are structured and how we do business. The steps that need to be taken are easy, simple and obvious, but will result in a transfer of power and wealth from the aristocracy to the masses, so my ideas are far from orthodox and won't be well received by those in power. The tyrants that have caused this mess will insist that the sky will fall without them there to hold it up, but these are obviously lies. This is the same way they have conned us into wars and huge corporate bailouts, using threats and fear. The politicians, the ruling class and the military industrial complex have brought us nothing but more problems which were dressed up as solutions. This is because real, honest solutions would leave them powerless and on even ground with the rest of us. The time has come for new solutions to stand in opposition of the status quo, the human suffering and environmental destruction that has taken place as a result of politics and savage military force is inexcusable and will not be sustainable for much longer.

The aristocracy that has kept us and our ancestors imprisoned under debt and propaganda is starting to lose their grip on the human consciousness. Their whole game is supported by us, the very people that they are viciously oppressing and we are finally starting to see through it. We need to stop working for them and start working for each other, and that message is spreading all over the world as average people are taking the revolution into their own hands. People are using their creative time and energy to develop solutions for the problems being faced by the working class. The only way to solve these problems is by creating our own solutions that will actually empower us, instead of just accepting the solutions that the ruling class offers. Any policy that the ruling class wishes to put in place is only to suit them and further exploit the Average people, so we cannot depend on them for any kind of assistance whatsoever.

When the declaration of independence was first signed in 1776 it only protected the white property owners who made up the colonial elite. There was no mention of the freedoms guaranteed to American citizens in the original constitution. It wasn't until oppressed colonial citizens took to the streets in protest and formed armed militias that the politicians of the time actually drafted the bill of rights in 1787. The bill of rights is the document that has officially recognized our natural born freedom of religion, the right to bear arms and the rights of the press, among others. Although many of the so-called "founding fathers" where the elite of their time and didn't have much sympathy for the working class, some of them did understand the importance of rebellion in a free society. Despite being a slave owning aristocrat, Thomas Jefferson was one of those people, in response to one of the antiestablishment riots in early America he said "*I hold it that a little rebellion now and then is a good thing, it is a medicine necessary for the sound health of government. God forbid that we should ever be twenty years without such a rebellion*" [1].

I'm not condoning violent action in response to our current oppression, I'm just saying that it's within our rights as members of a free society to DISOBEY the established order to maintain and advance our level of freedom. It is in fact the only way that any progress has been made for freedom in America or anywhere else. Without protest and rebellion white males would be the only people that had any rights at all. Luckily for us this isn't the case, America has a long history of brave intelligent people who led peaceful antiestablishment rebellions. This is why America has flourished so much in its short history, because of the average citizen's insistence on freedom and equal rights. The ruling class would have never handed those rights over if the public had not demanded them in protest. Currently their greatest power over the rest of the human population is the idea that we no longer have to fight for our rights and our freedoms.

When I began writing this book many years ago, the topics discussed herein were very underground and you had to look pretty hard for research. Likewise, it was rare to come across other people who understood what was going on. Now you can find these topics in the mainstream news every day, in the lyrics of chart topping songs, in the themes of blockbuster films and documented on websites all over the internet. The revolution of the mind that I discussed in the beginning of this book has already begun to take form, and a more peaceful and empowering attitude is seeping into the mainstream culture. Sure, things may seem bleak if you're approaching this information for the first time, but if anything, this knowledge should give you hope that a better world is possible and that human nature is not rooted in violence. We must not get discouraged by minor setbacks, and we cannot expect the world to be saved overnight. We are facing an enemy with multi-generational goals, so in order to keep up we must think just as long term. We can win this, and the fact that your reading this right now, shows that we are already #winning.

"The people who are trying to make this world worse are not taking the day off. How Can I?" — *Bob Marley (Reggae Musician)* [0]

65. About the Author – John G. Vibes

Since as far back as I can remember I largely rejected the cultural traditions that I was born into, because they seemed unnatural, irrational and oppressive. School was difficult because even from a young age I refused to conform and somehow understood that I wasn't going to learn anything of value in school. Most of my teachers in elementary school resented me because I would bring in books on topics that I was interested in and I would read them to myself while the class was going over their indoctrinating lesson. By the time high school came around I was so sick of the whole thing that I spent my class time sleeping, drinking and doing drugs, and from time to time I would still read. The oppressive nature of the school system only pushed me to hold greater resentment against authority and mainstream society. Unfortunately, that resentment pushed me toward some naive conclusions.

Although I had my suspicions about society and the status quo, I was still heavily conditioned by media and operating on a fairly low level of consciousness. I was still seeing the world in black and white terms and was pushed towards ideas like Satanism and Communism, because I was so turned off with the typical mainstream culture that I was subject to, that I just ran in the total opposite direction for solutions. Like many of the pitfalls I encountered, this was a necessary adventure along my path, and vital to my learning experience. Those interests led me to a wide variety of philosophical studies, but nothing would really make sense to me until many years later when I had enough information to get a clear picture of how things really worked. Most of my adolescence was filled with misplaced angst and overindulgence, which I hear is fairly typical. Regular drug tests pushed me towards heavy alcohol and pharmaceutical use, so although I was using psychedelics and researching philosophy I was still very clouded because of the mind numbing chemicals that I was putting into my body and the media that I surrounded myself with. Through those years I was faced with many synchronistic situations that slowly led me toward a more conscious lifestyle and informed perspective, but it would be many years before I broke free from the state of sleep that I was in.

There is no doubt that every single one of us has our whole perception of reality crafted by our environment and the things we experience, I'm obviously no different. Like most of the people on the planet I was born into a life of serfdom and grew up being constantly reminded about the struggles and obstacles that came along with financial slavery. Many times I was shown firsthand the senseless violence of war and the threatening oppression of the legal system, as you can tell my story is not unique, almost anyone can relate. The issues that have impacted my life and the ones I discuss in this book affect everyone, they are not limited to my experience.

Things did begin to get a little bit out of the ordinary when I started working at a funeral home at the age of 17. Looking back it's hard to imagine that I was drawn to that kind of profession, but at the time I was a very confused person. I ended up spending about 6 years as an apprentice mortician and those were quite possibly the most turbulent times of my life. I'm sure that the late teen to young adult phase is no cakewalk for anyone, but my job and my drinking problem seemed to at least keep things interesting.

They say you should never regret anything, and for the most part I agree, but if I could take back anything I wouldn't have let my drinking get so out of hand. At the time I was very ignorant, and underestimated the toxicity of alcohol due to its cultural acceptance. I was left with health problems that I'm still trying to sort out today. I was never an aggressive drunk, but that doesn't mean that I wasn't an extremely stupid drunk that caused a lot of trouble for myself and other people. Believe it or not it would take an enlightening shamanic experience to make me realize that I was destroying my body and that I should probably phase out my alcohol use. After 7 years of drinking hard liquor on a daily basis it was a lot easier to quit then I ever thought it would be, and with every day that passed I became more conscious of what was going on around me.

Due to my own personal experience and my earlier research into philosophy I was always untrusting of power, government, war, finance, religion and authority in general, but I didn't have enough of the specific background information to fully understand the true nature of our reality. I had a very limited knowledge of occult history for most of my life and was heavily sedated by chemicals and cultural assumptions that I greatly underestimated due to my ignorance. That all began to change when my physical and mental health started to deteriorate from alcohol abuse, heavy smoking and extremely poor eating habits. I was partying constantly because I was so disgusted with society and the life that seemed to lie before me, because it just seemed so confusing and backwards. I saw a world consumed with greed, violence, pain and misunderstanding for no apparent reason. This wasn't the kind of world I wanted to live in. I didn't want anyone to be subject to violence and I didn't approve of the status quo, but I was so convinced that this was the only world that was possible that I made no attempt to do anything about it and led a hedonistic lifestyle in order to fill a void in my soul.

During that period I was immersed in the heavy metal circuit in Baltimore and although mostly everyone was distracted by sex, drugs n rock n roll, I synchronistically met some activists and artists who were using the scene as a social platform. My new friends and acquaintances taught me all sorts of new information about the monetary system, social engineering and specifically the new world order. After putting a few tidbits together with the research I had done in the past, light bulbs went off all over the place in my head and I began to scour the internet for more information. There I found piles of documented evidence that supported what I knew all along but had no clue how to put into

351

words. Eventually after enough research, it became easier to find the words and I could accurately explain to myself and others why I disapproved of the status quo and exactly who was responsible for perpetuating it.

Unfortunately, even with my newfound knowledge I was still making poor decisions and still had a very negative outlook. My whole worldview was still heavily conditioned by years of media, schooling, and cultural norms. I was still looking at things in a very nihilistic way, where I had no understanding of the higher spiritual levels that existed or the unbelievable things that could be achieved through love and human cooperation. I really hate to be cliché here, but I was to learn all of this at my first hippy festival. I'm going to spare the names, dates and places out of respect for the promoters, but ill share the basics of what happened. This event was something that I had never experienced before and I had no clue what to expect. It ended up being a whole weekend almost completely removed from the mainstream American culture which had held me prisoner for most of my life.

My many adventures and realizations over that weekend would have a huge impact on my future path and encouraged me to delve deeper into the counter culture. After the enlightening weekend I had at that event. I spent the rest of the summer touring similar festivals on the east coast, seeking to clock more time outside of the mainstream culture and return once again down the rabbit hole. That summer my travels brought me to an outdoor rave that was on the water. That was probably one of the best parties I had ever been to, until around 3am when fire trucks, cop cars and other emergency vehicles began to surround the event. Things became very frantic at that point and I decided that I should leave the area where everyone had assembled and find another way out. Just before the area was raided I saw a fishing boat and began to shout to them for help and they came ashore to see what was going on. I offered them 20 dollars to take me and my friends out of harm's way toward where we had parked our car, and luckily the agreed to help us.

That certainly wasn't my first close call with the Gestapo that summer. After a few of these encounters I came to realize that the counter culture truly was outlawed in this Orwellian society I had come to find myself in. I always had a deep suspicion of authority, but now that I had the proper information and witnessed this peaceful culture being demonized by those authoritarian forces, I understood the reality of how our "civilization" operates.

In addition to the personal realizations that came to me at that show I had also made connections which would eventually help me establish myself as a rave promoter. At one of these events I met a promoter from Philly who said he hosted parties at a place called "Gods Basement" and that I should check it out sometime. If it wasn't for that synchronistic random encounter it is highly possible that I never would have wrote this book, thrown a single rave or even met my wife. Without Gods Basement and the time I spent there I can't even begin to imagine what my life would be like today. While I had been to some club and underground events in the past, Gods Basement was my official introduction into the underground rave scene.

When I started partying at Gods Basement, I was still in that part of my life where I was drinking on a daily basis and working at a funeral home in Baltimore. Nearly every day after work I would stop at local bars to kill time before traffic died down and most times I ended up at a place called The Black Hole. Eventually I took on a second job there working the door during rock and hip hop shows to make some extra money. Eventually, The Black Hole began getting involved in raves after a friend of mine made a suggestion to the owner. I helped book and promote a few shows there when things were starting up but was always helping other crews, doing my own shows never really crossed my mind at that point. After a while I began to spend most of my time in Philly and New York networking and promoting for shows at Gods Basement and the The Black Hole, with my wife Kali. At the time we had just recently met, but now we are happily married and I don't know what I would do without her.

Gods Basement was one of the main party spots on the east coast when I began promoting, and The Black Hole was still getting itself established and building its base crowd. Gods Basement is still to this day one of the most awesome venues I have ever been to, and I feel extremely lucky for the time I was able to spend there. As they say though, all good things must come to an end. When Gods Basement came under fire I learned just how corrupt and one sided the media is first hand. At the time I was familiar with media bias but I was still under the impression that the talking heads on the news were just mistaken with good intentions. However, as I would learn, the media consistently and deliberately constructs lies, falsifies reports and intentionally spins stories in order to uphold the status quo.

I'll be the first one to admit that wild things happen at raves, but they still offer a much safer and more peaceful environment than the average rock or hip hop concert that is advertised on mainstream television and radio. Gods Basement was eventually closed after an ignorant and close minded mother who didn't want her 18 year old child going to the events, reported the underground venue to the local news. Instead of playing an active role in her child's life and attempting to understand what was going on in her child's mind, this parent decided to force her will onto an entire culture. With her face and voice disguised, she appeared on the news calling for the shutdown of Gods Basement. This bigoted testimony was presented with fake video footage of kids doing various drugs, but long time patrons of Gods Basement could see that the clips which showed this were not even filmed at that venue. After the initial story ran, the NBC news channel received so much feedback defending rave culture that they were forced to run a second story to apparently show the other side of the argument.

As expected, that second segment was a total whitewash, where all legitimate complaints about the hit piece from the day before were mocked and marginalized, leaving the viewer with a skewed version of events. The fact that the promotion crews involved with the venue ran regular charity events and gave back to the community was completely left out of the reports and when it was time for the crew to make a statement their words were distorted and put in a context that made us look careless and unintelligent. The lies and attacks from the media eventually did result in the downfall of Gods Basement. When things got too crazy in Philly, I returned to Baltimore with a new direction and new connections that I developed working as a street promoter for Tru Skool Productions, the crew that ran Gods Basement.

By spring of 2008 I began to start thinking about doing my own shows because there were some elements that I had witnessed in the parties up north, which were lacking from the events in Baltimore and DC. The shows up north had a more underground feel, with themes, hard dance music and decorations, whereas the parties in my area were club events, not raves. So I approached the The Black Hole with my plan and by June of that year I began hosting my own underground themed events under Good Vibes Promotions. The name was just something that came naturally to me, almost at the same time that I had decided to start a crew.

From the first show on things were great, the parties were awesome, crowds came out of nowhere and packed the place every month, things were looking very promising. The only problem we really had was that the venue was in a residential area and we got harassed by the cops on a pretty regular basis. The place never backed down though and launched their own lawsuits on the police department armed with video evidence and countless eyewitnesses on their side, including myself. Unfortunately, years later the police launched a full scale raid and shut down the business, bringing an era to an end and putting many nonviolent human beings in cages. This situation was of course one of the many times in which I experienced the corruption of the legal system first hand.

In the beginning, I knew I enjoyed themed events but I was having a lot of trouble coming up with themes on my own. The names for the first few events that I hosted actually came from friends, for some reason my creativity seemed to be blocked. This was around the same time where I had really been getting deep in my activist research, spending up to 6 hours a day or more studying the things I have discussed in this book. It must have been very obvious to everyone around me that occult history and activism had pretty much consumed my interest, because many of my friends suggested that I themed my events around the things I was researching. The idea was brilliant and suddenly I no longer had any problem coming up with creative ideas for my shows. I did parties about sacred geometry, the Wall Street bailouts, free "end the fed" shows on tax day and many other events aimed at subtly educating the people who came out.

Eventually I was able to get a website set up thanks to the generosity of the raver who set up the domain and taught me the basics of the software. The website allowed me to host hundreds of educational activist documentaries and post independent news in an organized format on a daily basis. The website really took my research to a new level and eventually resulted in the book that you have just read.

I'm not the best writer in the world, I'm certainly not the best rave promoter and I'm not any smarter than your average person either. I have just spent my life confused about the social structure and why people behave the way they do, so I have continued to seek answers with every passing day. As time passed and I began to piece together more information I realized that most of what I was taught throughout my whole life was untrue. I had always suspected this but since I didn't have all of the information, I wasn't able to fully understand or specifically describe what I knew in my soul. I have always had a mentality that was in line with the principals of non-aggression and I was always aware that the major establishments in society didn't live up to those standards. For most of my life that vague idea was more or less the extent to my understanding of geo political and financial events. That all changed when I started researching things more thoroughly and came across the ideas and pieces of information that are contained in these pages.

Many synchronicities that I experienced during my adventures in the counter culture are eventually what led me to begin writing this book. I never had many resources or big time connections so when I began to think of new ways that I could contribute to the freedom movement, writing seemed like the only real option financially and logistically. Faster computers for video editing, music production software or podcasting equipment were not a financial possibility for me, but luckily writing doesn't cost anything. I knew that my path would be some form of art, because as I expressed many times I feel that human creativity is the only way to put an end to the violence and lack of compassion that is so prevalent in today's culture.

After I released my first book in 2011, I began writing articles for various alternative media sources. After about a year it became apparent that I had chosen a con artist as a publisher, causing me to become very discouraged with that path, so I began getting more involved in public activism. By 2012 I became a daily writer for Intellihub.com, one of the world's leading alternative media sources. Around that same time I took on a role as the executive producer of the Bob Tuskin radio show. In 2013, I began taking on more public speaking appearances. Prior to that I had only held seminars at the annual Big Dub Candy Mountain Festival, an outdoor rave event filled with many people that I would consider family. My first two speaking appearances in academic settings came in 2013, with appearances at the Free Your Mind Conference in Philadelphia and the Porcupine Freedom Festival in New Hampshire.

I also acted as a volunteer for all of these events, and eventually became one of the lead organizers for the Free Your Mind Conference. In 2014, Alchemy of the Timeless Renaissance, the book I had worked on for many years, is finally being released in an authorized form. Now I am working on writing more books, putting together events like the raves that I host with Good Vibes Promotions, and also organizing academic events like the Free Your Mind Conference.

Thank you for taking the time to read this book!

John G. Vibes

Made in the USA
Middletown, DE
03 September 2016